THE OPERAS OF PUCCINI

Giacomo Puccini in 1923

THE OPERAS OF
PUCCINI

William Ashbrook

*With a new foreword
by Roger Parker*

CORNELL UNIVERSITY PRESS

Ithaca and London

To Maria Bianca Ginori
and
To Florence

First published by Cornell University Press in 1985.
First printing, Cornell Paperbacks, 1985.

International Standard Book Number (cloth) 0-8014-1820-8
International Standard Book Number (paper) 0-8014-9309-9
Library of Congress Catalog Card Number 84-72674
Printed in the United States of America

The paper in this book is acid-free and meets the guidelines for permanence and durability of the Committee on Production Guidelines for Book Longevity of the Council on Library Resources.

Foreword to the 1985 Edition

ROGER PARKER

As the Italian critic Massimo Mila once pointed out, Leporello's comment in *Don Giovanni* when the stage band strikes up with a tune from *The Marriage of Figaro* seems as relevant as any to our problems when we approach Puccini with the least objectivity. "Questa si la conosco poi troppo!" he says: "Yes, this one I know rather *too* well!" The familiarity of Puccini's music—or at least parts of it—is undeniably a difficulty, particularly as we often hear it in contexts that do not have the air of "high culture" about them. Critics and scholars tend to react in one of two sharply divergent directions. For one group, the enormous public popularity of such operas as *Bohème* and *Butterfly* places them above criticism, in a kind of empyrean from which doubt, reason, and historical inquiry are excluded. But for another, this same success is the cause of automatic suspicion, the suggestion usually being that the composer must have cut artistic corners in the pursuit of immediate effect.

Certainly the latter group are more numerous and influential in some musical circles, and the history of writings on Puccini would feature a long list of denunciations. This began almost from the beginning. The *Rivista Musicale Italiana*, Italy's most prestigious musicological journal, published a highly critical assessment of the composer as early as 1894, and in 1912 the young Italian critic

Fausto Torrefranca devoted a full-length book to Puccini which is almost entirely negative. As Torrefranca says in the Preface, he chose Puccini because "he seems to me the composer who personifies with greatest completeness the decadence of today's Italian music, and who represents its cynical commercialism, its lamentable impotence, its celebration of the international vogue." More recently there have been other famous attacks: Stravinsky referring to *La Fanciulla del West* as "a remarkably up-to-date TV horse opera," and Joseph Kerman calling *Tosca* "that shabby little shocker." Almost everyone, it seems, has a bon mot against Puccini. My own favorite, probably because I have never been sure quite what it means, is attributed to J. B. Morton: "Wagner is the Puccini of music."

Against this tide of abuse, there have been remarkably few reasoned defenses. Mosco Carner's biography is of course a considerable landmark, and remains the single best account of the composer's life in any language. Carner also considers the work in some detail, but his canvas is broad and (some would say) he is hampered by his tendency to psychoanalyze Puccini from a distance. There was certainly room after Carner for a monograph that concentrated on the operas and their genesis from a sympathetic but not uncritical standpoint, and the gap was filled convincingly in 1968 by William Ashbrook's *The Operas of Puccini*. Ashbrook is, as his "Personal Note" tells us, undeniably a Puccini enthusiast, one who after a lifetime of listening still has an appetite for the latest *Bohème* or *Turandot* and who continues to be moved and impressed by the music. He is also a scholar with a broad knowledge of earlier Italian opera (his magnificent book on Donizetti was reissued in 1982 in a revised edition), and, so important for the Puccinian, he is deeply involved with the Italian language and Italian culture.

With these credentials, it would be strange if every page did not offer some original insight or felicitous summing-up. The genesis accounts, though necessarily not exhaustive (one could easily write an entire book on the genesis of *La Bohème*, for example), are models of clarity—no easy matter, for Puccini was an obsessive reviser who plagued his long-suffering librettists with minutiae. The discussions of the music are particularly revealing in their assessment of character and motivation, and show a sensitive understanding of the libretto and its effect on dramatic ambience and pacing, a matter that obsessed Puccini but at which he almost always excelled. One marvelous bonus is the attention Ashbrook gives to the autograph scores. These are in many cases documents that reveal an opera in the making and that offer us insights into the creative process as well as help with interpreting individual passages. How revealing, for example, it is to know that Puccini originally intended the climactic reprise of *E lucevan le stelle* at the end of *Tosca* to be sung by the heroine! The fact that most of us will surely be pleased that he changed his mind does not affect our altered perception of the meaning of the reprise. On a more technical level, we can learn that *Che gelida manina* (from Act I of *La Bohème*) was originally conceived in C major rather than D-flat major; this may cause us to rethink our ideas on the tonal planning of an act that begins and ends in C.

Readers will wish to know how far modern scholarship on Puccini has overtaken *The Operas of Puccini*. The answer is very little. A book on Verdi reissued from 1968 would have missed a vast literature, with international conferences, specialized journals, a mass of scholarly articles, and editions of the correspondence appearing at an alarming rate. But with Puccini the old scholarly indifference still remains. True, a Critical Edition is now under way, but the main collection of letters is still the *Carteggi Pucciniani* (1958), and there have been relatively few biographical or analytical initiatives during the last fifteen years.* Ashbrook may well stand corrected on a few minor points, but on the whole his information remains unchallenged. About the sensitivity and authority of his musical judgments there was never any doubt. This book, evidently born out of love for the composer, will I am sure inspire and inform many seeking to understand his music more fully.

---

*Notable contributions include: Giuseppe Pintorno, *Puccini: 276 lettere inedite: Il fondo dell'Accademia d'Arte a Montecatini Terme* (Milan, 1974); Cecil Hopkinson, *A Bibliography of the Works of Giacomo Puccini* (New York, 1968); Claudio Casini, *Giacomo Puccini* (Turin, 1978); and Arnaldo Marchetti (ed.), *Puccini com'era* (Milan, 1973). The *Carteggi Pucciniani* are edited by Eugenio Gara (Milan, 1958).

Acknowledgments

There are many people who have contributed much to making this book possible.

Chronologically, my earliest indebtedness is to Lucrezia Bori, whose Mimì and Magda first won me to Puccini and confirmed me in a life-long addiction to opera. Next, I should try, and must inevitably fail, to thank Max de Schauensee adequately for the insights and operatic lore he has unstintingly shared with me for nearly thirty years.

In the specific work upon this book I am particularly grateful to Maestro Raffaele Tenaglia, associated with Casa Ricordi since the days of Puccini. His assistance while I went through the autograph materials in the *caveau* of the Casa Ricordi was invaluable; he deciphered and elucidated obscurities, drawing on his rich personal experience, and lent me rare scores from his important collection. The Contessa Gaddi-Pepoli still lives in the villa La Piaggetta, built by her father, the Marchese Carlo Ginori Lisci. As her guests, my wife and I shared both unforgettable hospitality and her detailed memories of the Puccini family. The opportunity to spend two months on the shores of Lago di Massaciuccoli, directly across the lake from Torre del Lago, was a privilege.

I must also thank Maestro Salvatore Orlando of Livorno and Torre del Lago for sharing with me his recollections of Puccini, and

Maestro Alberto Cavalli for showing me the Puccini manuscripts at the Istituto Musicale Luigi Boccherini in Lucca. The assistance of Edward Waters and the staff of the Music Division of the Library of Congress was most helpful. And special thanks to Mary Ellis Peltz for making the resources of the archives of the Metropolitan Opera House available to me.

Ross Allen, of Bloomington, Indiana, has given much of his time to discuss Puccini with me and to read several sections of the book. I must thank him not only for many valuable suggestions but also for his generosity in sharing books, scores, and records. Dean Streit of New York City helped me by locating useful material for me.

I am indebted to Giovanni Martinelli and to Edward Smith for calling my attention to an anecdote concerning the composition of *Turandot*.

For help in preparing the manuscript, I want to say a special word of thanks to Donna Denny and to G. G. Taylor.

I owe a special debt to Manuela Kruger of Oxford University Press for all her understanding and patience in seeing this book readied for press.

Quite simply, without my wife's help and patience there would have been no book.

William Ashbrook

Terre Haute, Indiana
31 August 1967

Permission

Permission to reproduce the musical examples (with the sole exception of those from *La Rondine*) has been kindly granted by Casa Ricordi, the proprietary owners. Permission to quote from *La Rondine* was given by the Casa Musicale Sonzogno and Universal Editions.

Contents

A Personal Note

I can truthfully say I cannot remember a time when I did not know Puccini's music. My earliest memory is of coming into a room where my mother sat next to a big mahogany box. A man I couldn't see was singing. If at first I was most curious how the singer came to be in the box, I soon forgot that puzzle when my mother deflected my curiosity from the hand-wound Victrola by telling me the man was a poet in a Paris garret. I particularly remember how the soaring phrases near the end made me tingle. I had to hear them again. And again. For days I made myself a nuisance by insisting on hearing "C'ruso."

I still have that single-sided record of Caruso singing the Narrative from *La Bohème*. Although now the surface is badly scratched and pocked, I would not willingly part with the disc that first exposed me to the contagion of opera.

Puccini's music has many special associations for me. The first opera I saw, *La Gioconda*, much impressed me, but I cannot say it moved me. I did not have that experience until the following year when I saw my first Puccini opera—*Bohème* of course. The Mimì was Lucrezia Bori. Though I have since seen many excellent Mimìs, Bori's interpretation is still, for me, unsurpassed. No one else has projected as believably the mixture of timidity and eagerness in the first act. I remember well how she stood behind the tree in Act 3 and conveyed her shock as she overhead Rodolfo tell Marcello that she was fatally ill, not by a movement or gesture but by the sudden rigidity of her figure. Most of all I remember the last act. No other Mimì has suggested more movingly, or more delicately, that she is dying. Here Bori seemed to have difficulty focusing her eyes, and from time to time she would wipe the perspiration from her neck. (Later I learned that Bori had visited a hospital to observe—most sympathetically—patients with terminal tuberculosis.) This *Bohème* moved me to tears and, unable to find my handkerchief (I was eight), I cried into my scarf. For me that performance is always associated with the smell of wet wool.

Butterfly always makes me think of the summer I was married, and we knew that soon I would have to join the army. We had summer jobs in a fairly isolated part of the New Hampshire mountains. It was a sentimental summer, and the recording of *Butterfly* I packed up on my back from Twin Mountain became the symbol of it.

The following year I was training with a regiment stationed in the mountains of Colorado. My wife had a primitive apartment in a town about eighty miles away. Naturally, among the sparse furnishings was a small phonograph. I could get a pass only every other weekend. That period is associated with Bori's recording of *Ore dolci e divine* from Puccini's *La Rondine*, in which Magda describes how she met and parted from a young man at a Paris dance hall. On impulse I wrote to Bori, telling her that the record meant a great deal to us, and by return mail we had her photograph as Magda and written across it: "May there be many *ore dolci e divine* for both of you."

During the summer of 1966 we spent two months on the shores of Lago di Massaciuccoli, within sight of Puccini's villa at Torre del Lago. The house we stayed in was one Puccini often visited, and we saw photographs of him in the garden where we were staying. To live in this place, which remains much as it was in Puccini's time, and to hear his music there was to feel an almost uncanny sense of his closeness, as though he might at any time materialize in his hunting boots carrying his gun. Staying there brought moments of his music sharply to mind. The fishermen calling across the lake in the early morning sounded just like those off-stage voices near the beginning of the last scene of *Butterfly;* the full moon, huge and silver, rising over the reeds of the lake shore must surely have been in Puccini's mind when he wrote the Invocation to the Moon in the first act of *Turandot*.

These reminiscences are here to make one basic point about the operas of Puccini. Even those people who know nothing about music in a technical way find in them points of direct contact, moments of identification that stir them deeply. Operas by other composers may stir audiences deeply too, but the music of Puccini is particularly accessible to a large portion of the public. As Giulio Gatti-Casazza, former general manager of the Metropolitan Opera and a longtime friend of Puccini, said in a speech shortly after Puccini's death: "*Bohème*, *Tosca* and *Madama Butterfly* . . . are operas that speak above all to the emotions of the public and speak in a voice that is original, moving, penetrating, and sincere."*

I have admitted a partiality toward Puccini, but in the following pages I have tried to give an objective account of his operas. Only recently a prominent American critic dismissed Puccini's work as "slick trash." Although undeniably sincere, such a sweeping judgment is too flip. All it really does is indicate something of the taste of the person making it. Such an evaluation does not, of course, describe Puccini's music in any helpful way. My purpose is to help the average opera-goer or record listener regard Puccini's operas as they are, not to worry about what they are not, nor to use them as a basis for psychoanalytical interpretation.

Some people who have examined the Puccini manuscripts in the *caveau* of Casa Ricordi, comparing them with later printed scores, have charged the publishers with gratuitous manipulation of the material. These charges seem to imply that Ricordi's have been guilty of gross carelessness, of a lack of editorial scruple, in preparing material for the press. These charges are based on a false assumption about the relationship of the autographs to the printed material.

It is not my intention to argue that the printed scores are free of all errors, for that would be assuming human infallibility. It is patently obvious, on the other hand, that the autographs are not sources to be accepted unquestioningly. To cite the most obvious reason, each of the autograph full scores contains material that has been omitted or modified at some later date. These modifications may

* The minutes of this speech are in the archives of the Metropolitan.

be as minor as a change of a single word or they may be much more extensive. For instance, the autograph of *Manon Lescaut* contains the original (now discarded) finale to Act 1; there is no trace of the one substituted for it. Again, the autograph of Act 2 of *Bohème* does not include Mimì's description of her bonnet, which Puccini added to the opera after the first performance, a matter of ten pages in the printed full score. And then, the autograph of *Madama Butterfly* is chiefly that of the version at the La Scala *première*, which was subsequently withdrawn; of the drastic changes made for Brescia or the even later changes there is no trace. All this clearly demonstrates that Puccini's autographs represent merely one phase in the evolution of his scores and should not be taken as final authority for any detail.

Research on operas would be vastly simplified if composers never modified their material once they wrote it and if there were no such things as incendiary bombs to destroy invaluable evidence. In his way, Puccini was a perfectionist who felt free to improve his work, basing his judgment on rehearsals and performances, even years after the opera was first given, or accepting the opinion of someone he trusted, as when he accepted Toscanini's suggestion to lighten the orchestral texture of *Manon Lescaut*.

How did Puccini revise his scores after he delivered the autographs to Casa Ricordi? He used various methods, the most important being to make corrections upon the proof sheets. Unfortunately, the proof sheets with the alternations in Puccini's hand were destroyed in an Allied bombing raid upon Milan. Sometimes he suggested changes by letter or by postcard. For instance, on a postcard he asked that Rinuccio's aria in *Gianni Schicchi* be transposed up half a tone.* Other modifications he demanded in person; when Puccini was in Milan, where he maintained an apartment at Via Verdi 4, close to La Scala and Ricordi's office, it was an easy matter for him to deal directly with his publishers. Puccini's personal handling of revision creates the problem of leaving little documentary evidence.

There is, however, ample evidence that Puccini scrutinized his scores very closely and that he kept tinkering with them over the years. It seems reasonably safe to assume that very few errors would escape his notice. If changes have crept into the scores since 1924, then the editors at Ricordi's are responsible for them. The single

---

* The aria is in A major in the autograph; it was printed in B flat.

exception to this is *Turandot*. Because Puccini died before the opera
went into rehearsal, the necessary modifications were authorized by
Toscanini. One of these changes was to lower the tessitura of the
final part of Act 1: in the autograph, everything from *Non piangere
Liù* to the end of the act is a half tone higher than in the printed
score.*

I know that this is how Puccini worked, because I was fortunate
to have at my side every day as I examined the autographs Maestro
Raffaele Tenaglia. As co-operative a helper as one might wish and
a man whose quick and vigorous mind belies his more than eighty
years, Tenaglia has been with the firm since 1913. He became a
specialist in deciphering Puccini's frequently messy scrawl and
played a central part in preparing *Il Trittico* and *Turandot* for publication. As a matter of record, Puccini wrote to Tenaglia on receiving the parts of the *Trittico* for the Roman production, thanking
him for the correctness of his work and adding that this was the
first time he had received his music so free of errors. From Tenaglia
I got a detailed description of Puccini's punctilious way with proof
and of his habit of continually suggesting modifications.

---

* Toscanini here was merely carrying out Puccini's own instructions, for on 21
February 1924 the composer had written to Valcarenghi, one of the directors of
Casa Ricordi telling him to ask the copyist "to transpose all the finale of Act 1
down a half-tone, because as it is it is too high." (*Carteggi Pucciniani*, p. 548.)

THE OPERAS OF PUCCINI

I

PUCCINI AND HIS FIRST OPERAS

Le Villi to Manon Lescaut

Giacomo Puccini was born in the Tuscan city of Lucca on 22 December 1858. Music was in his blood, as four generations of Puccinis before him had been composers at Lucca. Lucca did much to shape his character, and all his life he preferred to live within its province. His cronies, as opposed to his professional friends, were almost all *lucchesi*.

The character of the town is individual. Ringed with thick walls, the old city with its narrow streets is a circumscribed world. The inhabitants live at close quarters. They are closely bound by family ties and concerns. Until recently only a handful of them has known much prosperity. The typical *lucchese* might strike an outsider as miserly, but he regards himself as frugal and sensible. Although Puccini has often enough been described as tight-fisted, he was merely exhibiting a trait prominent in his fellow townsmen. The people of Lucca are intensely proud of their cultural inheritance, but reluctant to spend much money on it.[1] Puccini's sense of identification with the town and region ran deep and survived squabbles and scandal. For years it was his habit to drive over from Torre del Lago to sit at the intellectuals' café run by his old friend Alfredo Caselli in the Via Fillungo to catch up on the local gossip.

---

1. Although there is a stone marker on the house where Puccini was born (30 via di Poggio), Lucca has never erected a monument to him.

3

Giacomo was five when his father died, leaving his widow with six children and six months' pregnant with the seventh. The boy grew up in straitened circumstances. Since the name of Puccini was automatically associated with music in Lucca, everyone expected that Giacomo when old enough would assume the traditional family position of organist in the cathedral of San Martino. His mother, Albina, who came from a musical family as well as marrying into one, insisted that he should have a good basic education before he started serious study of music. Drawing no doubt on extensive experience, she clung to the belief: *puro musico, puro asino*. Giacomo was an indifferent student in secondary school, his robust sense of humor frequently involving him in spectacular pranks. He was restlessly biding his time until he could enter the Istituto Musicale Pacini.[2] There his principal teacher was Carlo Angeloni, whose instruction was not limited to music.

Angeloni was an enthusiastic hunter, and in young Giacomo he found an eager novice. The chief sport of the region was the waterfowl abounding in the marshes surrounding Lago di Massaciuccoli. Hunting was a life-long passion with Puccini. Those who hunted with him have told me that he was never an outstanding shot and that he was given to minimizing his *padelle*, or misses. He loved the rituals and companionship of hunting. He enjoyed going out on the lake early in the morning before the mists had lifted, when everything was hushed. He was particularly proud of his prowess in silently approaching sitting birds and getting as close as possible to them before they took wing. Waterfowl was not his only game, although it remained his favorite. When he became famous he was often invited by the Collacchioni[3] to hunt on their preserve in the Tuscan Maremma. Here he could hunt for deer and hare, but the most famous prey was the once abundant wild boar. Clearly, hunting played an important part in Puccini's life. It afforded him a release from the pressures of his career and from domestic tempests; it was his antidote to the strain of playing a public role before stran-

2. The Istituto Musicale was then named for Giovanni Pacini (1796-1867), a prolific composer of operas all but forgotten today. Pacini delivered the oration at the funeral of Puccini's father. Today the music school has another name—since 1943 it has been called the Istituto Musicale Boccherini, after Luigi Boccherini (1743-1805), a native of Lucca.
3. Senatore Giovanni Battista Collacchioni (1810-95) held a large hunting preserve in the once-wild Maremma. A vivid picture of this hunting life is to be found in Mario Puccioni's *Cacce e cacciatori di Toscana* (Florence, 1932), a book which contains an entertaining chapter on Puccini as a huntsman.

gers; it was an escape into a world of easy masculine comradeship; it allowed him to rediscover himself.

Hunting established a rapport between student and teacher, and Puccini became an alert pupil at the Istituto Musicale. Angeloni's approach to teaching composition made a lasting impression upon Puccini. As a preparation for a particular assignment, Angeloni advocated the analysis of scores. Throughout his career Puccini regarded keeping abreast with current musical trends as a necessary part of the practice of his profession. He is known to have studied carefully the scores of his leading contemporaries: Debussy, Strauss, Stravinsky, Schönberg, and Hindemith.[4] He made no secret of this ingrained custom, and there are those who have scolded Puccini for his "eclecticism," forgetting that anyone composing music within a tradition is to some extent eclectic—a term that only in the twentieth century has become pejorative. Throughout his career Puccini continued to follow Angeloni's precept: a composer's vocabulary should be of his time, his idiom personal. An unbiased examination of Puccini's scores shows how well he remembered that precept.

While Puccini remained at the Istituto Musicale, he contributed what he could to his family's meager income by playing the organ at church services and by playing for dances held in the Casino at nearby Bagni di Lucca. As he grew older, he found he still depended on noisy, distracting surroundings for stimulation. He preferred to compose not in private but, at night, in a room surrounded by card-playing cronies who kept up a running fire of conversation. This relaxed, convivial atmosphere released his imagination. He would sit at the piano, often with a hat pushed back on his head, always with a cigarette dangling from his mouth, searching out a melody or a harmonic progression. From time to time he would insist that the group listen to a passage before he jotted it down in his sprawling hand. While he needed this friendly confusion as background when he was conceiving musical ideas, he required seclusion for the concentrated work of developing and orchestrating them.

While still a student at the Istituto Musicale, Puccini first felt a strong impulse to become a composer of operas. When he was

4. Puccini was not, of course, alone in studying the scores of his contemporaries. For example, I have been told by one who attended a recent congress at Prague in honor of Janáček that in a place of honor in the Czech composer's library was a copy of the German edition of *Butterfly*.

seventeen, he and two companions walked the three hours' distance to Pisa, where *Aïda* was having its first local performances. Some years later he told his friend Carlo Paladini, a journalist from Lucca whose reminiscences of Puccini are an important source of information about his early years, that the performance of *Aïda* had opened up a new world to him. Yet there were other pressures pushing him in the direction of the operatic stage. Writing operas was a family tradition with the Puccinis. Giacomo's great-great-grandfather, another Giacomo (1712-81), composed or collaborated in thirteen operas; his great-grandfather Antonio (1747-1832) was responsible in whole or in part for twelve; his grandfather Domenico (1771-1815) wrote five; but even more significant, the only opera by Giacomo's father, Michele Puccini, was performed in Lucca on 6 February 1864, about two weeks after the composer's death. It is likely that the boy, even though he was only five, attended this performance of his father's one-act opera and that it made some impression upon him. Further, as a boy Giacomo was in daily contact with men who composed operas, from Pacini to Angeloni. If that performance of *Aïda* at Pisa opened up a new world for Giacomo Antonio Domenico Michele Secondo Maria Puccini, he was already baptized, bred, and conditioned to it.

Fired with the ambition to write operas, even then still the chief path to wealth and fame for an Italian composer, Puccini needed more training than Lucca could offer. A most likely site for advanced study in music was the Milan Conservatory, the operatic capital of northern Italy. A particularly pressing argument for Milan could be made because of Alfredo Catalani, who had gone to the Conservatory there in 1875 and by January 1880 had had his first opera produced.[5] In the autumn of 1880, thanks to a grant from no less than Queen Margherita of Italy, obtained through the intercession of a lady-in-waiting, the Marchesa Pallavicini, Puccini was able to go to Milan and pass his entrance examination at the Conservatory. He pursued his musical studies with Amilcare Ponchielli and Antonio Bazzini. Some of the fugues and other exercises of these days are now in the library of his old music school in Lucca. They are conscientious student work, an effective contra-

---

5. Alfredo Catalani (1854-93). In 1880 Catalani's *Elda* made a rather dim impression, but in 1890, revised and re-christened *Loreley*, it won a notable success. He also published some chamber music. One of Catalani's early published works is a *Chanson groënlandais*, today familiar in another guise as Wally's aria, *Ebben, ne andrò lontano* (*La Wally*, Act 1).

diction to the often repeated anecdotes of Puccini as a lazy, slipshod student who deceived Ponchielli by turning in the same exercises over and over again.

The curriculum of the Conservatory included, among more usual courses, one in poetic and dramatic literature. Puccini's notes for this course survive.[6] It must have been deadly. At one point Giacomo wrote: "Ciao, professore . . . io dormo." On another page: "Ohimè!!!! Ahì!!! O dio!!! Ajuto per carità!!! Basta!!! È troppo!!! Muojo!!! Va un po meglio!" ("Good-by professor . . . I'm sleeping. Alas! Ouch! O God! Help, for goodness sake! Enough! It's too much! I'm dying! It is going a little better!") The professor for this course, which Giacomo took in 1882-83, was Lodovico Corio. Although Puccini developed a keen instinct for the stage, he found pedantic theory and abstractions on the subject stultifying.

As a student in Milan, Puccini made important friendships. At first he saw a good deal of Alfredo Catalani, but with time their relationship deteriorated. Catalani was a sickly intense man, fired with fierce ambitions: in those days Puccini was high-spirited and carefree. As long as Puccini was poor and consulted Catalani's advice, they got on well enough. When Puccini's operas were produced and especially after his success with *Manon Lescaut* (1893), the thirty-nine-year-old Catalani, dying of tuberculosis and exacerbated by the lack of wide acceptance of his operas, saw Puccini as the leader of a conspiracy against him, a conspiracy in which he saw the hand of Giulio Ricordi, the head of the publishing house, determined to establish Puccini as heir apparent to Verdi.[7]

Another acquaintance Puccini made during these student days was Pietro Mascagni (1863-1945). Five years younger than Puccini, Mascagni came to study at the Milan Conservatory, impatient to crash the bastions of La Scala and the Milanese publishers. Finding that he was required to follow a traditional course of study, writing counterpoint exercises and the like, Mascagni soon fled and took a job as conductor for a small touring company. During his stay in Milan, Mascagni had shared Puccini's garret apartment on the Vicolo San Carlo. Their student days in Milan, a Bohemian

6. These notes are at the Istituto Musicale, Lucca.
7. There is some justification for Catalani's view. For a time, Ricordi insisted that any theater which asked to produce Verdi's *Falstaff* also had to accept *Manon Lescaut*. Ricordi used this tactic with Covent Garden in 1894.

existence with little money and plenty of high spirits, created a bond that kept Puccini on friendlier terms with Mascagni than he enjoyed with most other composers of his generation. To call these terms "friendlier" is not to suggest they were always cordial by any means or that by the early 1920's the two men, for all their sense of a certain parallel between their careers, had not grown decidedly cool toward each other. Certainly the wives of both composers, each perfectly convinced of the primacy of her husband's position, did nothing to help their future rapport. For instance, in May 1921 Elvira Puccini was so incensed by a rumor that Mascagni would be appointed a Senator before her husband that she threatened to renounce her Italian citizenship and emigrate.[8]

Of his instructors at the Conservatory, Ponchielli exerted the greatest influence on Puccini. Although Ponchielli was a busy man —occupied with his own compositions, a post in Bergamo, and editing for the music publisher Giovannina Lucca, in addition to his duties at the Milan Conservatory—he was genuinely interested in his young pupil and helped Puccini much at the outset of his career. For instance, convinced of the promise in Puccini's graduation composition, a *Capriccio sinfonico*, he did much to ensure its favorable reception. Ponchielli's friendly concern accounts for the fact that Puccini's composition was warmly reviewed by a leading Milanese critic, scarcely the usual expectation for a graduation exercise. From Giacomo's point of view, Ponchielli had the important recommendation of being a respected and successful composer of operas.[9] Puccini's studies with Ponchielli left their mark on the younger man's music.

In July 1883, thanks to Ponchielli, Puccini made two acquaintances that were to have important consequences upon his career as an opera composer. The first of these was Giulio Ricordi (1840-1912), the head of the most influential music publishing firm in Italy. A great deal of the history of Italian opera throughout the nineteenth century is closely allied with Ricordi's, publishers of much of Rossini, Bellini, Donizetti, and all of Verdi. Puccini's association with the firm and family came to be close indeed, all but one

8. Carlo Paladini, *Giacomo Puccini*, edited by Marzia Paladini (Florence, 1961), p. 158.
9. The principal operas of Amilcare Ponchielli (1834-86), with the lone exception of *La Gioconda* (1876), are practically unknown outside Italy. They are: *I Promessi Sposi* (1856, revised 1872), *I Lituani* (1874), *Lina* (1877), *Il Figluol Prodigo* (1880), and *Marion Delorme* 1885). Besides his operas, Ponchielli won great but short-lived success with a ballet, *Le Due Gemelle* (1873), and a hymn in memory of Garibaldi (1882).

of his operas—*La Rondine*—bearing their imprint. Although Puccini's first meeting with Signor Giulio dates from this time, their professional connection did not begin until the following year.

Also through the offices of Ponchielli, Puccini was introduced to his first librettist, Ferdinando Fontana (1850-1919). Fontana was improvident and proud, an inveterate meddler in politics, but most important for Puccini he was an excitable eccentric who impulsively agreed to supply Puccini at reduced rates with a libretto, enabling the fledgling composer to enter a competition for one-act operas sponsored by the Casa Sonzogno.[10] Typically, it was Ponchielli who interceded with Fontana for the bargain libretto, and once this was arranged Puccini and Fontana set to work at once. Originally their work bore the hybrid title *Le Willis;* when Puccini enlarged his score to two acts the name became the more Italian *Le Villi.*

Le Villi

For his subject Fontana turned to a romantic German legend dealing with an innocent girl who is abandoned by her fiancé, dies of grief, and returns with the spirits of other jilted girls to dance the unfaithful young man to his death. If this story sounds familiar, it is because it is almost identical with Gautier's scenario for the ballet *Giselle.*

The details of the composition of *Le Villi* are difficult to reconstruct because few of Puccini's letters from this time survive. One, written to Fontana dated 30 August 1883, shows Giacomo was wasting little time. Besides asking for a few modifications in the text—how mild Puccini's tone is here in contrast to his later demands upon his collaborators—he adds one important particular: "I have been to Signor Giulio [Ricordi], and I have played Anna's *romanza* for him. He was most happy with it."[11] Anna's little aria of the forget-me-nots is one of the few bright spots in a dim score, in its contours clearly looking forward to Puccini's later melodic style. Considering the firmness of Ricordi's faith in Puccini over a

10. Sonzogno's competition, for which the scores had to be submitted by 31 December 1883, was the first of several held by the recently formed publishing house. There was a second competition in 1888, won by Mascagni's *Cavalleria Rusticana.*
11. Printed in *Carteggi Pucciniani*, edited by Eugenio Gara (Milan, 1958), p. 9. Unless otherwise indicated, all references to letters come from this collection. The translations are mine.

number of lean years, he must have heard in this aria a new and distinctive personality he believed well worth cultivating. A composer himself (under the pseudonym J. Burgmein), Ricordi was an unusually astute judge of promising young composers. But not infallible, for one day he turned away Mascagni with his manuscript of *Cavalleria*, one of the most profitable properties of the century.

Puccini composed his opera by establishing the vocal line and harmony first, then elaborating and completing the score as he orchestrated it. This practice he was to follow for the rest of his days. Since he apparently returned to Lucca some time in September 1883, most of the work on the original version of *Le Villi* was accomplished there. Lucca was to hold more than one attraction for him. He could live at home for practically nothing. His mother's health had been damaged by her long struggle with poverty, and Puccini had a typically strong Italian attachment to his *mamma*. There came to be still another attraction. Elvira Gemignani, the wife of a wholsale grocer and mother of two children, was two years younger than Giacomo, and since Lucca was an unusually close community for its size, he had probably known her as a child, when she was still Elvira Bonturi. During this autumn of 1883 Puccini contributed to his family's income by giving music lessons, and, as seems more than probable, Elvira became one of his pupils.

Puccini barely made the deadline of the Sonzogno competition with his score. But when the results were announced, Puccini's name was not mentioned. His score was so nearly indecipherable that the judges scarcely examined it. But what seemed like a disaster on his first attempt at operatic composition turned out more favorably than if he had won.

A number of important people, feeling that an injustice had been done in the upstart Sonzogno's contest, interested themselves in Puccini's behalf. Not the least of these was Fontana, who worked to have the opera produced so he could salvage his reduced fee for the libretto. Certainly Ponchielli was anxious to see his pupil succeed. Oddly enough, Ponchielli was a member of the commission that passed over Puccini's opera, but perhaps this very mild-mannered man did not succeed in influencing his colleagues.[12] Giulio Ricordi was won over to the young composer's cause to the

12. The other members of the commission were Cesare Dominceti, Franco Faccio (the famous conductor), Pietro Platania (a composer), and Amintore Galli (an instructor at the Conservatory and musical director of Casa Sonzogno).

extent of promising to supply libretti printed free for the *première*.
Besides these, Puccini gained the advocacy of Arrigo Boito, a powerful figure in Milanese musical circles, whose support helped influence a number of aristocratic *dilettanti* to help underwrite the
450 lire needed to pay for a performance. As for Puccini, his whole
future depended upon a successful production of *Le Villi*.

Thanks to the efforts of these people, *Le Villi* was performed as
part of a triple bill at the Teatro Dal Verme, Milan, on 31 May
1884.[13] The opera won a considerable success with both public and
critics. There were encores—the intermezzo entitled "La Tregenda"
(The Witches' Sabbath) had to be played three times—and Puccini
was called again and again before the crowded house. Among those
present was Pietro Mascagni, now playing the double-bass in the
pit.

The warm reception for *Le Villi* gave Puccini's career a real
impetus. Most important, it won for him his first contract with
Ricordi; according to its terms he was to expand *Le Villi* to two
acts, the firm was to publish the score, and he was to compose a
second opera, also to a Fontana libretto, which would have its
première at La Scala. The vital term in the contract from Puccini's
point of view was the stipulation that Ricordi's would pay him a
monthly stipend of 200 lire a month in lieu of an advance, the total
amount of this stipend to be repaid at some unspecified future date.
At one stroke Puccini's future seemed secure. He had been confirmed in his chosen career. The 200 lire a month was little more
than meager support, but it was a steady source of income guaran-
teeing him the opportunity to compose.

Yet another sign that Puccini was becoming a name to reckon
with in the musical world was Franco Faccio's decision to perform
the *Capriccio sinfonico* on 6 July 1884 at a concert in Turin, given
in conjunction with an Exhibition there. Franco Faccio (1840-91)
was then the foremost Italian conductor, in charge of La Scala performances from 1871 to 1889, and he had the prestige and authority
later associated with Toscanini. His support helped spread Puccini's
name, but the lift this recognition should have given Puccini was
considerably dampened by the death of his mother on 17 July.
Giacomo mourned his mother deeply and sincerely.

One consequence of his mother's death was the removing of the

13. The first performance of Puccini's first opera was conducted by Arturo
Panizza; the cast consisted of Regina Caponetti (Anna), Antonio d'Andrade
(Roberto), and Erminio Pelz (Guglielmo Wulf).

major obstacle that kept Giacomo and Elvira Gemignani apart. No one seems to know precisely when, whether it was this year or the next—such events are frequently not precisely documented— Elvira abandoned her husband for Puccini, taking with her her daughter Fosca (born 1880), but leaving her son Renato (born 1883). This step, whenever it took place, was not without consequences in the close-knit community of Lucca. The partisans of Giuseppe Gemignani never forgave them.

Puccini's revisions of *Le Villi* were completed by the fall of 1884. The new two-act version was first given at the Teatro Regio, Turin, a theater whose important associations with Puccini's career include not only this performance but the *premières* of *Manon Lescaut* and *La Bohème*, for the traditional opening of the season on Santo Stefano, 26 December 1884.[14] Both Puccini and Fontana went to Turin to oversee the new production. Although they were upset by the haphazard staging, the listless chorus, and the poor acoustics of the theater, they hoped to duplicate their earlier success. The opera was applauded, but without any of the enthusiasm, the special warmth that greets the first appearance of a promising new talent, that had given the performance at the Dal Verme in May its special cachet. Probably those who heard both the earlier production and this one were disappointed that Puccini's revisions were not more extensive. On 24 January 1885, less than a month after the Turin production, *Le Villi* was introduced to La Scala, with Puccini himself in charge of the stage direction.[15] The critics were severe, finding the orchestral features overemphasized; but the public was less harsh, allowing the opera to attain a run of thirteen performances. On some evenings the bill was completed by a ballet, *Messalina*.

What sort of an opera is *Le Villi?* The answer must be: a work of promise, one with moments of surprising surety of effect, but ultimately disappointing. Listening to *Le Villi* today, one cannot help being aware of its frequent foreshadowings of the later Puc-

14. At Turin, *Le Villi* was sung by Elena Boronat (the sister of the more celebrated Olimpia), the tenor Filippi-Bresciani, and the baritone Agostino Gnaccarini.
15. The La Scala production of *Le Villi* was conducted by Faccio. Romilda Pantaleoni (1847-1917), who two years later was the Desdemona in the *première* of Verdi's *Otello*, sang Anna. Andrea Anton (Roberto) and Delfino Menotti (Guglielmo Wulf) completed the cast.

cini; again and again it anticipates *Manon Lescaut.* Yet the audiences who first heard it listened with a different orientation. The
repertory at La Scala during the season of 1884-85 included Boito's
Mefistofele, Donizetti's *La Favorita.* Meyerbeer's *Il Profeta,* the
première performances of Ponchielli's *Marion Delorme,* and Bellini's *I Puritani,* besides *Le Villi.* In such company, *Le Villi* must
have seemed new, noisy, and rather nervous.

The sad truth seems to be that for all its interest to students of
Puccini, *Le Villi* cannot sustain more than an occasional revival. It
received its greatest chance to establish itself when it was given at
the Metropolitan in 1909, conducted by Toscanini and sung by
Frances Alda, Bonci, and Amato. If talents like these could not give
it permanent life, the fault lies in the opera itself.

Undoubtedly much of the blame is Fontana's. His dialogue is
turgid and riddled with clichés. His sense of what is dramatic is so
uncertain that he stresses decisions already made rather than the
conflict leading up to them. He reduces the action almost to in-
comprehensibility by eliminating such important episodes as Roberto's infidelity (described in spoken narration) and Anna's death
(although her funeral procession is seen behind a scrim during the
first entr'acte). There is only one adjective to describe Fontana's
libretto—inept.

Puccini's score is far stronger than the text, but to say this is by
no means to imply that *Le Villi* is a neglected masterpiece. Certain
impressions about the music emerge at once. The rhythmic vitality
of the score is its most consistently Puccinian feature. Although
much of the score is orchestrated with a coarser hand than in Puccini's later work, there are certain tricks of part-leading in the
woodwinds and of alternating instrumental groups that reveal the
composer at once. Surprisingly, the melodies of the score, with the
exception of the *Ländler* chorus, and the arias for Anna and Roberto, are not the point of greatest resemblance to the later Puccini.
In *Le Villi* many of the melodies are shorter, more fragmentary,
less cohseive, than those he came to write. There is a French texture, resulting from the bright orchestral palette, the rhythmic *élan,*
and the melodic contours. Some of the orchestral entr'actes sound
on close examination like something out of an Auber overture orchestrated by a talented pupil of Bizet.

What gives *Le Villi* an historical importance beyond its purely
musical interest was pointed out by Puccini himself in a letter to

Clausetti, dated 9 August 1895. "*Le Villi* initiated the type that today is called '*mascagnano*' and no one gives me credit for it. I am in a moment of bitterness." Granted there is a decisive difference in genre between the subjects of *Le Villi* and *Cavalleria*, but in other aspects the resemblances are clear. Remember that Mascagni was familiar with *Le Villi*, having played in the orchestra at the *première*. He could not fail to be impressed that the most successful part of the score was the orchestral intermezzo, which became an entr'acte when the score was enlarged to two acts. When Mascagni entered the second Sonzogno competition for a one-act opera, a circumstance sure to bring *Le Villi* to mind, he wrote an opera that included an intermezzo.

Although many phrases from *Le Villi* might be placed beside phrases by Mascagni and reveal resemblances, two comparisons of Puccini's score and Mascagni's *Iris* (1898) make the point.

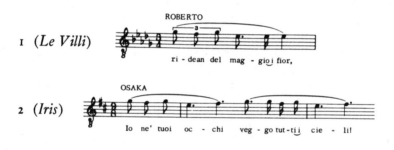

And, again:

Even more striking anticipations of Mascagni occur in the first entr'acte to *Le Villi*, "L'Abbandono" (The Abandonment), where certain progressions and dynamic contrasts looked forward to *Cavalleria*.

5 (*Le Villi*)

The significance of *Le Villi* lies not just in these passages which foreshadow Puccini's later style, but in its influence on the structure and style of Mascagni.

Puccini uses double titles for two consecutive entr'actes of *Le Villi*. Besides their descriptive titles—"L'Abbandono" and "La Tregenda"—he labels them "Parte Sinfonica": "Primo Tempo" and "Secondo Tempo." Although these names indicate Puccini's hope to capitalize on the favorable reception of his *Capriccio sinfonico*, they are misleading since there is nothing traditionally symphonic about this music. Instead of real thematic development and transformation, the principal melody of the first part is repeated, its contours intact, in varying instrumental colors and tempos. The second part sounds like a section from an operatic ballet in the French tradition. So important are the balletic features of the score that Puccini calls the score an *opera-ballo*.

Undoubtedly the so-called symphonic passage in Puccini's score attracted a good deal of attention. Word of it even reached the ears of Verdi, who wrote to a friend on 10 June 1884:

> . . . I have been hearing many good things about the musician Puccini. I have seen a letter that praises him highly. He follows the modern tendencies, which is natural, but he adheres to melody that is neither old nor new. It seems, however, that the symphonic element is dominant in him!—no harm in that. Only one must tread cautiously in this path. Opera is opera: symphony is symphony. And I don't believe it is good practice to insert a slice of symphonic music into an opera just for the pleasure of making the orchestra prance . . .[16]

Verdi's observation applies to an abstract principle more than to the example of Puccini's *Le Villi*. Puccini's entr'actes are descrip-

16. Reprinted in *Carteggi Pucciniani*, p. 12.

tive music: the first has choral parts and describes Anna's funeral procession; the second is dance music and recurs in the finale of the opera, thereby becoming an integral part of the score. It is difficult to believe that if Verdi had seen *Le Villi*, rather than hearing about it at secondhand, he would have made these observations.

The term "intermezzo," given wide circulation by Mascagni's example from *Cavalleria*, was not in general use for excerpts of this sort when Puccini composed *Le Villi*. After the furore over *Cavalleria*, intermezzos became practically a *sine qua non* of veristic opera.[17] Puccini's fondness for them continued after *Le Villi*, as the scores of *Manon Lescaut*, *Madama Butterfly*, and *Suor Angelica* show. Even in *Turandot*, the scene for Ping, Pang, and Pong that opens Act 2 is an intermezzo, but more in the musico-dramatic tradition of the eighteenth century.

Puccini never came to feel as badly about his first opera as he did about his second. *Le Villi*, in spite of its wretched libretto, is a creditable work. Surely, few first operas written by composers fresh out of the conservatory have received such attention in important theaters.

The "autograph" of *Le Villi* preserved at Ricordi's is a disappointment to anyone hoping to find out much about the development of the score. A good deal of it is not in Puccini's hand, but in that of a copyist, lending weight to the story of the illegibility of the manuscript Puccini submitted for the competition. For another thing, the expansion of the opera into two acts was performed upon the autograph. Therefore it contains the tenor's *romanza* (*Torna ai felici dì*), which was added to the two-act version, and it bears on its final page: *Fine, s/ Giacomo Puccini, San Martino in Colle, 28 8bre 84*, the date on which Puccini completed the orchestration of the two-act version.

A few details are provocative. Bound in with the score is a cover sheet for Anna's aria which is dated August 1883, a reminder of Puccini's performance of this aria for Giulio Ricordi shortly after it was composed. In the accompaniment to this aria, Puccini has indicated some changes in the string parts, but whether these were made for the first or second version it is now impossible to tell. One

17. The verismo school of opera featured abrupt, violent plots, often dealing with humble characters. The best-known examples of this school are Mascagni's *Cavalleria Rusticana* and Leoncavallo's *I Pagliacci*. For a discussion of the relationship of *Tosca* to this school, see pp. 80 ff.

tenuous clue may afford some indication to the sequence of composition. In one place Puccini has indicated a part to be played by
the ophicleide; in another a part for the "corno basso" or bass
horn.[18] Both the ophicleide and the bass horn were used for the
same function: the bass of the brass section, in the days before the
tuba or bass trombone became fixtures in Italian theater orchestras.
If it were possible to establish whether Puccini thought of using the
ophicleide before the bass horn, or the other way round, this fact
would give some insight into the sequence of composition.[19]

Edgar

According to the agreement reached by Ricordi with Puccini in
June 1884, the librettist for Puccini's next opera was again to be
Ferdinando Fontana. How long it took Fontana to produce the
libretto of *Edgar* is not precisely known, but Puccini received it in
May 1885. Nor is Puccini's reaction to a first reading of this example of Fontana's handiwork precisely known. For a while at
least, he seems not to have been dissatisfied with it. But his later
experiences with this libretto were to cause Puccini such disappointment that it taught him one of the most important lessons of
his artistic career. Never again would he take on a libretto without
reserving the right to refuse it or to order whatever changes he
thought necessary.

Fontana, for his point of departure, used Alfred de Musset's
closet drama, *La Coupe et les lèvres*. The title of the play alludes to
the proverbial "many a slip." Fontana's choice of Musset's play
even as a point of departure constituted a major slip. The play was
never intended for the stage, being principally a study of a self-
destructive hero, one of Musset's *débauchés* who suffers from *le
mal du siècle*. Unerringly, Fontana jettisoned the best parts of Musset and retained the worst—the spasmodically melodramatic parts.
And what Fontana used he frequently abused by further exaggerat-
ing the already overwrought.

Fontana departs from Musset at many points. He switches the
setting from the Tyrol (too reminiscent of the Black Forest of *Le*

18. Verdi wrote parts for the "corno basso"; now they are played of course by
the tuba.
19. Maestro Tenaglia told me that at Ricordi's London office there is a set of
"retouched" parts for *Le Villi*, but these I have not seen.

Villi?) to Flanders *circa* 1302. Musset gives his intemperate hero the name of Frank; Fontana, on the other hand, calls his equivalent of that character Edgar, but then Fontana turns around and gives the name of Frank in his libretto to quite a different character (Fidelia's brother, who is Edgar's rival for Tigrana's favor). Fontana's reassignment of this name creates confusion for those who seek to disentangle the libretto's rather obscure relationship to its source. Further he re-christens the two contrasting ladies of the plot, pointing up their dissimilarity not very subtly by calling them Fidelia and Tigrana.[20]

The composition of *Edgar* coincided with one of the bleakest periods of Puccini's life. His personal life was troubled by the scandal inevitable upon his setting up a menage with Elvira. Funds were short. Out of the 200 lire a month from Ricordi's he had to support not only Elvira and her daughter Fosca but do what he could for his younger brother Michele, then studying music in Milan.[21]

In November 1885 Puccini wrote to Fontana: "I am not working much, but I have done all the beginning and I am up to the Tigrana-ish entrance. The little off-stage chorus has gone very well, as has the entrance of Zaroë and the tale of the almond tree."[22] He is anxious about some modifications to the second act, claiming he cannot proceed without them. By the following January he gratefully acknowledges the receipt of the changes. (Many writers on Puccini have stated flatly that Fontana refused to make any changes at all in his text, but this letter[23] proves that was not the case.) Puccini goes on to report that he is working "tenaciously," that he has started on the Funeral March (Act 3) and completed the gypsy song (later removed from Act 1) and the tenor's *romanza*, although he has made a cut in the preceding recitative as it was "eternally long."

In May 1886 Puccini wrote to Giulio Ricordi to ask for another

20. In the play their names are Deidamia and Belcolor. The latter is an Italian courtesan, but this Fontana found either too tame or else it offended his patriotic sensibilities. Tigrana is a Moorish temptress, complete with dembal (a sort of lute).

21. Michele Puccini, born three months after his father's death, had a tragically short life. After being unable to carve a career for himself in Italy, he emigrated to the Argentine, where he died of yellow fever in 1891, aged twenty-seven.

22. Zaroë is the discarded name for Fidelia, whose aria about the almond tree begins: *Già il mandorlo vicino.* Puccini later cut a second verse to this aria. Fontana was fond of introducing sympathetic heroines in a flowery context. Anna in *Le Villi* first appears with a bunch of forget-me-nots.

23. *Carteggi Pucciniani*, p. 21.

year's extension of his remittance. "The opera is well along," he reports, but "in one year, as you will understand from your experience, it is impossible to finish an opera of such scope and of such difficulty as this one." He is, so he says, happy with his work so far, and he hopes Ricordi will be satisfied with it.

The orchestration of *Edgar* occupied Puccini for a year. He had left Lucca during the summer of 1886, probably because Elvira's pregnancy was becoming noticeable.[24] On 12 September 1886, the date at the beginning of the autograph full-score of *Edgar*, they were at San Antonio d'Adda, a small town not far from Bergamo and near to his librettist Fontana, who lived for some years in an easy-going *pensione* owned by Antonio Ghislanzoni, the author of the Italian poem of *Aïda*. Ghislanzoni's establishment at Caprino Bergamasco is indicated as the spot where Puccini completed the four acts of *Edgar* in September 1887.

Although the public announcement of Puccini's first contract with Ricordi (in the *Gazzetta Musicale* for 8 June 1884) said his next opera would be given at La Scala, and although the opera finally had its first performance there on 21 April 1889, other places were considered for *Edgar*'s launching. In 1886, the conductor Luigi Mancinelli,[25] who for some seasons directed the Italian season at the Teatro Reál in Madrid, wrote Puccini to inquire if *Edgar* was available for performance there. The following year Puccini let Mancinelli know when *Edgar* was finished, adding that a proposed Roman production had gone up in smoke when an opera by a local composer was selected instead. The possibilities of a Madrid production of *Edgar* were to become a matter of great eagerness and even greater frustration during the next five years.

In November 1887 *Edgar* was first under consideration for Madrid. Puccini's hopes skyrocketed because the company there was first rate.[26] But in those days the repertory was not decided upon by the musical management, the final word residing with the aristo-

24. Antonio Puccini, the composer's only son, was born at Monza, 23 December 1886.
25. Mancinelli (1848-1921) was one of the better Italian conductors of his generation. He conducted in Madrid 1887-95, in London 1887-1905, and at the Metropolitan 1893-1903. His opera, *Ero e Leandro* (with a libretto by Boito that had previously been set by Bottesini), was staged in Madrid (1897), at Covent Garden (1898), and at the Metropolitan (1899).
26. Appearing at Madrid in 1887-88 was Eva Tetrazzini (1862-1938), the elder sister of the more celebrated Luisa. Others in the company, which Puccini described as "stupendous," were the dramatic tenor Eugenio Durot, who sang Edgar successfully at Lucca in 1891, and the mezzosoprano Amalia Stahl.

cratic commission holding the royal patent. Apparently these gen-
tlemen found *Edgar*, which contains a scene with the hero disguised
as a monk attending his own funeral, inappropriate fare. Puccini did
not blame Mancinelli for this disappointment. Forced to wait a full
year, while his prospects seemed cheerless, his hopes of eventual
prosperity elusive, he was sustained only by his allowance from
Ricordi. Part of the summer of 1888, he spent just over the Swiss
border, living frugally at San Simone. The clouds parted, so he
thought, late in the autumn when he learned that *Edgar* had finally
been included on the *cartellone* of La Scala for the coming season
of 1888-89.

The *première* of *Edgar* took place on Easter Sunday,[27] an unusual day for a performance. As he was later forced to admit, Puccini knew this botched subject was not suitable for him, and he
awaited with trepidation the verdict of the audience. From all accounts the audience was courteous, they clapped politely when
they applauded, but the reception was undeniably mixed. The first
and third acts went reasonably well; the second and fourth aroused
no response. Although Puccini was called out several times both
during and after the performance, he realized that the opera was
clearly unsuccessful. In no sense, though, was *Edgar* an utter fiasco;
there had been just enough favorable reaction to half the opera to
deceive Ricordi and Puccini into believing *Edgar* could be salvaged
by revision. This turned out to be a thankless task.

During May 1889 Puccini was engaged in correcting the proofs
of *Edgar*. Ricordi placed the job of making the piano reduction
in the hands of Carlo Carignani (1857-1919), a function he was to
fulfill repeatedly for Puccini over the next twenty years. Carignani
was a *lucchese*, one of Giacomo's companions on the famous walk
to see *Aïda* at Pisa. He had moved to Milan, where he supported
himself chiefly by teaching singing. He made his reductions sometimes from the pencil sketches, sometimes from the autograph full-
score. Tenaglia told me that Puccini said of Carignani: "He knows
my intentions better than I do," a remark to be taken with a large
grain of salt. The piano score of the four-act version of *Edgar* was

27. The *première* of *Edgar* was conducted by Franco Faccio, then in his last
season at La Scala. He died two years later at the Monza insane asylum. The cast
included Aurelia Cataneo-Caruson (1864-91) as Fidelia, Pantaleoni in her second
Puccini role as Tigrana, the Rumanian tenor Gregorio Gabrielesco as Edgar,
Antonio Magini-Coletti (1855-1912) as Frank, and Pio Marini as Gualtiero. On
the whole, the cast fared better with the critics than the music did.

printed by Ricordi's in an edition of just two hundred copies, making it one of the rarest of Puccini's printed scores.

Although during 1889 Puccini began to work on his next opera, *Manon Lescaut*, that in no way meant he had given up hopes for *Edgar*. The indecisive *première* of *Edgar*, which achieved a run of just three performances, produced a crisis for Puccini. At a meeting of the board at Casa Ricordi many protests were made against Puccini as a bad investment, and it was claimed that the 200 lire a month paid him was so much wasted money. Giulio Ricordi argued with his board, alone maintaining his faith in Puccini's promise and forcing them to agree to continue Puccini's allowance until his next opera was produced. Then if things did not improve, well—Puccini had better find a new career. Ricordi's persuasiveness was well founded on the fact that the firm was practically a family business in those days, but Giacomo had a champion when he needed one most. As a gesture of faith in his protégé, Ricordi sent Puccini, in the company of Faccio and the stage designer Hohenstein to Bayreuth in August 1889 to see *Die Meistersinger*.[28]

During the last months of 1889, Puccini worried over the libretto for *Manon Lescaut* and made frantic efforts to revise *Edgar* in hopes of a second La Scala production for the season of 1889-90. Puccini's changes did not yet include reducing the opera from four acts to three. Although *Edgar* had been announced again at La Scala, Puccini's hopes collapsed when the dramatic tenor de Negri,[29] who was to have sung the role of Edgar, fell ill and had to cancel the balance of his season at La Scala. There was also talk of *Edgar* for the San Carlo in Naples, but this production did not materialize either. A third proposal to give the hapless *Edgar* that year proved fruitless when the commission of the Teatro Reál in Madrid again turned thumbs down. No wonder Puccini was writing to his brother Michele in South America to see if there were chances for a prosperous future there! Not only was Puccini depressed by this constellation of disappointments, but Ricordi was gravely concerned for his morale. The damage affected both Puc-

28. Ricordi's had acquired the Italian rights to Wagner's works in the fall of 1888, when they bought out the famous publishing house run by Giovannina Lucca. The quality and frequency of Wagnerian performances increased sharply in Italy as a result.
29. Giovanni Battista de Negri (1850-1923) was a serious rival to Tamagno in the early productions of Verdi's *Otello*, so much so that the public of the Teatro Carlo Felice, Genoa, preferred de Negri in the role. He left the stage in 1898.

cini's self-esteem and, more important, his purse, for each of these productions, had they materialized, would have brought the composer two or three thousand lire.

In July 1890 the prospects of *Edgar* at Madrid brightened again, thanks to Mancinelli, prodded by Ricordi, but just when everything seemed moving at last, the production was cancelled. This third disappointment in Madrid turned out to be just a postponement, as Ricordi turned on his full powers of persuasiveness. Madrid finally heard *Edgar* in March 1892, but not before still another round of revisions.

The spring of 1891 was an anxious time for Puccini. He was confronted with the necessity of finding a reasonably permanent home for himself, Elvira, and the children. For some time Elvira and Fosca were in Florence with her married sister Ida, while Giacomo and Antonio stayed in Lucca with his sister Tomaide. Things grew strained. Elvira's sister Ida kept her unnerved with gossip about Giacomo's alleged infidelities, which his daily, fond letters denied; meanwhile, Giacomo's strait-laced sisters filled his ears with their disapproval. During April and May there seems to have been a two-pronged campaign to break up their relationship. Only with the greatest difficulty did they manage a few days together at San Martino, a few miles above Lucca, but when the landlady discovered Elvira was not Giacomo's wife—gossipers saw to it she found this out—she told him firmly she could not tolerate such things beneath her virtuous roof. It was shortly after these harassments that Giacomo made the heaven-sent discovery of Torre del Lago.[30]

Torre del Lago was a remote hamlet in those days, just a handful of houses on the reed-filled shores of Lago di Massaciuccoli. It got its name from the tower of the gatehouse[31] to a villa, built in the middle of the nineteenth century by a Swiss sportsman and acquired near the end of the century by a Signor Orlando, a marine architect in Livorno. For years the lake had belonged to the Minutoli Tegrimi family of Lucca, but in 1887 the hunting rights were acquired by the Marchese Carlo Ginori Lisci. Puccini rented his

---

30. This episode is documented at moving length in George Marek's *Puccini* (New York, 1951), pp. 78-85, but in his concern with Elvira's difficult character, Marek does not give sufficient stress to the relief of their moving to Torre del Lago that summer of 1891.

31. The tower was destroyed by German artillery during World War II; it has not been rebuilt.

first house in Torre del Lago from one of Ginori's gamekeepers.[32] With its plentiful waterfowl and its isolation, Torre del Lago became Puccini's favorite place, one he praised in extravagant terms and was always restless to return to. Part of its attraction for Puccini, though, was that he found it when he needed it so badly.

Moving to Torre del Lago seemed a good omen for Puccini, at least temporarily. One of the first bits of good fortune was the production of *Edgar* at the Teatro Giglio in Lucca.[33] In the fall of 1891 there were thirteen performances to ringing enthusiasm. In a town the size of Lucca then, a run of thirteen performances means that audiences kept coming back to hear the opera again and again. Whatever the gossips of Lucca might say about Puccini as a man, they had capitulated to him as a composer.

These Lucca performances of *Edgar* were the last of that opera in its four-act guise. At Torre del Lago, Puccini revised his score once more, dropping the original ending of Act 3 and replacing it with the final pages of Act 4—the murder of Fidelia by Tigrana. This conversion of the work into a three-act opera entailed discarding the rest of Act 4.[34] The first performance of *Edgar* in its new version took place at Ferrara on 28 February 1892, with Puccini on hand to oversee the production. At Ferrara, *Edgar* earned "a real public success."[35] Buoyed by these two good receptions, Puccini went almost immediately to Madrid, arriving there by 8 March. The situation was discouraging: the chorus and orchestra were listless, and Giuseppina Pasqua found the role of Tigrana uncomfortably high for her low mezzo-soprano. Worst of all, an article appeared in one of the chief newspapers making sport of Fontana's libretto. To add to it all, Puccini fell ill with complications resulting from his chronic troubles with his teeth. When the first performance finally took place, having been postponed for

32. Puccini's first house at Torre del Lago is not the Villa Puccini shown to visitors there. That villa, Puccini's third residence at Torre del Lago, was built with the royalties from *La Bohème* and *Tosca* on the site of Puccini's first house, the so-called Casa Venanzio.

33. At Lucca *Edgar* was performed by the soprano Luisa Gilboni and the tenor Durot. Today the Teatro Giglio is called the Teatro Puccini.

34. One of the passages excised from Act 4 of *Edgar* is familiar in another context. The accompaniment to the duet for Edgar and Fidelia, *Ah, nei tuoi baci*, turns up with a new vocal line as the beginning of the duet, *Amaro sol per te* in Act 3 of *Tosca*. Many of the commentators on Puccini to the contrary, Cavaradossi's *O dolci mani* does not come from the old Act 4 of *Edgar*.

35. Giulio Gatti-Casazza, *Memories of Opera* (New York, 1941), p. 40. The impresario for this season at Ferrara was Gatti-Casazza's father.

four days, even the great Tamagno[36] could not save the performance from a chilly reception.

Although Puccini returned to Italy to lose himself once more in
the composition of *Manon Lescaut*, he had not definitely abandoned *Edgar*. In January 1901 he tinkered with the score again,
and once more in February and March 1905, when he readied it
for his final effort to resuscitate it. This version, which is also that
of Ricordi's current scores, was first given at the Teatro de la Opera
in Buenos Aires, 8 July 1905, conducted by Mugnone.[37] Even the ad-
ditional contribution of Puccini's assistance at rehearsals failed to
breathe life into *Edgar*. After this, he allowed the opera to fade
from the repertory. The next significant performance of music
from the score occurred at Puccini's funeral in the Milan Cathedral
on 3 December 1924, when Toscanini directed the Act 3 Requiem
from *Edgar*, with Hina Spani singing the music of Fidelia.[38]

If the autograph full-score of *Le Villi* presents difficulties, that
of *Edgar* poses greater problems. There are four volumes, one for
each act, partially in a copyist's hand; in addition, there is an autograph score for Act 1 and Act 3. The date of 12 September 1886 is
found at the beginning of Act 1 of the autograph and that of September 1887 at the conclusion of Act 3. A further note, by someone else, reports that on 15 January 1901 the copyist's first three
acts and Act 4 of the autograph were sent to Puccini; a further

36. Francesco Tamagno (1850-1905) was the most spectacular dramatic tenor of his
day. His great fame rests on his having been chosen by Verdi to sing Otello in
the *première* at La Scala, 5 February 1887. The baritone Emilio de Gorgoza described to me the impact of Tamagno's upper register as he heard him sing an
Aida at the old Met. The tremendous projection of Tamagno's tones during the
Triumphal scene made the pince-nez worn by de Gorgoza, who was sitting in the
front row of the orchestra, vibrate perilously as the tenor's voice drowned out all
the other principals (including Nordica) and the chorus!
   Tamagno's companions in the Madrid *Edgar* were Eva Tetrazzini-Campanini
(Fidelia) and Giuseppina Pasqua (Tigrana). (Pasqua (1855-1930) sang Dame
Quickly in the *première* of *Falstaff*.) The performance of *Edgar* was conducted
by Mancinelli.
37. Giovanni Zanatello (1876-1949), another famous Otello, sang Edgar in Buenos
Aires. The year before he had sung Pinkerton in the disastrous *première* of
Butterfly.
38. On 6 April 1967 *Edgar* had one of its rare performances. It was given its
British *première* by the Hammersmith Municipal Opera Company of London,
using the 1905 version. The cast included Angela Rubini (Fidelia), Doreen Doyle
(Tigrana), Edward Byles (Edgar), Michael Rippon (Frank), and Graham
Nicholls (Gualtiero). The conductor was Joseph Vandernoot.

notation, dated 24 January 1905, says that Act 2 of the autograph
score was sent to Puccini. In addition to examining the manuscripts
still at Ricordi's, I have collated two printed scores—that of the
four-act version and that of 1905—with these manuscripts.

A brief description of the general tendency of the changes should
suffice. Primarily, there has been extensive pruning of passages of
various length throughout the score. The music of Tigrana has
undergone the greatest curtailment and a general shift toward
higher pitches, making the role more suitable for a dramatic soprano
than a mezzo. There are, further, extensive changes in the orchestration, frequently thinning the parts, especially those of the brass.[39]
The largest amount of new music is found in Act 2. One of the
new passages, the duet for Edgar and Tigrana, *Dal labbro mio*,
bears a specific date: 3 March 1905. Although *Edgar* can only be
described as the least successful of Puccini's operas, the manuscripts
are pathetic evidence of Puccini's repeated, scrupulous efforts to
salvage the work.

To discuss even briefly the music of *Edgar*, it seems sensible to
talk of the 1905 version, since the piano score of it is readily available and since it is frequently impossible to pinpoint at which of
many possible times Puccini made a particular revision.

In the light of *Edgar*'s reputation as a hopeless failure, listening
to it today makes for quite a surprise, as the score contains some
quite effective music. The Act 3 Requiem is genuinely stirring,
with its free-moving choral parts and atmosphere of deeply felt
emotion. The dramatic situation—Edgar's funeral is a pretense and
he is present in disguise—undercuts the sincerity of the music. The
sure handling of the Requiem reflects Giacomo's early experience
as organist and music student at Lucca, but its point of origin is the
introduction of the *Capriccio sinfonico* of 1883, but here it is
greatly amplified and developed. Fidelia's two short arias later in
Act 3 are eloquent, the inter-relationships of the phrases showing
Puccini's instinct for euphony. The music of Fidelia contains quite
a few florid passages—an uncommon ingredient in Puccini's scores
—yet the coloratura is not written to express coquettishness, like
certain flourishes of Manon and Musetta, but passionate intensity
and exaltation. This example is representative:

39. *Edgar*, unlike *Le Villi*, contains a part marked for the bass trombone.

Fontana's libretto has many defects, but none more serious than its failure to indicate any clear motivation for Edgar's violent impulsiveness.[40] Thus, much of Edgar's music seems bombastic. To this general charge there are two notable exceptions. This first of these is his aria in Act 2, describing his vision of lost innocence. The melody flows freely and expansively with the resilence characteristic of the later Puccini.

The other exception occurs in Act 3 at the point where Edgar, still disguised, taunts Tigrana for her lavish display of grief at the catafalque:

This might be described as the earliest demonstration of Puccini's knack for writing "mocking" music. A better-known example is Marcello's teasing of Benoit in Act 1 of *La Bohème* The ultimate distillation of this tone occurs in the music of Ping, Pang, and Pong in *Turandot*. Significantly, both these passages from *Edgar* Puccini revised in 1905.

The influence of Ponchielli is frequently met in *Edgar*. Some of the propulsive unison passages for the chorus have a blatancy that immediately brings some of Ponchielli's cruder pages to mind.

---

40. This defect also exists to some extent in Musset's play, but certain of the hero's lengthy speeches, ignored by Fontana, indicate this delinquency stems from his lack of belief in traditional social and religious values.

4

The large-scale rhetoric of the big ensemble in Act 1 with its soaring vocal lines shows another aspect of Puccini's debt to his master, (see Ex. 5 from *Edgar*). Still another Ponchiellian device, and one that Puccini was slower to outgrow, is the use of a fortissimo peroration—a loud restatement of familiar melodic material—to end a climactic scene or act. Most composers of the verismo school adopted this device, but its provenance is found in Ponchielli and the first two operas of Puccini. One has only to think of the final pages of *Cavalleria, Pagliacci*, and *Tosca* to find this device that Ponchielli used at the end of Act 3 of *Gioconda* and Puccini used to conclude Act 2 of *Edgar*.

Although the opera begins without a formal prelude,[41] Puccini composed extensive orchestral passages to introduce the second and third acts. These are not descriptive music to accompany action, like the entr'actes to *Le Villi*. Nor do they describe a particular time and place, like the prelude to Act 3 of *Tosca*. Instead, these preludes express general emotional states, quite in the traditional vein of mid-nineteenth-century romantic opera.

Clearly, since the libretto of *Edgar* did not deeply move Puccini, it prevented the release of his powerful lyrical impulse. The characters, with the exception of Fidelia, are crudely drawn and generally unsympathetic. We never see, for instance, how Edgar was first attracted to the over-charged Tigrana; we find him, rather, at almost their first exchange addressing her as "Demonio!" The plot allows for few moments of lyrical expansion, and only rarely for the comparatively leisurely development of individualized emotions, but it is notable that these few moments of lyrical expansion result in the best music of the score. For all its shortcomings, *Edgar* is filled with conscientious, if rarely inspired, craftsmanship. No composer who did not understand his craft could have written *Edgar*.

41. For the Madrid production of 1892 Puccini wrote a 108-bar prelude describing the coming of spring. The unpublished ms. belongs to Maestro Natale Gallini of Milan.

5

FIDELIA
ff
allarg.
Ah!
TIGRANA
sguar - di, ah la man
EDGAR
Di col - - - pe no -
FRANK
portando
- can - to, qual fa - - - sci-no ar -
GUALTIERO
portando
- na - te! d'un vec - - chio la
CHORUS
Soprano
sì, con te ah! sì,
Alto
- tò, sì, con te o - - - gni
Tenor I
- tò, con te o - gni
Tenor II
portando
- tò, con te o - gni
Bass
- tò, ah! sì, o pa - dre, o - gni cuo - re con
8
allarg.

It is important to remember that *Edgar* precedes the *verismo* explosion touched off by *Cavalleria*, that it belongs to the late twilight of the over-exploited tradition of romantic melodrama, the tradition that had brought Verdi to the apex of his prestige. Keeping abreast of the musical tendencies of his day was a lifelong preoccupation with Puccini, and some pallid glimmers of that preoccupation are discernible in *Edgar*. The major musical event in Italy during the years Puccini composed *Edgar* was the *première* of Verdi's *Otello*. The title role of Edgar is written for just the sort of dramatic tenor Verdi requires in *Otello*, and it is no coincidence that Tamagno, de Negri, and Zenatello, all three famous Otellos, played important parts in Puccini's hopes for *Edgar*. Unfortunately, the young Puccini lacked Verdi's mastery of his idiom, and, worse, Fontana was no more a Boito than Musset was Shakespeare!

Manon Lescaut

Edgar had barely been produced before Puccini began his search for a new subject. This time he did not want a text foisted upon him by a Fontana, but one he chose himself, one well adapted to the musical idiom he was coming to recognize as his own. A number of causes prompted Puccini's haste. He had to retain the support of Giulio Ricordi at all costs. At thirty, with Elvira and two growing children to support, Puccini needed the confirmation of an unmixed success to justify his continuing his career.

The first new subject that attracted Puccini was *Tosca*, but six years were to pass before he definitely decided to use it. Many things may have contributed to Puccini's setting it aside in 1889: Sardou may have been reluctant to yield the rights to a composer then unknown outside Italy; in any event, Puccini soon decided the subject was not then the right one for him. And while Puccini was scouting new ideas, Ricordi was not idle. As a collaborator for his young, unproven protégé he turned to the distinguished dramatist Giuseppe Giacosa (1847-1906). Although Giacosa was later to become the co-author of the texts of *Bohème*, *Tosca*, and *Butterfly*, his first connection with Puccini was less fruitful. Giacosa prepared a sketch with a Russian setting, but Puccini found it insufficiently poetic, unattractive, altogether too gloomy. From Chiasso in Switzerland, Puccini wrote to Ricordi on 19 July 1889 to explain his reasons for rejecting Giacosa's scenario. This letter contains two key phrases. The first shows the lesson Puccini had learned from *Edgar:* "Supposing I had to compose an opera I did not *entirely feel?*" The other explains an even more persuasive reason for Puccini's refusal of Giacosa's scheme: "I will have *Manon* in August."[42]

This *Manon* that Puccini expected in August 1889 was a libretto by Ruggiero Leoncavallo (1858-1919) based on Abbé Prévost's novel. At this stage of his career Leoncavallo had not become known as a composer—*I Pagliacci* was still three years in the future. He first came to Ricordi's attention as a writer of libretti. In that guise, he had been put to work to concoct, at Puccini's suggestion, a text of *Manon.* Leoncavallo's connection with this enterprise lasted only a few months, as he and Puccini could not agree on the management of certain key situations.

It is clear that the idea of writing an opera based on the novel began with Puccini, undismayed by the thought of competing with Massenet's earlier *Manon* (1884). Ricordi was bothered by this thought, but Puccini reminded him how often a single subject had spawned multiple operas, adding that particularly an inconstant girl like Manon could serve more than one man. Puccini had first read the novel; apparently he did not see Massenet's score until the libretto for his own opera was already well under way. Once he had seen it, he realigned the acts to make his treatment less like Massenet's.[43]

Undiscouraged by his failure to arrive at a satisfactory plan with Leoncavallo, Puccini turned next to the dramatist Mario Praga,[44] counting on him for solid dramatic construction; for the versifica-

42. In *Letters of Giacomo Puccini,* ed. Giuseppe Adami (Philadelphia, 1931), pp. 71-72.

43. Not until after Puccini's opera had been staged did Massenet's *Manon* have its Italian *première,* which occurred at the Teatro Carcano, Milan, on 19 October 1893. Massenet's opera enjoyed a triumph, thanks to the passionate singing and equally passionate acting of Adele Stehle (1865-1945) as Manon and Edoardo Garbin (1865-1943) as Des Grieux. This pair, who were married shortly after, did Puccini yeoman service in the early rounds of his operas in Italian theaters—most particularly on the occasion of *La Bohème* in Palermo, April 1896. Stehle's place in history is further secure as she sang in the world *premières* of *I Pagliacci* (Nedda) and *Falstaff* (Nanetta).

44. The date of Praga's entry into the arena of *Manon Lescaut* is obscure. Nearly thirty years after the event, he told Adami that he could not remember whether it was in the spring or fall of 1890. The fall of 1889 seems a more likely date, because the project had developed far enough for Puccini to begin orchestrating Act 1 in "March 1890," according to Puccini's own note in the autograph score.

tion, Puccini left the choice of a collaborator to Praga, who at once nominated Domenico Oliva. Praga and Oliva soon came up with a four-act design:

Act 1: the meeting of Des Grieux and Manon
Act 2: the lover's modest apartment
Act 3: Manon living in luxury with Geronte
Act 4: the death of Manon in Louisiana

The second act of this scheme was discarded, probably early in 1891, as too closely resembling Massenet's second act. The decision to drop a whole act from his libretto was more than Praga had looked for. He bowed out of the arrangement, to be followed shortly by Oliva.

As early as June 1890 Puccini had been in despair over this libretto that kept having to be done and redone; in October 1890 Oliva had told Ricordi that he had never dreamed that writing a libretto could be so difficult. Although Puccini had begun to orchestrate the first act in March 1890, the whole project was in such a state of upheaval that he did not complete Act 1 until January 1891.

That Ricordi was able to resist the temptation to throw over the whole project is a credit both to his patience and to his belief in Puccini; it also reflects his decision that the only possible way to retrieve his by now considerable investment in Giacomo was to plow ahead. Accordingly, he drafted Giacosa, a respected member of the literary community, to mediate with Praga and Oliva, who had signed a contract with Ricordi, and Luigi Illica (1857-1919), a newcomer to the ranks.

Illica was an ingenious hothead—he had lost part of an ear in a duel—but he was also an experienced librettist, just then preparing two texts for composers under contract to Ricordi. These were the libretti for Catalani's *La Wally* and Franchetti's *Cristoforo Colombo*.[45] Once Illica began his work on *Manon Lescaut* he revised parts of Praga and Oliva's work and added a whole new scene —the Embarkation (Act 3).[46] By the time the libretto was com-

45. Illica's other chief libretti, besides those he wrote for Puccini include: Franchetti's *Germania*; Mascagni's *Iris*, *Le Maschere*, and *Isabeau*; Giordano's *Andrea Chénier*; Gnecchi's *Cassandra*; and Montemezzi's *Hellera*.
46. Praga's Act 3 (the scene of Manon *chez* Geronte) was changed to Act 2 after the suppression of the scene in the lovers' modest dwelling.

pleted, the end of June 1892, Ricordi, Giacosa, and Puccini himself
had all had a hand in it. With so many writers holding shares in the
libretto, it is small wonder that most of the summer was spent
haggling over rights. Thanks to Giacosa's intervention, the question was settled. It was agreed that no one's name would appear on
the printed libretto. Something bearing the names of all the participants—Leoncavallo, Praga, Oliva, Illica, Giacosa, Ricordi, and
Puccini—would have been a laughing-stock. A libretto that took
three years and seven men[47] to complete is no laughing matter.

Puccini completed *Manon Lescaut* in October 1892. Exceptionally for him, he composed Act 4 before Act 3,[48] an accommodation
on Puccini's part to reassure Ricordi that the score would be finished in time for the *première*.

The *première* took place at the Teatro Regio, Turin, on 1 February 1893. Turin was Ricordi's decision, for he knew that the
stage at La Scala would be busy at that time with the rehearsals
of another new work his firm was bringing out—Verdi's *Falstaff*
(La Scala, 9 February 1893). *Manon Lescaut* won a triumph. The
audience was still shouting enthusiastically long after the final curtain fell. In one night all Puccini's sacrifices for the past decade
were justified.[49]

The critics found much to praise, particularly the effective orchestration and the rich outpouring of melody. They found Puccini's style consistent, his sense of the theater irresistible. Every

47. Eventually there were eight. In November 1922 Puccini asked Adami to
supply a line to replace one of the textual repetitions in Manon's Act 4 aria.
48. The terminology of the acts as known today was decided after the autograph
was completed. There, the Geronte scene and the Embarkation are identified,
respectively, as Act 2, part 1, and Act 2, part 2. They were joined by the intermezzo (which seems more logical in this discarded context than the present one).
   Why did Puccini decide to divide these scenes into separate acts? Probably because he felt the total playing time—65 minutes—was more than an Italian
audience of 1893 could endure. Eleven years later at the *première* of *Butterfly*,
Puccini grievously overestimated the audience's tolerance by asking them to remain in their seats an hour and a half.
49. The *première* of *Manon Lescaut* was conducted by Alessandro Pomé. The
title role was sung by Cesira Ferrani (1863-1943), a native of Turin and a great
favorite there; she was also to be the first Mimì in *La Bohème*, but not before she
had introduced her Manon to Rome and Buenos Aires, singing that role almost
300 times in the course of her career. Others in the cast were: Giuseppe Cremonini (Des Grieux), Achille Moro (Lescaut), Alessandro Polonini (Geronte),
Elvira Ceresoli, who later became an outstanding Ortrud (the Singer), and Roberto Ramini (in the three roles of Edmondo, the Ballet Master, and the Lamp-
lighter).

one clearly recognized the appearance of a major figure upon the musical scene.

As Puccini took bow after bow from the stage, he knew his star had risen. And not a minute too soon. In the years between his first appearance as an operatic composer with *Le Villi* and the night of the *première* of *Manon Lescaut*, no fewer than three major rivals had won the favor of the public. Mascagni's *Cavalleria Rusticana* (1890), Leoncavallo's *I Pagliacci* (1892), and Franchetti's *Cristoforo Colombo* (1892) seemed to offer formidable competition. Although Puccini had started the race for fame before any of them, recognition came to him last. A number of years would pass before he outstripped them.

As might be expected, considering its mixed parentage, the *Manon Lescaut* libretto presents some problems. Its chief defect is the gap between Acts 1 and 2, caused by dropping out Praga's scene of Des Grieux and Manon in their unpretentious house;[50] with that scene dropped, the audience sees Manon run off with one man in Act 1, and the Act 2 curtain rises to show her the bored mistress of another man—the same man who was prevented from abducting her in Act 1! The lack of continuity between the last two acts is almost as obvious. At the end of Act 3 the lovers are tearfully reunited on board ship, and at the beginning of Act 4 they are seen lost and dying of thirst in the interminable "desert" of Louisiana!

Besides this looseness of structure, the characterization offers problems. The character of Lescaut, in particular, seems inconsistent. In Act 1 his avarice permits him to encourage Geronte in his design to kidnap Manon, Lescaut's own sister,[51] and in the opening of Act 2 he tells Manon that he has made friends with Des Grieux and is teaching him to gamble so that her former lover can win her back and support her in style. Really, all this is not as inconsistent as it sounds. Lescaut is avaricious, but he has a soft heart; in fact his character much resembles that of his sister Manon. Such unity of action as *Manon Lescaut* possesses is decidedly implicit ra-

50. Puccini was well aware of the difficulty. Early in his collaboration with Illica, probably in the spring of 1891, Puccini suggested a garden scene, "a vision of *freshness* and *profuse blossoms*," where Manon and Des Grieux "would play like two children in love." "But," he adds, "the finale would present difficulties."
51. In Massenet's *Manon*, Manon and Lescaut are cousins.

ther than explicit, but this shortcoming of the libretto seems no deterrent to audiences who applaud the opera in the theater.

These weaknesses aside, there is considerable merit to the libretto of *Manon Lescaut*, particularly when it is compared with the bombast of *Edgar*. For the first time in a Puccini opera, the characters express personal feelings in individual terms. They do not discuss abstract emotions, like the father in *Le Villi* or like Edgar.

Each act is constructed of little details that build up a strong sense of time and place. Most of these are Illica's contribution, since he knew how to apply naturalistic techniques to any period or level of society. Consider the scene of Manon's elaborate toilette near the beginning of Act 2; here the artificial atmosphere is established by the mention of curls, powder, white for the eyelids, jonquil perfume, and beauty-spots. Illica builds up details to create a very different effect in Act 3. The sergeant calls out the roll of prostitutes sentenced to deportation—Rosetta, Madelon, Manon, Ninetta, Caton, Regina, Claretta, Elisa, Giorgetta. As they cross the stage to the waiting ship, their individual demeanor is described in the stage-directions; and as they pass, the chorus comments half-mockingly, half-sympathetically on the spectacle. This scene adds a sociological dimension to Manon's fate. We see her not as an abstract type, but as part of a world made up of bravado, wantonness, suffering, and despair. The embarkation scene with its highly individual use of the chorus is one of the most original in opera.

For all the powerful effect of Act 3, Act 4 represents a miscalculation. Designed by Praga, it ill serves his reputation as a dramatist. Des Grieux and Manon in bad shape straggle in, they despair, Des Grieux goes off to search for water, Manon realizes she is going to die and doesn't want to, Des Grieux returns without water, Manon dies. Bluntly put, that's all there is to it. There is a single mood, a single color, no spectacle to engage the eye, no contrast.

Some of the blame for the monotony of the scene is Puccini's. He had the right to demand changes in the libretto, but he was satisfied with it as it was. He may have been too involved with all the troubles with the libretto; he may have been too pressed for time, since Ricordi was adamant about the date for the *première*. It is, after all, Puccini's first full-scale death scene;[52] he had yet to

---

52. Anna in *Le Villi* dies offstage; Fidelia in *Edgar* is stabbed by Tigrana and dies immediately, without uttering one syllable.

find the possible limits for scenes of unrelieved pathos. The problem really lies in the characters of Manon and Des Grieux. They are not complex enough to be truly tragic. For all their charm, they are both weak and impulsive. Their sufferings are real enough, but they do not awe us.

Later, Puccini became aware of the problem and tried to do something about it. From the already short act,[53] he cut Manon's aria, *Sola, perduta, abbandonata*,[54] believing that amputation would improve things by getting them over sooner. But then Puccini came to realize that omitting this aria made the act *seem* longer, as the suppression of the aria intensified the monotony by removing a vocal and emotional climax. For the famous thirtieth anniversary production of *Manon Lescaut* at La Scala, conducted by Toscanini during the 1922-23 season, Puccini insisted on reinserting the aria, having retouched it and added a new ending.[55] The Manon of that emotional occasion, Juanita Caracciolo (1890-1924), made a deep impression with her singing of the aria.[56]

There is no doubt that the merits of the libretto of *Manon Lescaut* far outweigh its shortcomings. Following the revelation that was Boito's magnificent libretto for Verdi's *Otello*, it was at long last generally recognized that a successful opera had to have a well-constructed libretto of some literary merit. The day of the literary hack who manipulated outworn conventions and debased clichés to jerrybuild a libretto was over. For 1893, the libretto of *Manon Lescaut* is a superior product.

If the libretto of *Manon Lescaut* is a clear improvement over Fontana's gallimaufry for *Edgar*, so is Puccini's score a long step in

53. According to Luigi Ricci's *Puccini interprete di se stesso* (Milan, 1954), the composer's timing for Act 4 of *Manon Lescaut* was 18 minutes.
54. For a number of years this aria was omitted from the printed scores, but it was restored about 1923.
55. Those who like to jeer at Puccini draw the snide conclusion from these later alterations to his scores that his motives were less artistic than mercenary: a move to extend the duration of his copyrights. Such a conclusion is grossly unfair to Puccini, a conscientious craftsman who revised his operas on the basis of frequent experience of them *in* the theater. Besides, in Italy, his changes would not affect the copyright, which runs for 50 years after a composer's death. This charge has as little validity as the once familiar one that Puccini wrote arias to fit the dimensions of the 78 RPM phonograph disc. Since the phonograph did not become more than a curiosity until after Puccini had composed *Butterfly*, this charge has no merit.
56. Juanita Caracciolo did not live long to enjoy her triumph. When the anniversary edition of *Manon Lescaut* was repeated the following season, she was already mortally ill, and the role of Manon was taken by Gilda della Rizza.

advance of his last attempt. Even a casual listener finds the ingratiating melody, the many-hued orchestral palette, the rhythmic
clarity, and the harmonic suavity characteristic of Puccini. A closer
look reveals that for all the torrent of musical ideas—and not until
Turandot is there a comparable lavishness—there are some things
that show Puccini's hand had yet to gain complete suppleness.

Unlike the late operas, *Manon Lescaut* seems to be written in
terms of larger units, rather as though Puccini was constructing in
terms of large-scale "numbers" but mortising the sections without
any gaps of old-fashioned recitative. These larger units where Puccini sticks to a single tonality, tempo, and rhythmic pattern are
particularly obvious in Act 1. The A major *Allegro brillante* in
3/4 that opens the opera continues for over 100 measures; in fact,
the 3/4 meter, except for an occasional isolated bar of 4/4, goes on
right up to the entrance of Manon, or for more than 300 measures.
Later in Act 1, Puccini adheres to a 3/8 meter, with only one brief
interruption, for nearly 500 measures. G. B. Shaw in his review of
the London *première* of *Manon Lescaut* (1894) makes some interesting observations about the structure of Act 1.

> . . . The first act . . . is also unmistakeably symphonic in
> its treatment. There is genuine symphonic modification, de-
> velopment, and occasionally combination of the thematic
> material, all in a dramatic way, but also in a musically
> homogeneous way. . . .[57]

When I examined the autograph score of *Manon Lescaut*, I was
forcibly reminded of Shaw's comment when I saw one page (the
beginning of section 37 in Act 1) with the heading: *Scherzo!* Puccini's use of this term suggests he had some notion of symphonic
structure in mind. Although the opening *Allegro* of the act might
be seen as a first movement and the meeting of the lovers followed
by Des Grieux's aria as a sort of slow movement, the whole first
act of *Manon Lescaut* cannot be taken as a four-, five-, or six-
movement symphony. The real point is that the bulky units com-
prising Act 1, however one chooses to describe its structure, make
it a bit static, lacking in the quicksilver variety and economy found
in *La Bohème*.

For all its revelation of Puccini's sure way with blending and
modifying orchestral tints, *Manon Lescaut*, much of it at least, is

57. Bernard Shaw, *Music in London 1890-94* (London, 1950), III, 219.

scored with a heavy hand. (Yet, *Manon Lescaut* is less noisy than Edgar!) Admittedly his hand was eager and impetuous, but undeniably heavy. For those who sing the roles of Manon and Des Grieux the chief problem is not the *tessitura* (that part of a vocal range emphasized in a particular role), although this presents a few tricky moments, but the difficulty of projecting clearly at times over the tumult in the pit. Although the orchestration is heavy in the current version of the opera, it was still heavier in the original version.

In 1910 Puccini went to Paris, where the Metropolitan was playing a season at the Théâtre du Châtelet, to consult with Gatti-Casazza and Toscanini about the forthcoming *première* of *La Fanciulla del West* in New York. He was able to combine future plans with a review of his past by attending the performance of *Manon Lescaut* on 9 July, which introduced his opera to Paris and Lucrezia Bori to the Metropolitan's ranks.[58] Toscanini, who conducted *Manon Lescaut*, had on his own volition lightened the orchestration in certain places to achieve better balance and improved audibility for the cast. These modifications he showed to Puccini and won his agreement to these practical suggestions. Later, at the time of the thirtieth anniversary production at La Scala, Toscanini suggested still further changes. All these were incorporated into the new edition of the opera published by Ricordi to coincide with the anniversary.

Although *Manon Lescaut* shows us where Puccini's hand is still lacking in its later cunning, there are some things he already could do very well. One of the attributes shared by the great masters of the musical theater is the ability to make, when desirable, almost instantaneous transitions from one color or mood to that of the next episode. Mozart's finales afford prime examples of this art, as do the scores of Wagner and the later Verdi. In the operas of Massenet, on the other hand, one episode is frequently separated from another by rests, producing this monotonous effect: one section ends—pause—the next begins. Two examples of Puccini's skill-

58. Bori (1887-1960) was not Puccini's original choice for role of Manon; he wanted Lina Cavalieri (1874-1944), remembering the effect she produced in the role in New York in 1907, but in the intervening years Cavalieri had made herself *persona non grata* with powerful figures at the Metropolitan. Bori was suggested as a replacement (*Manon Lescaut* had not been sung in New York the previous winter); she came from Italy and made a profound impression. Her New York debut was delayed until the fall of 1912, as she had prior engagements at La Scala. But it was *Manon Lescaut* that finally introduced her to the United States.

ful handling of transitions in his later operas are found following the septet that concludes Musetta's Waltz (*La Bohème*, Act 2) and following Calaf's *Nessun dorma* (*Turandot*, Act 3).

In *Manon Lescaut* a particularly effective transition occurs in Act 1 shortly before Des Grieux and Manon escape together. They sing a love duet, then the half-drunken Lescaut creates a disturbance, knocking on the table and shouting for wine. The lovers' duet is an expansive 9/8 melody in the key of B-flat which merges directly into an *Allegro* 3/8 in the relative minor.

I

As the tonic B-flat forms the minor third of the new key, the atmosphere shifts from one of warm ardor to one of surly agitation. The contrast of rhythm and harmony in these adjacent episodes is reinforced by the change from the lovers' long phrases to Lescaut's terse ones. The lush orchestration of the duet is followed by a staccato figure for the bassoon, illustrating Lescaut's pounding on the table.

Another striking transition is found in Act 3. As Des Grieux leaves the window of Manon's prison cell, their love theme (Example 6) sounds in the winds, horns, and strings. The melody is stated in full in G-flat major, the added trombones and trumpets underlining the climactic phrases. But instead of the final chord, a pistol shot rings out, coinciding with the beginning of a passage in an alien key (E minor). The pistol shot gives the alarm that foils Lescaut's plan to smuggle Manon out of prison.

2

For most listeners *Manon Lescaut* resembles the later Puccini operas because it contains examples of those short arias whose compelling melodies move with apparent freedom and abandon.[59] Although most of the melodic material of Des Grieux's *Donna non vidi mai* has been heard shortly before, but in a less brilliant key, with a different and less conspicuous melodic line, and much more discreetly orchestrated, the aria seems a spontaneous outburst of emotion.

3

59. Although the arias for Roberto and Anna in *Le Villi* have many forward-looking touches about their melodies, they are both strophic in form, an essentially static effect rarely used by the later Puccini. Magda's *Che il bel sogno di Doretta* (*La Rondine*, Act 1) is an instance, but here she is singing a strophic poem written by Prunier. Dick Johnson's *Ch'ella mi creda* (*La Fanciulla*, Act 3) is in two similar but subtly varied stanzas, as a glance in the score will prove.

Yet the aria has a clearly discernible structure. Just thirty measures long, it consists of three similar but not identical parts, each ending with a reminiscence of Manon's self-introduction (Example 7), and it concludes with three measures that form a sort of coda. The main flow of the melody is in the orchestra, although the voice frequently doubles it, often in asymetrical phrases. This aria has a tight organization, but the apparent freedom of the vocal line makes it seem spontaneous.

Another aria pattern is found in Manon's *In quelle trine morbide* (Act 2).

4

MANON

In quel-le tri-ne mor-bi-de nel-l'al - co - va do - ra - ta

This aria is 32 bars in length and is clearly divided into two halves: the first in E-flat 4/4 is Manon's response to her present situation with Geronte; the last in G-flat 2/4 is Manon's nostalgia for her liaison with Des Grieux. The shift of key is prepared for at the ninth measure when the original melody recurs without any preparatory modulation in G-flat. This transposition is psychologically sound: she begins to contrast the chilling present with the warmth of the past. In this aria the phrase lengths are more regular and balanced than those in Des Grieux's *Donna non vidi mai,* but Puccini creates the effect of spontaneity by shifts in tonality and in scoring. At the outset the voice is accompanied by syncopated chords, delicately scored for flutes, clarinets, and bassoon;[60] the strings enter to double the voice at the ninth bar, incidentally helping the soprano negotiate the unprepared modulation to G-flat. At the beginning of the second half, a melody is played by the piccolo and oboe in octaves, while the voice part is a succession of repeated D-flats. The last bars are sparsely accompanied by the strings, the vocal line ending on the note of the dominant.[61]

60. The soprano's unaccompanied attack on the first note of this aria can sometimes yield surprising results!
61. Ending a melody on the note of the dominant was a favorite device with Puccini. See the final phrases of *Che gelida manina, E lucevan le stelle,* and the *Butterfly* love duet. On the other hand, Calaf's *Nessun dorma* ends on the dominant of the dominant.

As far as their length and relative complexity go, the ensembles of *Manon Lescaut* set a standard that Puccini did not approach again for nearly twenty years. The ensembles in Acts 1 and 3 show a surety of construction and a unity of effectiveness that clearly surpass the efforts in this line by composers like Mascagni. In his next three operas Puccini wrote shorter and shorter ensemble passages; it was not until *La Fanciulla del West* that Puccini began to reassert his technical resourcefulness in this sphere.

The most distinctive aspect of *Manon Lescaut*, viewed against Puccini's total output, is the large number of melodies he uses thematically; that is, he repeats them, in whole or in part, at later points in the score to re-evoke a character, situation, or emotion. Furthermore, he employs considerable ingenuity in developing these evocative melodic scraps. This practice gives this opera an uncommon richness of "musical"—as opposed to "instrumental"— texture. Consider these examples. When Des Grieux first alludes to Manon's name in *Donna non vidi mai*, the orchestra follows his allusion with these notes:

5

This is the melodic germ from which develops Des Grieux's affirmation that his destiny is unalterably joined to Manon's.[62]

6

It would be unwise to assume that because Puccini introduces this melody and later presents it in its complete form that he is a leit-motivist of the Wagnerian type. Puccini's practice indicates

62. Manon also sings the melodic germ of this idea in the fifteenth bar of *In quelle trine*.

that melodic ideas are associated in his mind with verbal and dramatic cues rather than with abstract emotional states and that he preferred to plant the germinal idea in the listener's consciousness before he established its full significance. As a typically Italian composer and a pragmatic man of the theater, Puccini would not expect his audience to engage in the Wagnerian pastime of motive-snooping.

The most successful of Puccini's thematic ideas, the one he makes the most ingenious use of, is Manon's phrase of self-introduction.

7

This musical idea first appears in a more prominent context than does Example 5; these words are the first uttered by the prima donna and include the name of the character she is representing, which also happens to be the title of the opera. (Even an audience that understands precious little Italian can be counted on to grasp its significance.) To further establish this phrase, Puccini quotes it in Des Grieux's aria; indeed that whole aria is a passionate meditation upon it, making *Donna non vidi mai* a sort of tenor counterpart to *Caro nome*.

Example 7 recurs in many later guises. Many of these feature the first interval, which is sometimes heard as a major second, sometimes as a minor second. In Act 2 when Lescaut tells Manon of Des Grieux's reaction to her disappearance, Example 7 returns in its shortened form.

8

The effect is that of Des Grieux anxiously calling Manon's name, but as reported in Lescaut's ironical accents.

Later in Act 2 the theme returns in a much expanded form and produces now a lighthearted effect.

Laughing, Manon mistakenly believes she has taunted Geronte out of her life forever, unaware that he plans to have her arrested. A few pages later we hear an important variant of Manon's theme as she begs Des Grieux to forgive her thoughtlessness.

That this is properly a variant of Manon's theme and not a new musical idea is shown by the tell-tale descending second and by the situation: Manon is really trying to be a different, a more serious person at this moment. This variant, in amplified form, recurs with great prominence in the intermezzo and again in Act 4. The most telling use of Manon's theme opens that act.

Here the first two notes of the theme cast as minor chords become a dirge, a grief-stricken utterance of Manon's name. At the close of the opera the same sequence recurs to serve as her epitaph, revealing Puccini's nice sense of dramatic unity.

To some extent, Puccini's use of recurring themes may be a by-product of his Bayreuth trip of 1889. It should be clear, though, that Puccini's use of thematic material rarely approaches Wagner's symphonic treatment of his leit-motives. Much more clearly imitative of Wagner are certain passages from the Act 2 love duet and the intermezzo of *Manon Lescaut*, where the chromatic restlessness and sequential structure inevitably suggest *Tristan*,[63] a resemblance that Puccini himself alluded to in a letter to Illica written in October 1892 (when the score of *Manon Lescaut* was nearly completed). After talking about some details of the love duet, Puccini says: "After that, make the small rebuke as little emphatic and as short as possible so as to come to the end of the duo. To do this would make the success of the piece possible; if not, it becomes the duet from *Tristan*."

The following phrases illustrate Puccini's *Tristan*-izing:

12

Considered in its place in Puccini's development, *Manon Lescaut* is a major achievement. While the opera contains some problems of structure and an occasional awkwardness that the more experienced Puccini learned to avoid, its greatest strength lies in the frequent glimpses it affords of a composer who can express highly dramatic situations with passionate intensity. The embarkation

63. It is not clear when Puccini first encountered *Tristan*. Its much-publicized Italian *première* (sung to a translation by Boito) occurred at Bologna, 2 June 1888. The Isotta was Aurelia Cataneo-Caruson, whom Puccini knew from her singing in *Le Villi* at La Scala. It is possible that Puccini's familiarity with *Tristan* was based not merely upon study of the score, but upon attending an actual performance.

scene, in particular, contains real originality of design; not many composers can cap an effective ensemble with a tenor aria.

In his score Puccini used some pieces of music he had originally written for other contexts. The Madrigal in Act 2 comes, incredibly enough, from the *Agnus Dei* of a Mass composed in 1880. Some details of the minuet Manon dances with Geronte in Act 2 have their source in Two Minuets for String Quartet that Puccini wrote about this time. *Crisantemi*, an elegy Puccini composed on the death of Duke Amadeo d'Aosta (18 January 1890), supplied material for the scene between Manon and Des Grieux at the prison window (Act 3) and for the death scene.

The autograph score of *Manon Lescaut* differs from the modern version in a good many details, but there is one major difference—the finale to Act 1. The original ensemble was quite a bit less complex and longer than the present one. The idea of altering this finale came originally not from Puccini but from Illica, who in October 1893 suggested replacing the old finale with something between Lescaut and Geronte that would better prepare the audience for the situation at the rise of the curtain in Act 2.[64] Rather cautiously Ricordi agreed to the suggestion, and as soon as Puccini returned from Hamburg (where he had gone to stage *Le Villi*), he inserted a new passage for Lescaut and Geronte, concluding with a new ensemble for Edmondo and the chorus (a reprise of Des Grieux's *Tra voi belle*) a matter of about eighty measures. This new ending to Act 1 was first performed at La Scala, 7 February 1894, when *Manon Lescaut* was given there for the first time.[65]

The autographs show a few other changes. *Tra voi belle* is now first heard in F; Puccini wrote it out in the autograph in F-sharp—a key-signature he rarely used. The Act 1 love duet for Manon and Des Grieux, *Vedete? Io son fedele*, gave Puccini a great deal of

---

64. Illica's concern was prompted by the Italian *première* of Massenet's *Manon*, and he was anxious to strengthen Puccini's opera to withstand the inevitable rivalry between the two works.

65. At La Scala, *Manon Lescaut* was first sung by Olga Olghina, Cremonini (the original Des Grieux), Tieste Wilmant (Lescaut), and Vittorio Arimondi (Geronte). The opera was so successful that it was performed nineteen times.

Olghina also created Manon in London. Shaw describes her in these terms: "A clever Russian lady with chiseled features and a somewhat courtly fastidiousness of manner, just a little too ladylike for Manon. . . ." Shaw, *Music in London 1890-94*, III, 223.

difficulty; he has glued pages together—always an indication of suppressed material—and changed things around a good deal. At the close of the duet, he cut out twenty pages of the autograph and indicated the music he inserted is "Nuovo," written emphatically in red.

Puccini made some changes after the first printed scores appeared in 1893. He made a two-bar alteration in Manon's line in her duet with Lescaut (Act 2). He added two bars near the end of Manon's pastoral arietta, *L'ora, o Tirsi,* and cut eight bars after it, just before Geronte's phrase "Galanteria sta bene." When he reinserted Manon's last-act aria in 1922, he omitted part of the stage direction that used to precede it. After Des Grieux's exit, Manon was to fall at full-length, backwards, her head upstage, and in this position utter the first words of the aria.[66]

The over-all appearance of the autograph of *Manon Lescaut* suggests that Puccini encountered no more difficulty with composing this music than he would with *La Bohème* or *Tosca.* Looking at it, one can see something of the emotional heat the music generated for the composer as his penstrokes become broader and more violent in such highly charged passages as the Act 2 love duet.

Although *Manon Lescaut* enjoyed a great success from the first in Italy, it took longer for the opera to make its way in other countries. Its London *première* took place on 14 May 1894 at Covent Garden, with Puccini present for the occasion.[67] Earning polite applause and a good review from Bernard Shaw were not enough to save the opera from the ignominy of just one further performance before being put aside for ten years. Shaw's discussion, dated 23 May 1894, surveys recent performances of *Cavalleria* and *I Pagliacci* as well as Puccini's opera and brings Shaw to two conclusions: "Italian opera has been born again" and "Puccini looks to me more like the heir of Verdi than any of his rivals."[68] In spite of Shaw's enthusiasm, the management of Covent Garden was so unimpressed with *Manon Lescaut* that they refused *La Bohème* when Ricordi's offered them the English *première* three years later.

Manon Lescaut was introduced to the United States in 1894 by a

66. This stunt anticipates Maria Jeritza's famous business of singing *Vissi d'arte* lying on her stomach.
67. Besides Olghina, the cast included Umberto Beduschi as Des Grieux and Antonio Pini-Corsi (1858-1918) as Lescaut.
68. Shaw, *Music in London 1890-94,* III, 217-24.

traveling Italian company, but it did not really establish itself in
North America until it entered the Metropolitan repertory on 18
January 1907, sung by Lina Cavalieri, Caruso, and Scotti. Puccini
was present on that occasion and reported that Cavalieri sang very
well indeed. The Metropolitan was also responsible for introducing
the opera to Paris in 1910. Puccini was present again, and much
impressed by Bori, the Manon. Although *Manon Lescaut* had its
Viennese *première* in 1908, the opera did not make a real hit there
until 1923, when as a sort of a pendant to the La Scala anniversary
production, it was sung by Lotte Lehmann and Alfred Piccaver.
Again Puccini was on hand. He reported that Lehmann was deficient in coquetry in Act 2, but magnificent in Act 4.

Surely, few composers were to oversee the musical and theatrical
details of new productions of their operas with more persistent care
and attention than Puccini.

2

THE BIG THREE

La Bohème, Tosca, Madama Butterfly

For his first five operas Puccini had little difficulty finding subjects. With one work finished and in performance, he would soon be working with his librettists on the next. Later, he was to experience considerable difficulty and frustration in finding subjects that suited him, but this was certainly not the case with *La Bohème*. He claimed he had worked seriously on the projected opera ever since the first performances of *Manon Lescaut*, adding that he had made no mystery of his plans. These remarks, published in the *Corriere della sera* of 20 March 1893, were occasioned by his discovery during a casual conversation with Leoncavallo that the composer of *I Pagliacci* had also started writing an opera *La Bohème*, both libretto and music.[1] Puccini's attitude on this coincidence was unembarrassed. "Let him compose, I will compose, the public will judge." A letter from Giacosa to the librettist Illica, dated 22 March 1893, backs up Puccini's claim: in it he acknowledges the receipt of Illica's prose sketch for *La Bohème*.

Leoncavallo's answer to Puccini's challenge was to urge the precedence of his project. In his turn, he claimed he had been engaged on it since the previous December, adding that during the rehearsals

1. Leoncavallo was his own librettist for *I Pagliacci* (1892), *I Medici* (1893), *Chatterton* (1896), *La Bohème* (1897), *Zazà* (1900), and *Der Roland von Berlin* (1904). He used the words of others for *Maia* (1910), *Gli zingari* (1912), and *Edipo Re* (1920).

for the world *première* of Verdi's *Falstaff* he had discussed with the baritone Maurel the possibility of his creating the role of Schaunard.[2] In the light of the subsequent history of the two *La Bohème*'s the question of precedence is unimportant. Puccini's version apeared more than a year before Leoncavallo's (first given in Venice, 6 May 1897) and has proven itself one of the most popular operas ever written. Leoncavallo's *La Bohème*, even though many pages have considerable charm and buoyancy, has never enjoyed more than an occasional revival. Suffice it to say, the relationship between these former friends deteriorated sharply: on Puccini's part to contempt; on Leoncavallo's to open hostility.

More important than the question of precedence, the possibility of a rival *La Bohème* stimulated Puccini—at least after July 1894, when Puccini got seriously to work upon it. The rivalry increasingly appealed to his sportsman's instincts. Too, Leoncavallo's choice of the same subject seemed a confirmation of Puccini's belief in its possibilities, much as the thought of Massenet's *Manon* had attracted him to that subject rather than deterring him.

It would be a mistake, though, to imagine that either composer's thoughts during the next three years were given exclusively to *La Bohème*. Leoncavallo, no less than his publishers (Sonzogno), was eager to consolidate the enormous success of *I Pagliacci*. On 10 November 1893, he brought out the first part of a proposed Renaissance trilogy, *I Medici*, at the Dal Verme in Milan. It was a disaster.[3] On 10 March 1896, just five weeks after the first performance of Puccini's *La Bohème*, Leoncavallo hastily introduced his *Chatterton*, which, like *I Medici*, he had composed before *I Pagliacci*. *Chatterton*, too, left the public sitting on its hands. Its production was an ill-considered attempt on the part of Leoncavallo and his publishers to counteract all the publicity Puccini was receiving in those days.

For his part, Puccini was unable to really settle down to his new

2. Victor Maurel (1848-1923) not only created the title role of *Falstaff*, but also Tonio in *I Pagliacci*. Leoncavallo's suggestion of Maurel for Schaunard seems odd, since Rodolfo—not Schaunard—is the leading baritone role in Leoncavallo's *La Bohème*, and suggests that Puccini's rival for all his talk of December had not proceeded very far with his project.
3. It proved a double disaster, since Kaiser Wilhelm II, hearing the Milanese production, formed a contrary opinion to that of the public and press and commissioned Leoncavallo to compose an opera glorifying the Hohenzollerns. *Der Roland von Berlin* did not appear until 1904; after a torrent of premature eulogies, it proved a resounding failure.

opera for more than a year after his challenge in the *Corriere della sera.* During the rest of 1893 and the first half of 1894 much of his time was taken up with traveling to supervise production of his operas in various operatic centers, among them London, Vienna, and Hamburg. For a time he even toyed with putting by *La Bohème* for something else, to the point of going to Sicily to consult with Giovanni Verga about *La Lupa*, a play of his then still unproduced.[4] On his return from Sicily, Puccini wrote to Giulio Ricordi that he was unimpressed with Verga's play; it was too full of talk and, more significantly, lacked "a single *luminous* figure who dominates the action." The significance of this remark comes clear when he goes on in the same letter—dated 13 July 1894—to announce his resolve to resume work on *La Bohème*. To think of Mimì, particularly at that moment in Act 1 when she stands in a nimbus of moonlight, is to understand that Puccini came to see in her precisely the luminous figure he was seeking. Certainly his discovery of the sort of character his creative imagination demanded is a far more valid reason for Puccini's taking up this subject than the thought that Leoncavallo was also working on it.

The writing of the libretto for *La Bohème* was entrusted to Giuseppe Giacosa and Luigi Illica. Their efforts, both diplomatic and literary, had contributed so signally to the success of *Manon Lescaut* that both Ricordi and Puccini embraced them as the ideal collaborators for the composer. Their working relationship, despite some alarming ups and downs, was to endure for another decade.

In this, their first work from the beginning for Puccini, Illica's responsibility was to make the prose sketches, while Giacosa was to produce the verses. Illica's original scenario is derived both from Henry Mürger's episodic novel, *Scènes de la vie de Bohème,* and from the five-act play, *La Vie de Bohème,* that Mürger wrote in collaboration with Théodore Barrière. Illica's original plan was as follows:

Act 1, scene 1: the garret
Act 1, scene 2: the Café Momus

4. As Verga (1840-1922) had written the story and play that are the source of *Cavalleria Rusticana,* Puccini's interest in *La Lupa* indicates a desire to work in the *verismo* vein.

Act 2: the Barrière d'Enfer
Act 3: the courtyard of the house where Musetta lives
Act 4: the garret

In the final arrangement the two scenes of the first act became Acts
1 and 2; the Barrière d'Enfer became Act 3; the scene in the courtyard was eliminated at Puccini's insistence and over Illica's outraged
protests. The text of the excised scene survives.[5] The episode adds
little to the action save the spectacle of Mimì in a fancy dress bor-
rowed from Musetta, dancing with a student, the Viscontino Paolo.
An equivalent to this courtyard scene is found in Leoncavallo's *La
Bohème*.

Prior to his fruitless visit to Sicily, Puccini had insisted upon
numerous changes to the libretto, among them the dropping of the
courtyard scene, but it was not until after his return that he really
settled down to work, that he began to exact detailed modifications,
much to the annoyance of Giacosa and Illica, who had hoped that
most of their problems were settled. Passages from the correspondence published in *Carteggi Pucciniani* give clues to the nature of
the changes in the libretto and to the points of particular difficulty.
Act 1 used to begin rather differently—originally it was Marcello
who entered with the food and money, not Schaunard as it became
—and, in its original shorter form, Act 1 contained no aria for the
tenor, no *Che gelida manina!* It was not until April 1894 that
Rodolfo's and Mimì's autobiographical arias took shape. For Act 2,
Puccini had a very different view of Musetta's character than that
sketched by Illica, and it was only after considerable turmoil that
Puccini's conception prevailed. Act 3 once began with some comic
episodes, but these were later discarded.

The greatest problems came with the last act. At one point Puccini envisioned it beginning with Mimì in bed, while Rodolfo wrote
at his desk, a plan that Illica successfully argued against because it
produced the impression that Rodolfo and Mimì had never parted.
As a substitute opening to Act 4, Illica suggested having the curtain
come up on Rodolfo alone, staring out the window as a gust of
autumn wind blows a letter into his hand, reminding him of Mimì
and providing a cue for an aria. This is more like, but less effective

5. The Italian text was printed in the periodical *La Scala* (December 1958). The
whole issue of December 1958 is devoted to Puccini in commemoration of the
centennial of his birth. An English version of the excised courtyard scene appeared in *Opera News* (4 February 1967).

than, the present arrangement with both Rodolfo and Marcello on stage at the opening of the act, both obsessed with thoughts of the girls who have left them. Then there were other difficulties with Act 4. Wanting to build up the role of Schaunard, Puccini suggested he be given a humorous *credo* in dispraise of women.[6] Later he decided this misogynous outburst retarded the action at a critical point. The act did not assume its present form, however, until another idea—a series of exaggerated toasts to be drunk in water—had been discarded. These final issues were not resolved until late in October 1895, barely three months before the scheduled *première*, and after Puccini had already completed the orchestration of the first three acts.

The world *première* of *La Bohème* took place at the Teatro Regio, Turin, on 1 February 1896, three years to the day after *Manon Lescaut* had made its first appearance. The first Manon, Cesira Ferrani, also was on hand to create Mimì.[7] The superstitious Ricordi was doing what he could to ensure that the success of Puccini's newest opera would equal that of his last. The person who could contribute most significantly to the outcome of the performance was, however, new to the ranks of a Puccini *première*. This was Arturo Toscanini.[8]

Puccini was lukewarm about the idea of holding another *première* at the Regio. His reluctance was based on practical considerations. He disliked the acoustics of the theater, even though some attempts had lately been made to improve them.[9] He distrusted pushing his luck twice in the same theater. Besides his superstitions, Giulio Ricordi had his hard-headed reasons for insisting on Turin. It was close enough to Milan not to be too difficult to get to, but far enough away—he hoped—to avoid a demonstration by the rival

6. The idea of employing a *credo* shows the powerful influence of the Verdi-Boito *Otello* on the younger composers. Scarpia has an aria in Act 2 of *Tosca* that fits into the *credo* tradition.

7. The balance of the cast for the first *La Bohème* included Camilla Pasini—not to be confused with her contemporary Lina Pasini-Vitale—as Musetta, Evan Gorga (Rodolfo), Tieste Wilmant (Marcello), Michele Mazzara (Colline), Antonio Pini-Corsi (Schaunard), Alessandro Polonini (Benoit and Alcindoro), and Felice Foglia (the Sergeant). Gorga's first name—Evan—is not a clue to Welsh extraction; it is a reduction of Giovanni Evangelista!

8. Arturo Toscanini (1867-1957) was twenty-nine at the time of *La Bohème* and was making his reputation as the outstanding conductor of his generation. His long relationship with Puccini was stormy at times, but his service to him was, quite simply, invaluable.

9. Puccini's repeated adjective for the Teatro Regio was *sordo* (muffled).

house of Sonzogno in behalf of its stable of composers, one of whom was Leoncavallo. There was no demonstration, but then neither was there the unalloyed success that had greeted *Manon Lescaut* three years before.

Most of the critics expressed their disappointment in the new opera, if not hostility toward it. Several of them felt that Puccini had taken a backward step from *Manon Lescaut*, that he had lost his way on the "path of progress." The reasons for the generally unfavorable tone of the reviews are not too difficult to find. For one thing, shortly before the first *La Bohème*, on 22 December 1895, Toscanini had opened the season at the Regio with the first Italian performance of *Götterdämmerung*. No wonder that the critics who had just braced themselves for the *longueurs* of Wagner were put off by the terseness of Puccini's newest score, particularly as there was more than a hint of Wagner in the pages of *Manon Lescaut* and none in *La Bohème*. Further, the cast was not ideal: the tenor was in vocal difficulties, the Marcello was brought in almost at the last minute to replace an inept predecessor. With Toscanini at the helm, though, we may be certain that the cast, whatever their shortcomings, gave the best they had. Still another element contributed its share to the misfiring of these performances. Delicately equilibrated as the score of *La Bohème* now is, Puccini had not yet put it in absolutely the final form we know today, and these differences were sufficient to dampen the effectiveness of Act 2 in particular. In any event, the public was more cordial than the critics and applauded the first run of performances warmly, if not enthusiastically.

Today the success of *La Bohème* is so incontestibly assured that it is difficult to imagine the relative coolness of its first reception. Then the qualities making it a success seemed novel and, to those expecting something different, disappointing. The virtues of *La Bohème* are its economy, its understatement, and, particularly, its unity and tight construction.

The economy of *La Bohème* is readily apparent when that opera is compared with *Manon Lescaut*. In *La Bohème* the musical unities —passages in a single key, rhythm, and tempo—are shorter and treated more flexibly. Although the transitions from one episode to another are quick in *Manon Lescaut*, they are masterly in *La Bohème;* a good example is the ease and grace of the transition

from the ensemble climax of Musetta's Waltz to the military band.
In *La Bohème* the exposition is handled more simply and naturally
than in *Manon Lescaut*. There is less rhetoric, both of text and
music, in *La Bohème*, where the musical climaxes are relatively
brief and the expansive moments are motivated consistently by
character rather than by some abstract emotional idea.[10] Again,
Puccini's orchestration in *La Bohème* is far less thick and more
adroitly colored.

The notions of economy and understatement are closely related.
Understatement is the keynote of Mimì's death scene, unlike
Manon's, where her suffering is graphically emphasized. The music
of Mimì's death scene, except for Colline's "Coat Song" and Mimì's
Sono andati?, is composed almost entirely of phrases heard earlier
in the opera, and these but sparsely orchestrated. Much of the conversation is reduced to brief questions and answers, just the way
people talk under such circumstances. This understatement builds
dramatic tension far greater than the means used to produce it. A
less obvious example of understatement and just as psychologically
sound is the love duet closing Act 1. In structure it is the reverse of
the usual love duet: instead of building up to a climax, it builds
away from one. The big phrase with the voices doubling the climactic melody comes near the beginning as Rodolfo, gazing at
Mimì in an aureole of moonlight, recognizes her not only as his beloved but as a source of poetic inspiration. This moment past, they
realize that they have, after all, just met, and that they have arrangements to make. After these conversational phrases over an
orchestral texture that grows increasingly delicate, their voices
combine once more at the close.[11]

The organic balance of the score is felt most strongly in the relationship between the first act and the last. They have the same
setting, the garret. Both Rodolfo and Marcello are on stage when
the curtain rises, and in both cases, Mimì appears well after the act
has started. There are liberal quotations of music from Act 1 in

10. An example of an outburst motivated by rhetoric is the unison passage in the
Act 3 love duet of *Tosca*.
11. Two common disobediences of Puccini's explicit instructions make the Act 1
curtain lose its poetry. The final notes sung carry the direction *perdendosi* (to be
lost in the distance). The poetry of the moment is heightened when the tenor
restrains his vanity and sings the lower E rather than the high C with the soprano. The public should clearly show its disapproval of the tasteless bellowing
that all too often ruins what can be one of the high points of the opera.

Act 4. This much is obvious to even the most casual observer, but there is more than this to give the score organic balance.

Consider for a moment the idea of Mimì as Rodolfo's poetic inspiration. She first appears at the moment when Rodolfo throws down his pen, unable to finish his article. Just when Rodolfo recognizes in Mimì the fulfillment of his dreams, the off-stage voice of Marcello shouts ironically: "Trovò la poesia" (He's found poetry); onstage this is not a joke but dramatic truth. The matter is made explicit when Rodolfo introduces Mimì to his friends in Act 2:

> RODOLFO: *Il suo venir completa*
> *la bella compagnia,*
> *perchè . . . perchè son io il poeta*
> *essa la poesia.*

> (TRANSLATION: Her coming completes this fine company, because . . . because I am the poet; she, poetry.)

Again, near the beginning of Act 4, Rodolfo throws away his pen when the thought of Mimì's unfaithfulness prevents his writing.

The idea that most closely unifies the opera is that of cold, with its associations with poverty, loneliness, illness, and death; implicit in this notion are the contrasting ideas of warmth, spring, gaiety, and love. In each act, cold is stressed. The garret is freezing until Rodolfo makes the symbolic sacrifice of his manuscript to the stove. In her autobiographical aria, Mimì expresses her longing for the warmth of spring and makes a poignant contrast between the lifeless artificial flowers she constructs and the fragrance of real flowers. The middle acts are both set outdoors, but what a contrast between the festive Café Momus and the scruffy cabaret of Act 3 in the early morning snow! Act 3 contains the most striking references to these ideas when Rodolfo and Mimì sing: "Soli d'inverno è cosa da morire!" (To be alone in winter is a thing to die of!). At the moment of her death, Mimì murmurs that her hands in the muff are warm now, and we remember with a contraction of the heart the beginning of Rodolfo's Act 1 aria, *Che gelida manina!* (What a frozen little hand). Although I have described these associations here in terms of the libretto, these cross references are made and stressed by the music as well.

One more unifying effect needs mentioning as its significance is often missed by audiences. I have already spoken of the importance of the nimbus of moonlight that surrounds Mimì near the end of Act 1. The counterpart to this moment occurs in Act 4, when Rodolfo uses Musetta's shawl to try to block out a ray of sunlight that falls across Mimì's face. Although Mimì has just died, Rodolfo is not yet aware of it. The phrase accompanying Rodolfo's action comes from Mimì's first aria.

These examples of structural cross reference and of economy and understatement could easily be multiplied. A consideration of them brings one close to the special merit that resides in *La Bohème*. The libretto has more virtues than meet the casual eye. There is little of the standard vocabulary of romantic melodrama—more than may be said of parts of *Manon Lescaut*. As a matter of fact, in *La Bohème* this old-fashioned style is parodied by Colline and Schaunard in their mock-duel scene: *Snudi il ferro!* (Unsheathe your weapon), etc. The vocabulary that Giacosa and Illica use is uncommonly large as libretti go; they avail themselves of the rich resources of Italian to describe objects precisely. They demonstrate a keen sense of the poignancy that resides in concrete allusion; see, for example, the text of Mimì's *Addio* (Act 3) with its mention of the gold ring, the prayer book, and the bonnet. The text is rich in metaphor and retains much of Mürger's high-spirited hyperbole. In this libretto Puccini had a text tailored and refined to his particular needs. It has made a signal contribution to the opera's popularity.

Few composers have a more easily identifiable style than Puccini's. Though many of its characteristics are discernible in *Manon Lescaut*—the melodic contours, the unflagging rhythmic vitality, and some of the harmonic trademarks—still it is in *La Bohème* that his style really emerges full blown, and often with a refinement that makes much of *Manon Lescaut* seems obvious and almost crude in comparison. Instead of analyzing the music of *La Bohème* act by act, it should be instructive to examine it in terms of the elements that form Puccini's individual style.

The predominance of melody for Puccini is beyond question. As a true Italian, his is primarily vocal melody. It is difficult to think of any prominent theme in the score that is not at some point *sung*. A typical Puccini melody is predominantly conjunct and has a clear rhythmic outline. Conjunct melodies—those moving stepwise or in relatively small intervals—occur in such familiar examples as:

One of Puccini's favored devices shows up clearly in Example 1 and Example 3; he advances the melody by "surrounding" a pitch.[13] Large intervals are surprisingly rare in *La Bohème*, Musetta's music providing nearly all the examples. Although Puccini usually employs large intervals in the vocal line for dramatic emphasis (as in Tosca's description of stabbing Scarpia in Act 3), such a passage as Musetta's "Vien, Lulù!" is motivated by her desire to call attention to herself:

12. A strange foreshadowing of Rodolfo's big phrase occurs at No. 20 in Act. 1. During the scene with Benoit, Marcello and the others twit the landlord about his amorous prowess. It seems strange to introduce one of the main melodies of the score by a comic variant. Perhaps Puccini was unconscious of the undeniable resemblance.

13. The most familiar example of a melody that moves by surrounding or bracketing a pitch is the opening of Butterfly's *Un bel dì.*

The chiefly diatonic character (that is, confined to the notes in the scale of a given key) of Puccini's melodies in this opera leads him frequently to write scale-wise passages:

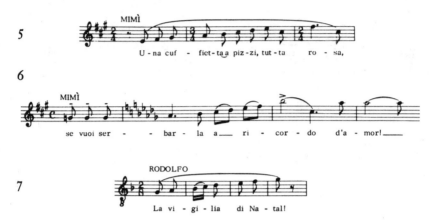

These examples all involve ascending scales, yet an even more famous phrase is the beginning of a descending E major scale:

Puccini uses vocal embellishments sparingly in *La Bohème*. Save for an occasional flourish for Musetta, he contents himself chiefly with grace notes that provide a mellifluous stress. This example comes from Rodolfo's Act 1 aria.

This scarcity of embellishment contributes to the conversational quality of many phrases. Puccini shapes them to the natural inflection of words in a particular dramatic context and seldom sets one syllable to more than one note. As a result, the text emerges clearly. As other writers on Puccini have pointed out, this conversational tone resembles the frequent practice of such French composers as Thomas and, particularly, Massenet, whose early works began to be introduced in Italy in the late 1870's, thanks to the prodding of Giovannina Lucca. A good example of Puccini's conversational style occurs shortly after Mimì's first entrance:

10

Such a passage, which an earlier composer might have set as arid recitative, here has charm and easy naturalness due to the clear melodic contours and the rhythmic directness. Example 10 points up another frequent trait of Puccini's melody; each phrase ends on two notes of the same value at the same pitch. Phrases that end this way are common in *La Bohème*,[14] as instances chosen at random show.

11

12

One can find more phrases with this sort of ending in Puccini's scores than in Verdi's, say, because librettists before 1890 used a higher percentage of masculine (one-syllable) rhymes than was usual later and because Verdi was trained in a tradition that often used ornamented cadences for phrases ending in feminine (two-or-more-syllable) rhyme.

The peculiarly Puccinian quality of these melodies resides in the great consistency of his practice, his adherence to a personal idiom. Consistency can easily make for monotony, but Puccini usually avoids this danger by maintaining rhythmic vigor and by control-

14. Puccini has used this characteristic ending of vocal phrases earlier. Seven of the first eight phrases of Des Grieux's *Donna non vidi mai* have this pattern. It is nearly as frequent in Cavaradossi's *Recondita armonia*.

ling gradations of orchestral color. Looking at his melodic consistency from another angle, we see that Puccini eschews almost everywhere the old-fashioned distinction between recitative and aria.[15] His extended solos often begin conversationally, as does *Che gelida manina*. His climactic phrases often have much the same contour as less prominent ones, but they owe their climactic feeling to being pitched high for the voice, to Puccini's custom of doubling the voice with instruments, and to some slackening of rhythmic tension, a combination that makes for a feeling of expansion.

A discussion of melody necessarily involves mention of rhythm: the tones in sequence that comprise a melody inevitably possess a rhythmic relationship. Necessarily, too, the rhythm of vocal phrases must exist in some sort of relationship to the rhythm of the orchestral accompaniment. At points where Puccini wants to stress the vocal melody these two rhythmic patterns coincide. At other points the predominant rhythmic pattern may be in the orchestra, while the vocal lines (usually in the same meter as the accompaniment) are heard against it. This practice can be illustrated by a passage near the end of Act 2. The orchestra plays the march-rhythm of the tattoo, as Rodolfo and his friends vainly try to find the money to pay their restaurant bill.

13

15. There is a passage in recitative at the end of Mimì's first aria, but here it is dramatically apt as an expression of her shyness and confusion.

Again, the predominant rhythm may be in the vocal melody, a secondary rhythmic impulse animating the accompaniment. This secondary impulse usually entails some stress of off-beats, imparting a
feeling of urgency to the music. A case in point occurs in Mimì's
first aria.

14

piac-cion quel - le   co - se   che han sì dol-ce ma - lì - a, che par-la-no d'a-mor,

A more complex example of Puccini's contrasting the rhythmic
impulse of the accompaniment against a variety of different patterns in the voice parts is found in the brief trio from Act 3.
Here, the rhythmic variety underscores the dramatic situation:
Rodolfo pours out his fears for Mimì's health, while Marcello
and the eavesdropping Mimì utter agitated asides. (See Ex. 15, A 62.)

In *La Bohème*, and in *Tosca* and *Madama Butterfly*, the two
operas immediately following it, the keynote of Puccini's ryhthmic
style lies in the relationship between the rhythm of the vocal
phrases and of the orchestra. Puccini had strong feelings about strict
rhythmical accuracy in interpreting his music. Any variation of
tempo, any slowing down or acceleration is precisely indicated,
otherwise he wanted no change. Although he rarely describes the
desired degree of change, he is everywhere adamant about the point
at which the alteration in tempo is to begin and how long it is to
continue. Consequently, his scores are filled with such directions as
affrettando, poco allargando, rallentando, followed either by a row
of dots to indicate its duration or by the marking *a tempo*. On a
related point Puccini was equally firm. As Luigi Ricci points out,[16]

16. Luigi Ricci, *Puccini interprete di se stesso* (Milan, 1954), p. 13. Ricci says:
"The crowned notes (*le note coronate*) in the middle of a phrase Puccini wanted
held *exactly twice their morphological value*. This is consistent with his view of
art: never exaggerate effects. No very long high notes, nor exaggeratedly loud,
violent, or aggressive notes. No notes held painfully long, so that to release them
produces an effect of utter exhaustion. Exactitude in what he had written: this is
what Puccini demanded."

15

Puccini wanted a *fermata*—a note marked to be held—expanded exactly twice its written value and no more, the practice of certain prominent singers to the contrary.

Puccini's harmony has several distinctive features. In *La Bohème* there is relatively little ambiguity of harmony, although Puccini was to become more venturesome in this matter later. He shows a

fondness for chords with an added seventh, ninth, or even thir-
teenth, but he uses altered chords rather sparingly in this score.
Much attention has been called to his use of parallel fifths at the
opening of Act 3, but an even more daring effect (for 1896) is the
suggestion of bitonality in chords describing Rodolfo's tearing his
manuscript across before he throws it on the fire. There are some
unresolved dissonances, as at the moment of Mimì's death, and some
unprepared shifts of key, as at Schaunard's shout of "Fandango!"
in Act 4. Perhaps his favorite harmonic device is the drawing out
of pedal points. At the beginning of Act 3, the cellos have a pedal
point that lasts for 114 measures. Against it, at one point, the piccolo sustains an inverted pedal point.

No aspect of Puccini's art shows closer attention to detail than
does his orchestration. His scores are peppered with directions:
divisi (to divide a section), *uniti* (to bring them together again),
con sordina (to use mutes), *via sordina* (to remove the mutes), and
so on. In Act 2 (at No. 14) the exit music for the children following after Parpignol shows Puccini's keen ear for effect. The chief
melody, a sort of miniature march, is given to the clarinets and
flutes, which are reinforced by the harp, glockenspiel, and xylophone, while the triangle, snare drum, and strings (which are instructed to play with the back, or wood, of the bow) emphasize
the martial rhythm. Not only is this resourceful scoring, but the
sounds blend to form an appropriate color that seems more than
the sum of its ingredients.

The frequent delicacy of Puccini's instrumentation in *La Bohème*
is well illustrated by the opening of Act 3. With such simple means
as staccato chords for flutes and harp in unison over a cello pedal
point, he suggests not only snow falling but the winter of the heart.
On the other hand, when Puccini wants to reinforce a melody he
frequently doubles the voice extravagantly. When Mimì and Rodolfo sing the melody in their Act 1 duet (Ex. 1), their voices are
reinforced by flutes, piccolo, oboes, clarinets, four horns, violins,
and cellos.[17] This is the obverse of delicacy, but its effectiveness is
difficult to resist.

The harp part in *La Bohème* reveals something of Puccini's ingenuity as an orchestral colorist. Far from looking on this instrument as a sort of orchestral guitar as did so many of his predeces-

17. It is only fair to note, however, that this example of redundant doubling lasts
only two measures.

sors, he uses it to describe the flickering of the fire in Act 1, the shimmering of moonlight, the fall of snow, and Mimì's slackening heartbeat just before her death. It is not the harp, however, that participates in one of Puccini's most graphic musical descriptions but two violins pizzicato against a flute chord that describe Rodolfo's flicking water on the fainting Mimì's face in Act 1.

Puccini avoids monotony of color by delicately adjusting the scoring of a repetition of a melody. For instance, the scale-wise melody (Ex. 5) associated with Mimì's bonnet is scored differently at each recurrence. First the voice is doubled by the clarinet, then by the harp and first violins; when Colline sings this tune, his voice is seconded by the cellos and bassoon. Puccini's skill at avoiding monotony shows up in the openings of Acts 1 and 4. The notes are the same, as is the rhythm and tempo, but by thickening the harmony and adding the brass at the opening of Act 4, Puccini transforms its earlier lighthearted air to one of strident desperation.

If any single consideration runs consistently through this discussion of Puccini's style in *La Bohème*, surely it is the fundamental point that all his effects are conceived as expression in musical terms of character, of atmosphere, and of dramatic action. There is precious little in this score that can be looked on as filling out a musical form for its own sake or as pursuing a musical idea at the expense of the drama—all of which is more than can be said for *Manon Lescaut*.

Those who approach opera as music first, second, and third, and only much further down the list rank the encumbrance of a libretto, are apt to find Puccini little to their taste; however, those who approach his scores through the characters and drama can come to appreciate his exceptional sensitivity to dramatic stimuli and his expert craftsmanship. Those who enjoy his operas as vehicles for singers are often oblivious to almost everything but the familiar arias or the occasional spectacular high notes. Their enjoyment overlooks the richness of detail and the fact that what is going on in the pit can often be just as stimulating as what is heard from the stage.

Although one may discern in *La Bohème* the dominant traits of Puccini's style, one should never forget his diligence at keeping his musical vocabulary abreast of his times (as he understood them) and at broadening the range of expressive means at his command.

Puccini's capacity to assimilate makes the study of his successive operas fascinating. Although they contain resemblances of idiom, each one has its individual color and personality.

The autograph score of *La Bohème* affords some interesting clues to the subsequent development of the opera. Bearing the date 10 December 1895 on its final page, it differs in quite a few details from the established version familiar today. Any differences between the autograph and present scores reveal changes Puccini made after 28 February 1896, for on that date he entrusted the autograph to Ricordi's. No subsequent changes appear in the autograph.

While some changes are minor—the alteration of a word or rhythmic pattern—others are more significant. In Act 1 a sweeping change involves the transposition half a tone upward of more than a hundred measures, including such a famous passage as the beginning of *Che gelida manina*, which used to begin in C major instead of the present key of D-flat.[18]

More drastic changes occur in Act 2. Puccini's dissatisfaction with this act is expressed in a letter he wrote to Giulio Ricordi on 30 March 1896, in which he speaks of it as "chilling" and as "needing a bit of air." In the autograph the whole episode of Mimì showing off her bonnet (beginning with Ex. 5) is missing, and therefore this is the "bit of air" Puccini later added.[19] Originally the action moved directly from the exit of the children scrabbling after Parpignol to Marcello's shout, as he catches sight of Musetta, "E a me un fiale di tossico!"[20] (And for me a phial of poison). The "chilling" effect Puccini referred to had occurred at the end of the act where Alcindoro, returning with Musetta's new shoes and confronted by the huge bill, spoke some lines. These lines do not appear in the autograph, but Puccini mentions their existence in his letter of 30 March to Ricordi. Puccini solved this problem by alter-

18. This transposed passage ends at No. 32 of Act 1 just before Rodolfo sings "In povertà mia lieta."
19. Apparently the "bonnet" addition was first sung in performance at Palermo (April 1896), where the opera created for the first time, wild enthusiasm. In the first printed scores this addition does not appear, nor do eight bars of counterpoint marked *Poco meno* that were inserted five bars before Rodolfo's "Marcello, finalmente!" Needless to say, neither do these eight bars appear in the autograph.
20. Just before Musetta appears, Marcello now says: "Ch'io bevi del tossico!" (Let me drink poison).

ing Alcindoro's lines to pantomimed action and by adding a six-bar *fortissimo* coda to the end of the act.[21]

In Act 3, it is quite surprising not to find the familiar business of Mimì deciding to eavesdrop behind the tree to overhear Rodolfo, but to discover that Marcello used to direct Mimì to hide, pointing toward three trees where she is to conceal herself. This change, then, is one of motivation and involves principally an alteration of words rather than the music.[22] Originally Marcello's words in the trio (Ex. 15) were different; knowing that Mimì can hear, he tries to draw Rodolfo farther away, saying such things as "Vien via" (Come away), "Taci!" (Be silent), rather than "Povera Mimì!" Certainly there can be little disagreement that Puccini's change here was all for the better!

Tosca

Shortly after the *première* of *Edgar*, Fontana first suggested to Puccini the idea of composing an opera based on Victorien Sardou's *La Tosca*.[23] On 7 May 1889 Puccini wrote to Giulio Ricordi that he was attracted to the subject because it was "neither of excessive proportions, nor an elaborate spectacle, nor such as to occasion the usual over-abundance of music." Puccini went on to urge Ricordi to take steps to obtain the rights from Sardou.[24] The route that led

21. A photograph of the final page of Puccini's autograph of Act 2 *La Bohème* appears as an illustration in *Casa Ricordi (1808-1958)*, ed. Claudio Sartori (Milan, 1958), facing p. 80. In this photograph the original last bars of Act 2 may be seen, minus the 6 measures that Puccini added in March 1896.
22. Toscanini's fiftieth anniversary broadcast of *La Bohème* (3 and 10 February 1946), later released on records by RCA-Victor, suggests there was still another variant for Marcello. Just before Mimì leaves to hide behind the tree, Francesco (later Frank) Valentino replaces the words in the present scores with these: "Ora andate a casa, per or gli parlerò, poi tutto vi dirò" (Now go home, for now I will talk to him, then I will tell you everything). I do not know the source for this unexpected alteration. It is, however, consistent with the present motivation of the scene and is followed by the trio in its customary form.
　　Toscanini makes another change for Marcello in Act 4. In the final phrase of the Rodolfo-Marcello duet, Toscanini allows the baritone Valentino to sing the lower G rather than the top E with the *fermata*.
23. Sardou's title contains the article "La," which was early dropped from the opera, which is properly called *Tosca*.
24. Sardou (1831-1908), dramatist and librettist, had other plays besides *La Tosca* turned into operas. At one point, Sardou tried to interest Verdi in his play *Patrie!* (1869), later turned into an opera first by Lauro Rossi and then more notably by Emile Paladilhe. *Piccolino* (1861) served as the basis for three operatic settings: one by Mme Frandval, another by Ernest Guiraud, and still another by

to Puccini's composing *Tosca*, however, contained a major detour.

At first, Sardou was reluctant to enter into negotiations. Further, Ricordi acted with no sense of urgency at the outset of the *Tosca* project. A year and a half passed before a librettist was assigned to reduce the play to the requirements of the opera stage, and then the librettist Ricordi nominated was not Fontana, but Luigi Illica. Fontana was furious, claiming he had been the first to suggest the subject, and resentful, feeling that he had been summarily eliminated from participation in Puccini's future works. He had been. In January 1891 when Ricordi put Illica to work on a *Tosca* scenario, it is not clear whether Ricordi thought of the subject as exclusively for Puccini, who was then hard at work on *Manon Lescaut*. Perhaps Ricordi regarded the *Tosca* project as an ace in the hole if the difficulties with the libretto of *Manon Lescaut* proved so insurmountable that it would have to be abandoned. At the time Puccini was collaborating with Illica on *Manon Lescaut* and it would be very surprising if he did not know what other plots Illica was working on concurrently, particularly as Puccini had raised the idea of *Tosca* in the first place.

In any event, Illica's sketch for *Tosca* lay dormant for three years, until January 1894, by which time Puccini had publicly committed himself to *La Bohème*. With Puccini otherwise occupied, Ricordi turned Illica's sketch over to Baron Alberto Franchetti.[25] Franchetti, two years Puccini's junior, had a name then on the lips of every Italian opera lover. His *Cristoforo Colombo*, celebrating the four hundredth anniversary of Columbus's exploit, had not only survived its ceremonial launching at Genoa (6 October 1892) but had made a major splash when it opened the La Scala season of 1893. For its spectacular scenes and massive choruses,

Johann Strauss (*Der Karneval in Rom* (1873). Before Umberto Giordano's opera of *Madame Sans-Gêne* had its *première* at the Metropolitan in 1915, Sardou's play of the same name (1893) was mined by Ivan Caryll for an operetta, *The Duchess of Dantzic*. Three other plays by Sardou—*Fédora* (1882), *Théodora* (1884), and *Gismonda* (1894)—gave rise to operas by Giordano, Xavier Leroux, and Henri Février.

As this evidence shows, Sardou had more first hand experience with operatic treatments of his plays than any other dramatist Puccini worked with.

25. Franchetti (1860-1942) composed eight operas: *Asrael* (librettist Fontana) 1888, *Cristoforo Colombo* (librettist Illica) 1892, *Fior d'Alpe* 1894, *Il Signor di Pourceaugnac* (librettist Fontana) 1897, *Germania* (librettist Illica) 1902, *La Figlia di Jorio* (librettist d'Annunzio) 1906, *La Notte di Leggenda* (librettist Forzano) 1915, *Glauco* (librettist Forzano) 1922. And in collaboration with Giordano, Franchetti composed *Giove a Pompeii*, 1921.

this opera earned for Franchetti a slightly malicious soubriquet—
"the Meyerbeer of modern Italy"—a label that referred not only to
Franchetti's fondness for large-scale effects but also to the fact his
mother was a Rothschild (Meyerbeer also came from a Jewish bank-
ing family). Fuller Maitland's estimate of Franchetti, written in
1906, squarely sidesteps evaluation: "that he . . . stands entirely
apart from the hysterical school of Young Italy should not be reck-
oned against him."[26]

After Franchetti's *La Figlia di Jorio* (1906) failed to accord with
the expectations aroused by the composer's collaboration with
d'Annunzio, his reputation went into an eclipse that neither his
last works nor subsequent revivals of his earlier successes dissipated.
(A recent Italian recording of excerpts from *Cristoforo Colombo*
suggests, however, that some pages of the score are eloquent.)

During the early months of 1894, the libretto of *Tosca* advanced
slowly as Illica was engaged on other projects, including *La
Bohème*. In October of that year Illica went to Paris to get the
needed approval of Sardou for the *Tosca* libretto he was preparing
for Franchetti. At that time, the eighty-one-year-old Verdi was in
Paris to supervise the French *première* of *Otello*,[27] and accompanying him as buffer was Giulio Ricordi. Sometime that month there
was a meeting between Sardou, Illica, and Franchetti. The accounts
of this meeting[28] do not make it absolutely clear whether Verdi and
Ricordi were present then or whether there was a second meeting
without Sardou. Considering Verdi's age, status, and dislike of
social encounters, it seems more likely that a second meeting took
place. In any event, Verdi expressed the liveliest interest in the
libretto and regretted that he was too old to undertake it himself.
Doubtless, Verdi's reaction caused the stock of the proposed *Tosca*
to rise sharply in Ricordi's eyes.

In January 1895 Illica wrote to Giulio Ricordi, recounting his
difficulties in working on *Tosca* with Franchetti, who perpetually
wanted revisions and kept pulling the work to pieces. This letter
contains a phrase striking in the light of future events: "I have a
sure way of making Franchetti work. . . . I talk to him about

26. *Grove's Dictionary of Music and Musicians* (ed. 1906), II, 95.
27. Verdi had written new ballet music for the Paris Opéra's *première* of *Otello*.
28. The usually cited account is that in Arnaldo Fraccaroli, *La Vita di Giacomo Puccini* (Milan, 1925), a not outstandingly reliable book, even though Fraccaroli claimed it was based on conversations with Puccini, his friend of long-standing. The Marchese Gino Monaldi, even less reliable a source, gives a brief account in his *Giacomo Puccini e la sua opera* (Rome, n.d.).

Bohème. Likewise to get Puccini working it suffices to talk to him about *Tosca!*"[29] Puccini would have heard from either Illica or Ricordi, or both, of Verdi's enthusiasm for *Tosca* in the preceding October. The subject came to seem ever more desirable to Puccini as he thought of one of his rivals working on *Tosca*, and especially one who could ruin the work with his compulsion to tinker. Furthermore Puccini could claim that he had spoken of *Tosca* and had wanted it long before Franchetti came into the picture. The usual reason given for Franchetti's renunciation of *Tosca* is that Illica and Ricordi, with Puccini's knowledge, systematically undermined Franchetti's confidence in the project, and then, when they had gained their ends, they promptly turned *Tosca* over to Puccini. There are, however, extenuating circumstances. Illica and Franchetti were at loggerheads over the management of the libretto; there was no doubt in the minds of Ricordi, Illica, and, above all, Puccini which of the rival composers was temperamentally better suited to make a success of the subject. However the transfer occurred, it took place during the summer of 1895, while Puccini was composing Act 3 of *La Bohème*. On 9 August he crows to his friend Carlo Clausetti,[30] then head of the Naples branch of Ricordi: "I will do *Tosca*, an extraordinary libretto by Illica, in 3 acts. Sardou is enthusiastic about the libretto."

Puccini did not commence the preliminary planning of his *Tosca* until *La Bohème* was on its own, but by way of preparation he made a special trip to Florence in October 1895 to see Sarah Bernhardt in Sardou's *La Tosca*. Puccini was so upset by her lifeless performance and by the coolness of the audience that he was afraid he had misjudged the play. He wrote of his misgivings to Ricordi, who by return mail assured him that Bernhardt's acting in the play in Milan had been incandescent, the audience wildly enthusiastic, going on to explain that the actress had fallen ill before she started out for Florence. Mollified, Puccini returned to complete the orchestration of *La Bohème*.

The work on his new libretto proceeded slowly. As before,

29. *Carteggi Pucciniani*, p. 113.
30. Carlo Clausetti (1869-1943) was the son of Pietro Clausetti, whose music publishing firm in Naples was bought out by Ricordi in 1864. On the resignation of Tito Ricordi, Giulio's son, from the firm in 1919, the direction of the whole operation was taken over by Carlo Clausetti, in conjunction with Renzo Valcarenghi. Clausetti was one of the staunchest friends and supporters Puccini ever had.

Giacosa was to versify Illica's draft, but Illica could not devote his full attention to *Tosca* just yet, as he had to see another of the operas he had worked on, Giordano's *Andrea Chénier*, safely through its rehearsals and *première*, which took place at La Scala on 28 March 1896.[31] Two weeks later Illica turned over his draft of *Tosca* to Giacosa, but Puccini did not read Illica's sketch then, as he was off in Palermo, overseeing the production of *La Bohème* at the Teatro Carolino. For these performances, the conductor was Leopoldo Mugnone,[32] who would officiate at the *première* of *Tosca*.

Giacosa read Illica's draft of *Tosca* with distaste. Always a deliberate, painstaking writer, Giacosa was reduced to moving at tortoise speed by a subject he found repugnant and anti-poetic. He was convinced the plot was not well adapted for operatic treatment as it contained so few opportunities for lyric and poetic relief. On 23 August he detailed all his reservations in a long letter to Ricordi, summing them up: "It is a drama of gross emotional actions, without poetry." These huffings off his chest, Giacosa reluctantly agreed to work ahead. The very day before Giacosa's letter to Ricordi, Puccini had written gaily to Illica to announce that he had begun composing *Tosca*.

On 22 August Puccini had no more in his hands than just the words of the first act, and even these he thought needed a little condensation, a little touching up. For minor repairs Puccini most often turned to Illica because he worked faster than Giacosa. Even with an incomplete libretto, Puccini could not restrain his eagerness to get started. The autograph score of Act 1 suggests that the first music of *Tosca* Puccini composed was the E major part of the duet for Tosca and Cavaradossi, beginning *Mia gelosa!* This passage is on separate sheets bound in with the rest of the act; the words to some of the phrases of the duet exist in three different

---

31. *Andrea Chénier* enjoyed a major success, but not the sort of love affair with the public that *Bohème* thrived upon. *Chénier* was the second opera by Umberto Giordano (1867-1948). His first, *Mala Vita* (Rome, 1892) was raw *verismo*, but lacked the musical substance to survive. Since Giordano established himself *after* Puccini had made his mark, the relationship between the two, while never intimate, was less thorny than the associations between Puccini and his earlier rivals. Gara describes the rapport between Giordano and Puccini as "cordial, almost affectionate."

Illica was also busy in March 1896 with other projects besides *Chénier*. He was involved with Spiro Samara's *Martire* and Franchetti's *Fior d'Alpe*.

32. Mugnone (1858-1941) was one of the most admired conductors of his day. He led the *première* of *Cavalleria* (1890). Puccini entertained great respect for Mugnone and his ability to make a performance come alive.

versions, an unusual situation in Puccini's autographs, which suggests the music antedates the words. Hearing the opera today, one cannot help but notice the unprepared modulation this passage begins with.

Although Puccini had made a beginning, he was not yet able to enjoy clear sailing. It was not until 18 November 1896 that Giacosa could inform Illica: "In a few days *Tosca* will be finished."[33] Early in December, Puccini left Torre del Lago for Milan, where he took part in a round of conferences with his librettists. Since these discussions were face to face there is no epistolary evidence of the points discussed. In February Puccini returned to Milan for more conferences and to supervise La Scala's first production of *La Bohème*.[34]

This second visit to Milan gave Puccini another chance with the librettists. Most of the rest of 1897, as far as one can tell from the unusually sparse documentation, Puccini was at Torre del Lago hunting or working on the piano sketches of *Tosca*. I have seen some of these sketches, consisting of the melodic line scrawled hastily, brief notes of accompanying figures or melodies, and the harmony indicated *en bloc*. In April of that year, Puccini made his second journey to England, but not to London. Liverpool was his destination, where the Carl Rosa touring company put on the British *première* of *La Bohème*, Covent Garden having refused to mount the opera when first offered it.[35] In late November Puccini made another trip, this time to Rome so that he might hear for himself the sound of the Roman church-bells from the platform of the Castel Sant'Angelo. It is perfectly consistent with Puccini's brand of operatic realism—almost always a concern for aural atmosphere—that he should personally visit the setting of the third act of *Tosca*

33 Giacosa here is referring to his finishing the versification of the libretto for *Tosca*.

34. Mugnone conducted the La Scala *première* of *La Bohème*. After his success with the score in Palermo the previous April, Puccini would consider no other, not even Toscanini, to introduce his opera to Milan. The distinguished cast included Angelica Pandolfini (Mimì), Camilla Pasini (the original Musetta), Fernando de Lucia (Rodolfo), and Edoardo Camera (Marcello). This edition of *La Bohème* enjoyed a run of sixteen performances.

35. The Carl Rosa *première* of *La Bohème* was sung by a resolutely un-Latin cast: Alice Esty, Bessie Macdonald, Robert Cunningham, William Paull, William Tilbury, and Arthur Winckworth. The Carl Rosa Company (in October 1897) introduced the score to Covent Garden.

La Bohème was first given during the Royal Opera Season at Covent Garden in 1899, with Melba, Zélie de Lussan, de Lucia, Mario Ancona, Marcel Journet, and Charles Gilibert; the conductor was Mancinelli.

to gather his impressions firsthand. Puccini first encountered the "pretino," Don Pietro Panichelli, on this trip to Rome, and the priest supplied him with helpful details, such as the pitch (low E) of the great bell of St. Peter's and the melody for the Act 1 *Te Deum.*

Since Puccini dated his autograph full-score, these dates supply some—but only some—help in determining when Puccini orchestrated *Tosca.* The opening page, which contains the three so-called Scarpia chords and nothing else, is dated January 1898. The following page bears this heading: *La Tosca, atto primo, agosto 1898,* while just before Scarpia's *Va, Tosca* there is still another rubric: *Tosca, Finale primo atto, Giacomo Puccini, Monsagrati, 18 agosto 1898;* at the end of Act 1 there are no dates. While this gives the impression that Puccini completed almost all the orchestration of the first act—thousands and thousands of notes—in less than a month, I think it far more likely that during this month of August he put in order passages that he had worked on earlier.

The first six months of 1898 had kept Puccini on the move. In January he was in Milan, in February he went to Paris to sign the contracts relating to the Opéra-Comique's production of *La Bohème,* slated for later that spring. In April he returned to Paris, where he was kept dangling for two months while the singers suffered from spring distempers and while Albert Carré, the stage manager of the Opéra-Comique, took his own sweet time. *La Bohème* finally made its Paris debut on 13 June 1898, more than a month later than originally scheduled.[36] With the Paris public *La Bohème* had a fine success; with the critics it encountered a chauvinistic disdain directed against almost all music not French.

Illica joined Puccini during this stay in Paris, and together they called on Sardou. Their meeting, postponed almost as many times as the performance at the Comique since Sardou was ill, was an effort to come to a final agreement about the handling of the last act of *Tosca.* These conversations were inconclusive as Puccini was back in Paris again the following January for further talks with Sardou. Sardou was an indefatigable monologuist rather than a

36. The first *La Bohème* at the Opéra-Comique was conducted by Alexandre Luigini, who insisted on the old-fashioned arrangement of having his music-stand back by the prompter's box so that he faced the audience. The performance was in French, the translation being the work of Paul Ferrier, and it was sung by Julia Guiraudon (Mimì), Jeanne Tiphaine (Musette), Alphonse Marechal (Rodolphe), Max Bouvet (Marcel), Jacques Isnardon (Colline), and, last but far from least, Lucien Fugère (Schaunard).

true conversationalist, an irrepressible source of dramatic "business" if not a profound dramatist. It was he who came up with the suggestion that Tosca's leap from the battlements of the Castel Sant'Angelo should terminate in the Tiber, and when Puccini objected that the river did *not* flow between the Castel and St. Peter's, Sardou blandly waved his hand, assuring Puccini that such a quibble was immaterial!

Puccini returned to Tuscany near the end of June 1898, but the heat was unbearable. He and Elvira found a villa in the hills above Lucca, at a little place called Monsagrati, in the commune of Pescaglia. Here Puccini settled down to serious work on *Tosca*, finding the hours from ten in the evening until four in the morning the most conducive to work because of the heat during the day. On 31 July he wrote to Ricordi, offering to send him all the music he had completed so far,[37] begging Ricordi not to look at it as the penmanship was very poor. Ironically Puccini continues: "I can't explain it, but as I get older I lose that skill in penmanship that was once such a conspicuous talent of mine." Perhaps the Milanese copyist's groans had penetrated to Monsagrati, for Puccini took special pains to write down the *Te Deum* conclusion of Act 1 as legibly as he could. Speaking of his work, he happily described it as going "più che benone" (more than swimmingly).

Puccini was a bit over-optimistic, as in September 1898 Giacosa is still grumbling about the text of Act 1. This letter shows that adjustments of the text still went forward even after the music was completed. The scrupulous attention to detail that went into the creation of *Tosca* arouses admiration for the patience of the collaborators. Apparently during the fall of 1898 things came to an almost complete standstill until problems of how to proceed were settled. In November, Puccini took another trip, this one to Rome to see the *première* of Mascagni's *Iris* at the Teatro Costanzi (22 November 1898), not only for the purpose of hearing Mascagni's score but to look at the prima donna, Ericlea Darclée,[38] whom Puccini decided to have as his first Tosca.

Puccini began to orchestrate Act 2 of *Tosca* on 23 February

37. In the light of the dates on the autograph of Act 1 of *Tosca*, Puccini's offer of 31 July to send what is finished confirms that Puccini had already done a good deal of work on Act 1 before August.
38. Darclée (1868?-1939) was a Rumanian soprano, who came to Italy from Paris in 1890. She first sang a Puccini role when she took over the role of Manon from Olghina at La Scala in 1894.

1899, and it engaged him until 16 July.[39] He completed the scoring
of Act 3, all but the Prelude, on 25 September, at 4:15 in the morning. As soon as each act was done, it was sent to Ricordi. After
getting the last act, Ricordi sent Giacomo on 10 October a mo-
mentous letter.

Ricordi was dismayed with Act 3, finding in it grave errors of
conception and structure. He had no complaints with Cavaradossi's
aria and the entrance of Tosca, or with the scene of the execution
at the end of the act. His fears focused upon the duet for Tosca
and Cavaradossi, which ought to have been "the true luminous center of the act." He is appalled to discover that Puccini could do no
better than adapt some music from *Edgar*[40] in the heart of the duet.
He distrusts the interruptions caused by Tosca's preoccupation
with the mock execution. But most of all he was disturbed that
what Illica had intended as a Hymn to Love and Art should be
reduced to a few measures. "Where," he demands, "is that Puccini
with the noble, warm, vigorous inspiration?"

Those who have commented on Ricordi's fatherly and deeply
concerned letter have overlooked the fact that Ricordi was basing
his judgment on only *part* of Act 3. Although Ricordi knew that
Puccini intended to provide a prelude, the publisher had not yet
seen it. The prelude bears the date 17 October 1899, a week after
Ricordi wrote his letter. Knowing how much the description of the
Roman dawn would help balance the act, Puccini answered Ricordi's letter immediately. Struck by Ricordi's earnestness, he expresses his faith in what he has composed. He defends his use of
the excerpt from *Edgar* by pointing out that though it comes from
the suppressed fourth act, he used it only because it was so full
of the poetic spirit that emanates from the words. He justifies the
fragmentation of the duet by assuring Ricordi of the psychological
truth of Tosca's preoccupation under such circumstances. As for
the so-called Hymn, he says he has yet to receive the words from
the poet, and indeed, in the autograph score the unison passage
(which we know as "Trionfar la nuova speme") has the notes but no
text. He continues:

39. The autograph score clearly states the date of 16 July 1899. Yet a letter in
Carteggi Pucciniani, p. 167, from Puccini to Ricordi, headed "*Monsagrati, luglio
1898, martedì*," contains this sentence: "Carignani has finished the reduction of
Act 2 and I will send it tomorrow." Thus, the standstill of the autumn of 1898 was
due chiefly to difficulties with Act 3.
40. See note 34, Chapter I, p. 23. Ricordi's letter is printed in *Carteggi Pucciniani*,
pp. 176-78.

The Act 3 duet has been the great reef. The poets have not been able to come up with anything good (I speak of the end [of the duet]), or above all, true: always academic stuff and the traditional amorous effusions! I have tried to get to the end without boring the audience too much and by avoiding everything academic.[41]

Further, he tells Ricordi that Mugnone, who will conduct the *première*, has heard the third act and is enthusiastic about it. He closes with an offer to come to Milan and play it for Ricordi—just the two of them at the piano.

The Prelude to Act 3 had been delayed because Puccini wanted a brief poem in Roman dialect to add to the atmosphere. For the shepherd boy's off-stage song he wanted a quatrain expressing romantic melancholy, but did not want it to allude directly in any way to the plot. As he often did when he had the music in mind but no words for it, he sent a sample quatrain to indicate the rhythm to Alfredo Vandini, one of Puccini's boyhood friends from Lucca who had settled in Rome. The words were supplied by a certain Giggi Zanazzo, but they were not inserted in the autograph score when Puccini delivered it to Ricordi.[42]

The two months before the *première* of *Tosca* were nervous ones for Puccini. Irritated at the enforced idleness now his score had been delivered, he started a brisk correspondence with Illica over the possibility of finding a new subject right away. If Puccini was excitable, his two librettists also managed to contribute their share to the rising tension. In *L'Illustrazione Italiana* there appeared over Giacosa's signature the sonnet from the last act of the libretto, beginning *Amaro sol per te*. Illica was enraged because the libretto was to be presented to the public as a joint effort and Giacosa's publication seemed an unnecessary provocation to the easily irritated Illica. Ricordi was hard put to it to calm the feuding librettists. As the date of the *première* drew closer, the focus of Puccini's, Ricordi's, and the librettists' anxiety shifted to Rome.

The reasons for Ricordi's decision to bring out *Tosca* in Rome have never been made public. That Franchetti and his partisans

41. *Carteggi Pucciniani*, pp. 179-80.
42. Perhaps the words were late arriving or perhaps Zanazzo's pretensions to claiming a full librettist's share in *Tosca* had to be put down before the words could be safely adopted; whatever the reason, just the notes of the shepherd's song appear in the autograph, not the words.

might make trouble if *Tosca* were brought out at La Scala would be an adequate reason for moving the *première* farther away from Milan than Turin. As the capital of Italy, Rome had its importance and its opera public was distinguished, even brilliant, and to bring out Puccini's newest opera there would be rather like acknowleging the composer as a national institution. Further, the public at the Costanzi had proved hospitable to new operas, for it was they who had greeted *Cavalleria* with unbridled enthusiasm ten years before. The most obvious reason for the choice, of course, is that each of the acts of *Tosca* is set in a prominent Roman landmark, and where else could this be better appreciated?

The cast chosen for the *première* turned out to look stronger on paper than it was. For Tosca, Darclée had the recommendation of being a proven success not only on stage but in the ranks of society, then a considerably more exclusive aggregate than today. Although she had made a name with new scores, having been the first to sing in *La Wally* and *Iris*, her reputation rested more securely on her achievements as Wagner's Elisabeth and Meyerbeer's Valentina. Puccini thought her appearance and voice excellent for Tosca, but privately he worried about her lack of temperament.[43] It was not to be until six months later in London that he found a Tosca who really pleased him—Milka Ternina.

The role of Mario Cavaradossi became something of a bone of contention. Caruso, who was singing that season at the Costanzi, desperately hoped to get the part. In view of his recent (1898) success in the *première* of Giordano's *Fedora* and of the enthusiasm he had lately aroused in Russia and South America, Caruso was confident that Puccini would name him for the part. Indeed, at that point the plum of singing a part in a Puccini *première* would have set a seal on Caruso's still emerging career. Puccini himself decided against Caruso. If today such a decision sounds like the height of folly, it is well to remember that in the late fall of 1899 Caruso could be construed as a bit of a risk. His vocal technique was not as secure as it became later, his acting was decidedly primitive, and he certainly did not have the *physique du rôle* for the aristocratic painter Cavaradossi. Puccini's choice was Emilio de Marchi (1861-1917). De Marchi had more than a dozen years of stage experience

43. In 1892, at the time of *La Wally*, Catalani had been upset by Darclée's coldness. He described her as a "coldness to make you despair, in spite of her beautiful voice," going on to say "she has no talent." Darclée sounds a bit like a Rumanian Emma Eames as far as temperament goes. Darclée retired in 1918.

and had recently made a great hit in *Gli Ugonotti* at La Scala. Although de Marchi's *métier* was singing the traditional romantic roles like Edgardo in *Lucia* and Manrico in *Il Trovatore*, he justified Puccini's faith in his healthy voice and handsome stage presence by winning the lion's share of the applause among the singers.[44]

The rehearsals were nerve-wracking. Tito Ricordi, Giulio's son, worked with painstaking care on the stage direction, but the singers found it difficult to concentrate as they kept receiving letters threatening them with public embarrassment or even physical injury. The conductor Mugnone, for all his talent and faith in Puccini, was a nervous, sensitive man. Imagine his terror when someone advised him—it is not clear just who—that if a bomb should be thrown in the theater he should immediately start conducting the National Hymn. In November 1893 a bomb had been hurled in the Teatro Liceo, Barcelona, during a performance of *Guglielmo Tell*, killing fifteen people. The fear of anarchists and their explosive ways had, if anything, increased in the years since that night. Even though there turned out to be no bomb, the words of advice to Mugnone vastly increased the tension of the *première*.[45]

Originally set for 13 January 1900, the performance was moved ahead one day to Sunday because of the ominous portents. The *première* of Puccini's latest opera was international news, attracting representatives of all the leading European papers and even some transatlantic ones. The audience was brilliant. Government was represented by Prime Minister Luigi Pelloux and by several cabinet ministers; royalty by Queen Margherita for whom all the talk of bombs was a bad omen; her husband, King Umberto, was assassinated by anarchists six months after the *première* of *Tosca*. This was the same Queen Margherita whose subsidy had allowed Puccini to attend the Milan Conservatory twenty years before. The world of music was represented by a full phalanx of Puccini's rivals, among them Mascagni and Franchetti. Not one of this last group would

44. For Scarpia, Puccini selected the baritone Eugenio Giraldoni. This singer came by his talents legitimately, as he was the son of two once-reknowned opera stars, the soprano Carolina Ferni and the baritone Leone Giraldoni. An imposing actor, he seems not to have made much impression vocally at the Roman *première*, for after the first La Scala performance Puccini described him as "much more effective, really much more!" Later Giraldoni became a Boris much in demand on Italian stages.

45. Besides Darclée, de Marchi, and Giraldoni, the original cast of *Tosca* consisted of Ettore Borelli (the Sacristan), Ruggero Galli (Angelotti), Enrico Giordano (Spoletta), Giuseppe Gironi (Sciarrone), Aristide Parassi (the Jailer), and Angelo Righi (Pastore).

have been permanently saddened if Puccini were to taste failure. Waiting for the performance to begin, Puccini discovered himself in the unenviable position of someone with two consecutive successes to his record and the whole world daring him to pull it off again.

The curtain had barely risen on Act 1 when the crush of late arrivals in the foyer, shouting and shoving to gain admittance and being loudly shushed in turn by those already in the house, caused such a tumult that Mugnone, resisting the temptation to break into the National Hymn, put down his baton instead. The curtain was lowered, and after some semblance of order had been restored, the performance began again—somewhat shakily. Many who were present that night remembered the audience as unusually restless and noisy. Pungent witticisms were frequent. Timing his appearance in a box to make the maximum effect, Mascagni was greeted by loud shouts of "Viva, Mascagni!" Against this background of barely concealed hostility the performance went on.

It is surprising, then, to learn that there was considerable applause and that several portions of the score were encored: both the tenor's arias, Tosca's *Vissi d'arte*, the finale to Act 1, and what must have seemed a vindication to Puccini—the Act 3 duet. The composer was called out by the audience twice after Act 1 and once after *Vissi d'arte*. On the other hand there was relatively little enthusiasm at the end of Act 2, and no mention is made of any calls at the end of the opera. At best, the reception could be called mixed.

Mixed, also, were the reviews. Today when new operas are relatively scarce and must stand the strain of being measured against both a long-established repertory and contemporary styles uncongenial to lyric expression, the critics from the composer's point of view must seem inordinately powerful and captious. In 1900, new operas were a more frequent event, and their chances of establishing themselves in the face of initial critical coolness were comparatively better. Not one of the critics who reviewed the *prima* of *Tosca* denied that there were effective pages of lyrical expansion. Most of them praised the adroitness of Puccini's orchestration. Many of them felt Puccini displayed a stronger dramatic sense than his earlier scores had demonstrated. Some of them were plainly put off by the sadism of the plot and complained of inequalities in the score, observing that the more violent the action the emptier the music. Only a few boldly stated the opera had little or no chance for survival.

For the first time in the reviews is there mention of a distinctive Puccini style. The game of spotting reminiscences is a favorite reviewer's pastime, and the resemblances of *Tosca* to *La Bohème* and *Manon Lescaut* were not neglected. One critic, Ippolito Valetta,[46] described Puccini's style at some length in the pages of the *Nuova Antologia*:

> Certain habits of harmonizing the scale, many successions of fourth chords, immense delays in resolving dissonances (one no longer speaks of preparation), rapid transitions of curious modulations, and contrasts of rhythm and frequent syncopations, jerks caused by strong accents on weak beats of a measure, this is the mobile or kaleidoscopic background that Puccini took pleasure in in *Bohème* and delights in in *Tosca*. No one will succeed in convincing me that it does not constitute, as one says, a *manner*. . . . Granted this system, few employ it with the ease and ability of Puccini.[47]

The libretto of *Tosca* differs markedly from that of *La Bohème*. Besides the obvious dissimilarity of the two sources, the task each one posed the librettists was opposite. With *La Bohème* their problem had been to expand the hints and ironies of Mürger sufficiently to allow for the emergence and interaction of character. The plot is tenuous—characters meet and part; the dramatic tension results from carefully regulated contrasts. With *Tosca*, on the other hand, their problem was to compress and yet to keep coherent Sardou's plot, an intricate example of what is ironically known as a "well-made" play. Where the text of *La Bohème* is a tissue of related images and metaphors, the text of *Tosca* is melodrama: raw responses to threats and violence, abrupt declarations of jealousy and desire, and terse talk about people and events not represented on stage.[48]

Many writers have spoken rather loosely about the veristic ele-

46. Pseudonym of Giuseppe Ippolito Franchi Verney, Count of Valetta (1848-1911).
47. Reprinted in *Carteggi Pucciniani*, p. 191.
48. Some of the people and events not represented on stage in *Tosca* are: the Marchese Attavanti, Cavaradossi's arrest, Angelotti's suicide, the scaffold, and the execution of Count Palmieri. Colautti's libretto for Giordano's *Fedora*, also based on a Sardou play, is if anything more notable than the book of *Tosca* for the variety, complexity, and dramatic importance of people and events the audience learns about only through hearsay.

ments in *Tosca*. Such talk can be misleading. Strictly, the school of
verismo in opera derives from the literary tradition of naturalism,
with its emphasis on the desperate conflicts of ordinary people
against a meticulously observed background. On the whole, it
seems more plausible to view *Tosca* as belonging to the tradition of
romantic melodrama, in the line of works like *Il Trovatore* and
La Gioconda, rather than as kin to the peasant drama of *Cavalleria*
and *I Pagliacci*. The traditional melodramatic aspects can be seen
in Scarpia's proposition, essentially that of di Luna and Barnaba,
and in Tosca's suicide, the parallel of Leonora's and Gioconda's.
The significant difference between the plot of *Tosca* and those of
Il Trovatore and *La Gioconda* is that Tosca murders the villain,
murders him in full view of the audience. In the usual literary sense
of the word, no one would call Sardou's play naturalistic.

If a distinction is drawn between the subject itself and the way
the subject is treated, then there is more justice in applying the term
"veristic" to *Tosca*. What some people find disconcerting and others
engrossing about *Tosca* is the diminution of the aesthetic distance.
An audience finds itself closer to the action of *Tosca* than is really
comfortable, much closer than it feels to the events of *Il Trovatore*
or *La Gioconda*. This is one of the perils of Puccini's approach, one
of the things that dismayed Giacosa. The audience's feeling of
closeness to the action strains credibility unless the roles, particularly those of Tosca and Scarpia, are acted with some plausibility
and conviction. Until Puccini experienced the revelation of Ternina
and Scotti in London, he had not realized how effectively his creations could be presented. Today a Callas and a Gobbi have proved
sensationally effective in these roles, but their interpretations are
based on their ability to characterize completely details of gesture
and action. When one thinks how much less specific detail of gesture and action is required in *Aïda* as opposed to *Tosca*, then one
can see that *Tosca* is veristic and *Aïda* is not.

Since the adjective "veristic" is almost always used too loosely to
be really helpful, there may be some justification for embarking on
a brief digression here to consider still another way this word is
used. Veristic is sometimes used to describe the style of singing demanded by *Tosca*, a style differing from, even opposed to, the
finesse and stamina demanded by the great Verdi roles. Verdi's
concept of the voice, generally speaking, developed out of the older
bel canto tradition, with its emphasis on agility, the long line, and

elegance of style. In Verdi's middle operas, there is an increasing emphasis on dramatic vehemence,[49] and it can be argued that it is from this tendency the veristic vocal style developed in its turn. With the sudden appearance of *Cavalleria* in 1890 and with the compelling example of Gemma Bellincioni, the original Santuzza, the veristic vocal style caught hold. No longer was there the emphasis on vocal refinement and studied technique, but on stentorian high notes, italicized declamation, extremes of vocal color (including the exploitation of the female "chest" voice), and on a whole repertory of extramusical effects, such as cries, gasps, and hysterical laughter. Some of the first-generation veristic singers, particularly the sopranos, were very exaggerated and their abused voices faded too soon. The extreme form of this vocal type has rarely appealed to English and American audiences, consequently mention of veristic singers is largely restricted to Italian writers who are more familiar with that species. Since the Italian repertory at Covent Garden and at the Metropolitan is more restricted than in its native theaters, there is less chance for singers specializing in only one of its branches to make a place for themselves in England and America, where singers survive on their versatility in a number of styles (even though their aptitude for some styles may be notably limited). Therefore, while it is safe to say that the demands of the roles in *Tosca* are closer to those of the veristic vocal style than the romantic, it is equally safe to say that English and American audiences very rarely have the chance to hear *Tosca* sung in that style, and they would probably disapprove of it if they did.

Now to return to the libretto of *Tosca*, many of the reservations Giacosa and Illica felt about it turned out to be unfounded. For instance, Illica was concerned that the plot contained so many scenes for just two characters, forgetting that this peculiarity of structure, if it is a disadvantage, has not hurt such different works as *Rigoletto* and *Tristan*. Illica thought there should be more big ensembles. *Tosca* contains only one, the scene of the *Te Deum* at Sant'Andrea della Valle in Act 1, and this is a rather one-sided ensemble, juxtaposing just one solo figure, Scarpia, against the chorus. Compared with *La Bohème*, *Tosca* contains fewer ensemble passages. While Tosca and Cavaradossi have two duets, there is none

49. Consider for a moment Manrico's back-to-back arias in *Il Trovatore*. The first, *Ah sì, ben mio*, requires vocal finesse; the second, *Di quella pira*, dramatic vehemence. Although one may find tenors who do well with one or the other, only very rarely does one find a tenor who sings both arias equally well.

for Tosca and Scarpia. The brief trio passage for the three principals in Act 2 turns out on examination not to be a real trio at all,
but a tune for the tenor with superimposed exclamations by the
soprano and baritone. While Illica was still working with Franchetti on the *Tosca* project, he sought to insert a quartet into the
torture scene. This unlikely notion was discarded immediately
when Puccini entered the picture. *Tosca* and *Butterfly* contain less
ensemble singing than any of Puccini's other scores because their
libretti more closely resemble the structure of stage plays than the
other texts he set to music.

One of the chief complaints raised by the librettists, seconded by
Ricordi, was against Puccini's suppression of the Hymn to Life and
Art they hoped to be the high point of Act 3. The chief recommendation for its inclusion was the praise Verdi gave it in Paris in
October 1894. Undoubtedly Verdi was moved by it since the
words apparently suited his own mood as he approached the end
of his long career. Puccini was wise to discard it because he felt
these sentiments were inappropriate to Cavaradossi, whose career
was not being terminated naturally after many years of glorious ac-
complishment, but prematurely, violently, and unjustly. Puccini
insisted that there should be greater emphasis on Cavaradossi's despair and suggested the key words: "Muoio disperato" (I die despairing), which were incorporated into the text of *E lucevan le
stelle.* Vincent Seligman remembers Puccini telling him that ad-
mirers of this aria "had treble cause to be grateful to him: for composing the music, for causing the words to be written—and for declining expert advice to throw the result into the waste-paper
basket."[50]

Some of the libretto's problems of credibility and structure are
inherited from Sardou's play. For instance, at the start of Act 1,
Angelotti appears in the church, searches for the key to the chapel,
and disappears into it to find the disguise of woman's clothing his
sister had deposited there. From his admission that in his foolish
terror he saw a policeman's jaw on every face he passed, we gather
that he is an escaped prisoner. And we are left to wonder about the
plausibility of his crossing half of Rome to reach a disguise hidden
in a semi-public place, when some simpler, less hazardous plan
would seem far more credible.

The dramatic structure almost breaks in half in the middle of

50. Vincent Seligman, *Puccini among Friends* (New York, 1938), p. 44.

Act 2. After Tosca has been goaded into revealing Angelotti's hiding place, Cavaradossi is released from his tortures and soon learns from Scarpia's order that Tosca has disclosed Angelotti's whereabouts. At this moment the problem of the first half of the action is solved: Tosca has secured Cavaradossi's freedom and Scarpia can arrest Angelotti. The logical continuation of this would be for Cavaradossi to turn on Tosca for betraying his trust, but this continuation is limited to one exchange, for the audience cannot witness sympathetic characters rounding off on one another without dismay or without feeling the accumulated tension dissipate. Some coup is needed. Something to put Cavaradossi back into Scarpia's power.

Providing the unexpected bit of news that winds things even tighter, Sciarrone bursts in to announce that the battle of Marengo has turned out contrary to the first report; at the last minute Napoleon has surprised and routed General Melas. The news of this defeat of the forces of reaction so excites Cavaradossi that he shouts: "Vittoria!"--which from Scarpia's point of view can be interpreted only as treason. Scarpia orders Cavaradossi hauled away for immediate execution. Once again Tosca is confronted with the problem of freeing Cavaradossi. But now for an entirely different reason. There has been a basic shift of motivation.

While it might be argued that Cavaradossi was not really freed by Tosca's informing, since he was obviously an accomplice to Angelotti's escape, yet to proceed along those lines would be anticlimactic. Sardou resorts to his shoddy coup, knowing that French audiences would respond to word of a Napoleonic victory in any context. In the play, the lavish use of historical detail better prepares the audience for this shift—Sardou counted on most of them to know all along who really won at Marengo. In the opera, however, where the background has been heavily pruned, Sciarrone's sudden appearance is mystifying. In the score, this moment is weak. The terse dialogue between Sciarrone and Scarpia is set to a chugging 2/4 passage that serves as a vacantly hectic buildup to Cavaradossi's cry of victory, a moment that allows the tenor to hurl high notes at the audience—hopefully an adequate recompense for an awkward moment of dramaturgy. Here, Puccini's music reflects his own sense of discomfort at the clumsy structure; his solution is to get over the awkwardness as rapidly and as inoffensively as possible.

In spite of its blemishes, the libretto is more effective than either of the librettists realized at first. Their letters in the days shortly after the *première* show they were stung by the charges of depravity and sadism leveled against their text. Puccini had more insight into its theatrical effectiveness than either Giacosa or Illica. It is wide of the mark to dismiss the plot as total claptrap and contrivance, for beneath its sometimes lurid surface *Tosca* exists as a fascinatingly representative product of the turn of the century. For all its veneer of elegant leisure, *la belle époque* was a period of deep social unrest, of political prisoners, and of corruption in high places. While these matters are the stuff of *Tosca*, they are not exactly unfamiliar in our times. And so without a too great wrenching of credibility, if with some dislocation of style, *Tosca* has been updated on occasion and played against a World War II background.[51] This suggests that beneath the melodramatic surface of *Tosca* there lurks a substratum of dramatic truth.

The score of *Tosca* contains many of the now-familiar traits of Puccini's style, but in a new emotional environment. The plot of *Tosca* differs from those of *Manon Lescaut* and *La Bohème*. In *Tosca* the lovers are victims of a repressive system personified by the villain Scarpia, while the earlier lovers had been primarily the victims of their own moral or physical weakness. This heightening of the conflict in Tosca requires a complementary heightening of Puccini's style. The moments of lyric expansiveness are in the familiar vein, brief arias and longer duets, but such moments constitute a smaller proportion of the whole work than in the preceding operas. Again Puccini uses recurring themes, fewer of them than in *Manon Lescaut* or *La Bohème*, but they undergo more transformation than those in the latter opera, less than those in the former. With the notable exception of the music for the arias and love scenes, Puccini's melodies in *Tosca* are less arresting for their own sake because many of them describe particular dramatic situations and depend on context for their effectiveness. As *Tosca* contains fewer attractive tunes and situations, most people tend to rank it below *La Bohème*, feeling that no matter how much one may be gripped by it, somehow one is less moved by it. If it is possible to resist the everlasting temptation to rank works—this obsession with

51. In a film version of *Tosca* entitled *E avanti a lui tremava tutta Roma*, the period of the action was advanced from 1800 to 1944.

masterpieces is frequently more inhibiting than helpful—it becomes easier to see how in *Tosca* Puccini was heading in new directions. He extends his resources by seeking more expressive ways to describe action and character; he experiments with vocal types new to him; he enlarges his orchestral palette, particularly in the range of somber, ominous hues.

Such actions as the precipitate but awkward entrance of the fugitive Angelotti, as Cavaradossi's mixing his colors before he starts painting, or even Scarpia's lustful lunges after Tosca are vividly described by Puccini. My favorite example of his new expressiveness in this line occurs in Act 2. While Scarpia writes the safe-conduct, Tosca—too numbed by her realization of her dreadful situation to think clearly of ways to avoid rape—blindly approaches the table for a sip of wine and suddenly catches sight of the sharp knife.

The F-sharp minor melody drags wearily, moving without any stress where it would customarily fall, but underlined by a second more regular melody, played in the cellos and bass clarinet, that rises and falls stealthily. These melodies in combination present us with both Tosca's numbed exhaustion and her half-conscious search for a means of escape. A variant of Example 1 appears in Act 3 when Tosca tells Cavaradossi how and why she murdered Scarpia, but here its form and character are greatly changed.

It is strongly accented, its tempo quickened, and its contours made bolder. Before it tottered, now it surges. It tells us that what had been Tosca's moment of black despair has become in retrospect a moment of triumph.

Puccini's skill at adapting melodies to suit a variety of moods is not always a matter of altering them drastically, but sometimes of modifying the scoring. Puccini makes frequent use of this melody from the Act 1 love duet:

3

This melody expresses ardent impetuousness and is scored for clarinet and bassoon over string arpeggios. Later in this act, when Tosca exits after her scene with Scarpia the melody returns in a grandiose form, fully scored and embellished by a counter-figure for the horns. Here it describes Tosca's sense of herself as a woman tragically wronged.

4

In Act 3 as Cavaradossi writes his letter of farewell to Tosca, the melody recurs fairly dripping with nostalgic tenderness, played by two solo violas and four cellos. Strongly contrasting to this is its next reappearance as Tosca enters like an eager Nike. Here it is highly developed, its surging sequences reminiscent of Tristan's entrance to join Isolde in the garden.

5

The complex character of Tosca gave Puccini a greater challenge than did either Manon or Mimì. While Tosca may seem less sympathetic than these earlier Puccini heroines, she is far more interesting. Consider for a moment how she is established at her first entrance.

6

To this broad melody (in the solo cello doubled by the flute and accompanied by string arpeggios) Tosca sweeps into the church. This melody describes her physical poise, her absolutely female presence. Her vocal line does not double this melody. She is peremptory, irritated at having been kept waiting, her prompt jealousy rising to the surface. In a few bars, Puccini has set before us the prima donna and the woman. Example 6 returns in *Vissi d'arte*, but here the vocal line is more closely adjusted to it. In this aria Tosca speaks as a woman; she is not acting, but revealing her basically devout and generous nature. With great skill Puccini paints her throughout the score, showing many facets of her volatile temperament and her ever-present sensuality. It is important to remember that in *Tosca*, for the only time in his career, Puccini presents the portrait of a mature Italian woman, a type one can imagine he knew and understood better than his more exotic heroines.

With this role, Puccini essayed what was for him a new vocal type. What he had in mind is revealed by a letter he wrote in a fit of discouragement over a poor production of *Tosca* in Pavia. The letter is dated March 1902.

> . . . *Tosca* has come out in a sad period. There are no artists any more! The present ones only produce 30 percent of what the composer conceived! It is too little. There aren't any longer the dramatic temperaments there used to be! My fault then has been to write an opera that will never have the interpretation it ought to have. The Marianis, the Durands, the Pantaleonis are meteors that have vanished.[52]

The three dramatic sopranos he mentions are linked in Puccini's mind by their associations with Ponchielli operas—Mariani-Masi

52. *Carteggi Pucciniani*, p. 219.

was the first Gioconda, Durand sang in the *première* of *I Lituani*,
Pantaleoni in the first *Marion Delorme*. (It is curious to see how
Ponchielli's influence survived more than twenty-five years in his
pupil's artistic consciousness.) What Puccini had in mind for Tosca,
then, was a voice with the power, stamina, and range to sing Gioconda, and he asked for a flaming temperament to match the voice.
This is the kind of voice needed to negotiate such passages as this
one from the torture scene in Act 2.

7

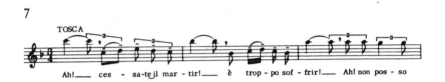

Ah!___ ces - sa-te il mar - tir!___ è trop - po sof - frir!___ Ah! non pos - so

Such a passage, sung full voice over heavy orchestration, is not for
vocal lightweights. Further, the ideal singer for Tosca needs a dark,
sensuous color in the lower octave. Many of her most expressive
and provocative phrases exploit this part of the voice.

8

flo - re - al___ i - ne - bria il cor.

9

par___ che le co - se a-spet - tan tut - te in - na - mo - ra - te il so - le?___

In Max de Schauensee's happy phrase,[53] the role of Tosca combines
fire and feminine languor.

For the role of Scarpia, Puccini experimented with another vocal
type new to him. It is unlike the more lyric roles of Lescaut and
Marcello. Scarpia, the forerunner of Rance in *La Fanciulla* and
Michele in *Il Tabarro*, is an extension of the vocal type Verdi used
for the role of Iago. The association between Scarpia and Iago is

53. Max de Schauensee, *The Collector's Verdi and Puccini* (Philadelphia, 1962),
p. 127. This little book contains more perceptive comment than many volumes
twice its size.

made explicit in Act 1, when Scarpia holds the Marchese Attavanti's fan and remembers Iago's use of Desdemona's handkerchief. Like Iago, Scarpia analyzes his own motives in an aria near the beginning of Act 2, but *Ha più forte sapore* is a pallid descendant of Iago's *Credo*. Scarpia's account of his life as a voluptuary is short—only thirty bars—and its choppy phrases lack the bitter irony and grandiose evil of the *Credo*. Scarpia's monologue is overshadowed, as Puccini feared it might be, by the *Te Deum* scene, where Scarpia's phrases have real lyric propulsion. On the other hand, Scarpia's moments of suavity likewise remind us of Iago with their sugary hypocrisy. Scarpia's invitation to Tosca to share his supper is in this vein.

10

Such moments as these never develop into sustained cantilena. His outburst later in Act 2, *Già mi struggea*, presents a severe challenge to a singer; the vocal line hammers relentlessly at the top register, while the singer must color his voice to show his barely restrainable desire for Tosca. At this moment Puccini has pushed the singer about as far as he can go without tumbling over into absurdity. The role demands an authoritative baritone voice with a powerful top up to G-flat.[54]

For Cavaradossi Puccini uses a vocal type he had exploited before, a *lirico spinto* tenor with facile upper notes. This role is lighter in its demands than that of Des Grieux, but heavier than that of Rodolfo. If the character of Cavaradossi seems overshadowed by those of Tosca and Scarpia, that is the penalty of a plot which puts the hero in jeopardy and sets the heroine to saving him. That Cavaradossi is an artist, Puccini convinces us by the warmth and ardor of his music; that he is an aristocrat, a *Cavaliere*, to judge from the music assigned him, must be taken on credit.

The chief redeeming feature of Cavaradossi's part is the famous

54. For Scotti, Puccini sanctioned a transposition that lowers the top G-flat along with the most grueling tessitura of the role. This transposition may be heard on Scotti's recording of *Già mi dicon venal* made for Victor on 30 March 1908. The transposition occurs in the phrase: "Se la giurata fede debbo tradir" at the 8th syllable.

scene near the opening of Act 3. Although this scene produces an impression of spontaneity, Puccini has gone to unusual lengths in his formal design. The episode is dominated by this famiilar melody:

11

After the description of the Roman dawn, it is played by the strings in unison, accompanied by the deep tolling of the *campanone* of St. Peter's. As Cavaradossi is led onto the platform, the flute and clarinet begin to double Example 11. There follows a short bit between Cavaradossi and the jailer. Cavaradossi begins to write his last letter to Tosca, accompanied by Example 3, but at the point his memories so overwhelm him that the pen falls from his hands, Example 11 reappears longingly (*vagamente*) in the clarinet.[55]

E lucevan le stelle begins as a bittersweet recollection of sensual life and ends as an expression of bleak despair at the thought of the death of the senses. In phrases each set to a single pitch, he begins his passionate recollection of Tosca coming to his arms. The restricted vocal line of the opening phrases expresses Mario's effort at self-control; his emotion rises as he takes up Example 11, for what is really the second verse of the aria. He speaks of their sweet kisses, their languid embraces; he remembers how impatiently he freed her lovely body of its diaphanous raiment.[56] The orchestra-

55. At Cavaradossi's entrance, Example 11 is heard in E minor, but it occurs in G minor during the aria. This relation of keys is reminiscent of *Manon Lescaut*, where the melody of *Donna non vidi mai* is introduced in G major, but the aria itself is in B-flat.

56. I give these lines of the text because their meaning is obscured in many prudish translations of the libretto. The singing of them is a great test of a tenor's taste and vocal skill.

There are those who speak with ill-concealed scorn of a hero who speaks of things of the senses as the moment of death approaches. They should re-read the text of Siegfried's *Heilige Braut* or some of Tristan's lines in the last act.

I have vivid memories of a performance of *Tosca* in Rome just a few months after the war in Europe ended. The cast included Gigli and Gobbi, and the Tosca was Pia Tassinari, married to the tenor Tagliavini, Gigli's alternate that season. After Gigli sang *E lucevan le stelle* there was a tremendous uproar in the audience. The Tagliavini fans booing the old lion Gigli, while the Gigli party tried to roar them down. Waiting for the verdict, Gigli stood patiently, looking at the stage. After some minutes, the conductor Basile gave the signal for the encore. With the stimulus provided by the highly partisan audience, Gigli's repetition of the aria was a master-lesson. The ovation he received at the end was thunderous—and unanimous.

tion grows more intense and heavy as Cavaradossi's mood darkens. Never has he loved life so much as at the moment when it must end. As the aria was preceded by Example 3 when Cavaradossi started to write, so it is followed by that theme in a varied form to accompany Tosca's entrance. The applause following the aria always tends to obscure the balance of this whole scene, but its formal design emerges without that distraction on phonograph records.

In the matter of orchestration *Tosca* marks a real advance for Puccini, calling forth a greater range of instrumental color than he had used before. For instance, the three chords that open the opera —a sequence of chords based on the whole-tone scale—are scored for full orchestra.

When Cavaradossi explains to Angelotti about the well, a variant of this chord-sequence occurs, but in an entirely different orchestral color and rhythm. Now the chords are given to three flutes and, for the top line, an oboe in unison with the celesta; the bass line is played by the bassoon, and the final chord is reinforced by a soft harp chord and drum roll. The effect is mysterious and ominous.

13

This sequence is varied again to accompany Tosca's business of placing lighted candelabra by Scarpia's corpse. Puccini has instructed these chords now to be played as softly as possible. The strings play the first two chords; the third combines three flutes (the upper harmony completed by the clarinet), and the harp, gong, and bass drum. The harmony of the third chord is here altered from E major to E minor. This sequence is repeated three times. It is followed by a sudden forte chord and snare drum roll. This chord is designed to accompany Tosca's dropping—not placing—the crucifix on Scapia's chest. The eerie orchestral color complements Tosca's compulsive ritual.

In *Tosca*, Puccini makes particular use of bells in a variety of sizes and pitches. In the church, a bell in F tolls the Angelus. Later in the same act, during the scene between Tosca and Scarpia, there is a much more elaborate effect of bells. Besides a four-tone chime for the bells themselves, Puccini imitates them in many ingenious ways. Once he uses pizzicato strings, then harp with staccato flute, and later a combination of staccato woodwinds, horns, glockenspiel, and pizzicato strings. Puccini's virtuosity is such that he produces the effect of the bells continuing their chime, but the fact is that many of the bell effects are produced by other means. In the finale to Act 1, Puccini uses an ostinato repetition of bells in B-flat and F to provide the ground bass, over which he erects the full orchestral texture of his ensemble. As this scene increases in sonority, he adds an organ and punctuating explosions of a cannon to the instrumental fabric. The greatest use of bells occurs in the Act 3 prelude. There are sheep bells and then church bells at a wide range of pitches. To produce an effect of "tinntinnabulation" Puccini writes for the bells in overlapping parts, most often heard in a sequence of three, four, and five strokes. When Verdi heard of all the requirements for bells in the scoring of *Tosca*, he is said to have shaken his head and mentioned what difficulties he experienced to get a single E-flat bell for the *Miserere* scene at the Roman *première* of *Il Trovatore*.

The changes in the autograph score of *Tosca* are relatively slight, but they shed insight on Puccini's pragmatic way with his scores.

For instance, when Tosca demands to know the price of Cavaradossi's release, the notes originally were:

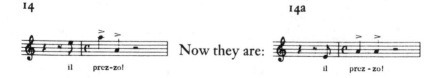

14   14a

il   prez-zo!   Now they are: il   prez - zo!

By removing the octave leap Puccini not only reduces the danger of what might sound like an outraged squawk, but he increases the intelligibility of a key word. Even more important, Example 14a more easily permits Tosca to express her loathing and contempt for Scarpia, by pitching the phrase nearer the middle of the soprano range.

Some of the changes in the text show Puccini's concern for appropriate expression. In Act 1 the Sacristan[57] covets Cavaradossi's hamper of food and asks if he is fasting. The painter's reply originally was "Pranzai" (I have eaten), but this was changed to "Fame non ho" (I am not hungry), an expression that strengthens the sense of class distinction between the aristocratic Cavaradossi and the Sacristan. In Act 2 one finds a stronger indication of this concern with propriety. Where Tosca now assures Cavaradossi, just released from the torture chamber, that the just Lord will punish Scarpia ("Ma il giusto Iddio lo punirà"), formerly she had these strong words: "Ma il sozzo sbirro lo pagherà" (But the filthy cop will pay for it). Not only is the expression unladylike, but dramatically unconvincing, since Scarpia is present on stage when Tosca addresses these words to Cavaradossi.

Besides these changes which remove inappropriate expressions, some omissions are designed to cut out empty rhetoric and tighten the action. Just before the E major passage of the Act 1 love duet, there used to be this bit of dialogue:

> TOSCA: *Oh, come la sai bene*
> *l'arte d'entrarmi in core!*
> CAVARADOSSI: *Non è arte,*
> *E amore è amore, è amore!*
> TOSCA: *Sì, sì, ti credo,*
> *Ma falle gli occhi neri!* . . .

(TRANSLATION: TOSCA: Oh, how well you know the art of penetrating my heart! CAVARADOSSI: It is not art, it is love, it is love! TOSCA: Yes, yes, I believe you, but make her eyes black! . . .)

Now this passage is much shorter.

> TOSCA: *Oh, come la sai bene*
> *L'arte di farti amare!*
> *Ma falle gli occhi neri!*

57. In the autograph, the Sacristan is always referred to as *'lo scaccino'* (the Sexton or Verger). His present title is regarded in Italy as more refined.

(TRANSLATION: Oh, how well you know the art of making
                 yourself beloved! But make her eyes black!)

This condensation concentrates Tosca's capitulation instead of dis-
sipating it in a bit of feeble protestation. Only five measures have
been removed here, but the gain in keeping up the momentum of
the scene is notable. The removal of this short passage illustrates
Puccini's keen sense of timing.

   In the Act 2 torture scene there is a somewhat similar change, but
here it is not a matter of a simple cut, but rather of altering the
vocal lines and text over one of Puccini's most heavily orchestrated
climaxes. Originally in response to Scapia's shouts of "Più forte!"
(Harder!) Tosca had bemoaned her too great suffering ("Ah,
troppo soffrir!"). Observing her, Scarpia used to repeat (twice!)
his earlier line about Tosca having never been so tragic on stage
("Mai Tosca alla scena più tragica fu!"); Puccini recognized the
ineffectiveness of the characters' commenting on their situation
rather than responding directly to it. Since the music at this point
scarcely permits cutting out a few measures, he changed Scarpia's
third shout of "Più forte!" to "Parlate!" (Speak!), thereby mo-
tivating Tosca's denial that she knows Angelotti's hiding place. This
change is a decided improvement.

   The most surprising change occurs in Act 3. When Tosca realizes Cavaradossi's execution has been a real one, not a pretense, she
exclaims "Finire così? Finire così?" (To end like this?). The autograph shows that next she was to sing a five-bar fortissimo reprise of
the melody of *E lucevan le stelle*, Example 11.[58] Cutting out Tosca's
lament not only removes the inconsistency of having her sing a
melody first sung when she was not on stage, but speeds up the
action at a critical point when a rhetorical outburst, even a short
one, would cause an unendurable delay.

   From these changes we can see how carefully Puccini gauged
the interaction of his characters and how painstakingly he sought

---

58. The melody of Example 11 is heard at the end of the opera. Some have ques-
tioned its appropriateness there, but their reservations might be lessened if they
knew that at one time Puccini planned to give that melody to Tosca, too. Puccini's
intention, then, seems to have been that the melody stood not just for Cavaradossi's love for Tosca, but for their love for each other. At the end of the opera,
Example 11 is a commentary on the destructiveness inherent in great passions.
This final appearance of Example 11 is the apotheosis of the Ponchiellian peroration; the melody is played by the strings, winds, horns, and trumpets in unison,
punctuated by drum rolls and cymbal crashes.

to maintain the dramatic impetus. There are those who claim that *Vissi d'arte* slows down the action at a critical moment. In his later years Puccini has been reported as sharing this opinion, but surely his first instincts were best. Some release of tension is mandatory in this scene of attempted rape, and since Tosca has had no big aria up to this point, a bit of sustained singing for her here supplies a needed aspect to the role. There is absolutely no indication in the autograph that *Vissi d'arte* was planned as anything but an integral part of this scene.

Maestro Tenaglia pointed out to me one error that crept into some scores, but it has since been corrected. It arose from an editor's misunderstanding of Puccini's harmonic intent. In Act 1, at the end of her *Non la sospiri*, Tosca has this phrase:

15   15a

Ar-de a   To - sca nel san-gue il fol-le a - mor!__

The last note of the phrase is supported by the chord of Example 15a. In some scores the final note of Tosca's phrase was printed as an A-flat, a far more ordinary effect than Puccini intended. I made a random survey of some phonograph records of *Non la sospiri* and discovered that Olive Fremstad, Ljuba Welitch, Zinka Milanov,[59] and Renata Tebaldi (in her second, "stereo" complete recording of *Tosca*) all sing the A-flat; while Geraldine Farrar, Germaine Lubin, Renata Tebaldi (in her first, "mono" complete recording of *Tosca*), and Maria Callas sing the F.

Madama Butterfly

In the weeks before the *première* of *Tosca*, Puccini had already started fretting about the subject for his next opera. For the first time in his career, he did not find what he was looking for almost

59. Since Milanov was a pupil of Milka Ternina, who introduced Tosca both to London and New York, perhaps her singing of the A-flat rather than the F in this phrase derives from Ternina.

immediately. From now on, he was to experience difficulties in this line. But if he could not start on his next opera, he could at least keep a careful eye on his old ones.

From Rome and the world *première* of *Tosca*, he went to Milan to await its introduction at La Scala. If Puccini's Roman experience had suggested that his success had aroused resentment, his Milanese experience did nothing to alter that impression. Gatti-Casazza, then the impresario of La Scala, remembered the night of 17 March 1900 as one of "great coldness and contrarities during the entire first act and in the second until *Vissi d'arte*, in which Darclée, who was in the good graces of the public, succeeded in overcoming the coldness. . . ."[60] The Milanese critics praised the production, but were for the most part hostile to the score. Puccini was particularly pleased with the conducting of Toscanini, who directed the opera for the first time on this occasion. Like *La Bohème*, *Tosca* did not become an overnight success; it took the score nearly a year to establish its wide popularity.

Shortly after this performance, Puccini went to Torre del Lago to inspect the new villa being built there according to his designs. This house is the present Villa Puccini, now a combination museum and mausoleum. It is built on filled land, fronting the lake, the site a gift from Marchese Ginori,[61] whose own villa, La Piaggetta, was then being built on the opposite shore of the lake. The Villa Puccini today is farther from the shore than it used to be as there are now a square and restaurant built on the filled land in front of it.

By the middle of May, Puccini was back in Milan, still anxiously searching for a new subject. At this time he exchanged a series of letters with Illica, discussing the possibilities of a comic opera on the subject of Alphonse Daudet's *Tartarin*. As frequently happened with Puccini, his initial enthusiasm would cool, and soon he would be considering other proposals. In June he left Milan for London, where *Tosca* had its Covent Garden *première* on 12 July 1900.[62]

60. Gatti-Casazza, p. 96.
61. Puccini dedicated the score of *La Bohème* to Ginori.
62. The first London cast of *Tosca* included Milka Ternina (1863-1941), whose Tosca Puccini called a "true creation," Fernando de Lucia (1861?-1925) as Cavaradossi, and Antonio Scotti (1866-1936) as Scarpia.
   Mancinelli conducted the Metropolitan *première* of *Tosca* on 4 February 1901. Giuseppe Cremonini (who had created Des Grieux in *Manon Lescaut*) sang Cavaradossi, with Ternina and Scotti repeating their London success. The rest of this New York cast included Eugéne Dufriche (Angelotti), Jacques Bars (Spoletta), Lodovico Viviani (Sciarrone), and Cernusco (the Jailer). Puccini did not come to New York for this performance.

This was the most successful production of the opera so far. The audience was genuinely enthusiastic, and at Mancinelli's urging Puccini took repeated bows.

The most important by-product of Puccini's London sojourn was his going to see a double-bill at the Duke of York Theatre. Rounding out the evening, after Jerome K. Jerome's *Miss Nobbs*, was a play written by David Belasco in collaboration with John Luther Long—*Madame Butterfly*. Puccini was much struck by the second play, particularly by the scene of the vigil—more than ten minutes during which Butterfly, Suzuki, and the baby wait a whole night for Pinkerton's return—and by the scene of Butterfly's suicide. Although Puccini's English was almost nonexistent, he found himself absorbed by the play, but not to the extent that Belasco reports in his unreliable autobiography. There he speaks of Puccini rushing up to him, weeping inconsolably, and demanding the operatic rights on the spot. Puccini was still considering other prospects before he definitely decided on *Butterfly*.

On his way to Italy from London, Puccini stayed for a few days in Paris. Here he made a point of consulting Zola about his sensational novel *La Faute de l'abbé Mouret*, a step he would scarcely have taken if he were wholly committed to Belasco's play. By mid-August 1900 he was toying with the idea of Marie Antoinette as a subject, a notion that had plagued him before and would again, but he had reservations about "the too old and over-exploited" subject of the French Revolution. In October, Puccini was in Brussels and sent Illica a pamphlet on Marie Antoinette. *Butterfly* was far from forgotten though, for on 20 November he wrote to Ricordi that the more he thought of it the more irresistibly he was attracted.

But before he finally started working on *Madama Butterfly*, an event took place that was an unpleasant omen. *La Bohème* was announced as the second opera of the 1900-1901 season at La Scala, with Toscanini conducting, Emma Carelli[63] as Mimì, and Caruso making his La Scala debut as Rodolfo. (Puccini and Caruso had somewhat patched up their difficulties over the *première* of *Tosca*, when Puccini heard Caruso sing Cavaradossi triumphantly at Bologna the preceding October.) *Tristan* was to have been given for

---

63. Carelli (1877-1928) was first a successful soprano and then an influential *impresaria*, in charge of the Teatro Costanzi, Rome, from 1912 to 1926. Her memoirs, *Trent'anni di vita del teatro lirico* (Rome, 1932) give her account of this *Bohème* production. See also Gatti-Casazza, and see Pierre V. R. Key, *Enrico Caruso* (Boston, 1922).

the opening, its first production at La Scala, but the illness of the tenor Borgatti[64] necessitated a postponement, and *La Bohème* was substituted for *Tristan*. This moving up of the performance added strain to an already tense situation. Caruso was nervous at facing the critical Milanese and had got off on the wrong foot with Toscanini by refusing to sing the high C in *Che gelida manina* full voice in rehearsal.[65] There were difficulties between Caruso and Carelli, both Neapolitans, and the soprano had no desire to be outshone by the tenor. Puccini was eager that his opera appear to the best advantage and personally supervised the rehearsals. In the strained atmosphere caused by strong personalities at odds, Puccini labored hard to animate the cast, even to the extent of calling a special rehearsal that lasted all morning and almost all afternoon on the day of the public general rehearsal. By the time the cast assembled for the opening, there was more than one obstinate and sulky person about.

But all the difficulties were not behind the footlights. As with the *Tosca* performances at La Scala the preceding March, there were those present who were determined to see the evening turn out badly. The partisans of Mascagni hoped that the success of that season would not go to *La Bohème* but to *Le Maschere*, which was to be introduced on 17 January 1901 not only at La Scala but at six other theaters the same night.[66] The opening *La Bohème* of 26 December 1900 was performed to "fatal silence" as Emma Carelli remembered. Puccini was so saddened and humiliated by the occasion that he fled to Torre del Lago for a few days' hunting to quiet his nerves. Although his opera was repeated nine times that season, the reception was never enthusiastic. Caruso's great success at La Scala did not occur until later that season, when he sang Donizetti's *L'Elisir d'Amore* on 17 February 1901. This *La Bohème* was the sixth production of a Puccini opera at La Scala; the seventh was to be an even more traumatic experience for Puccini.

Puccini returned to Milan shortly after the New Year (1901) to find a letter from Illica, suggesting that the bad reception of *La*

64. Giuseppe Borgatti (1871-1950) was the greatest Italian Wagnerian tenor of his generation. Before his identification with this repertory he sang in the *prima* of *Andrea Chénier* and in the first *Tosca* at La Scala (with Darclée and Giraldoni).
65. Caruso was so uncertain of his high C at this stage of his career that Toscanini insisted he transpose *Che gelida manina* down half a tone for these performances.
66. *Le Maschere* had only six simultaneous *premières!* The seventh, at the San Carlo in Naples, had to be postponed because of illness in the cast. This presumptuous launching did the attractive score, unfortunately burdened by a poor libretto by Illica, little service. Mascagni earned a good deal of ridicule over this opera.

Bohème at La Scala was caused by the public's annoyance with him for working so little. Justly irritated by this accusation, Puccini answered by asking, "But tell me who has given the stage in a few years three operas that travel about and stir up the theatres?? It is only the hatred of the critics for one who works and above all who earns money without turning over one penny (*un baiocco*) to their pockets."[67] In his turn, Illica was put out with Puccini for his lack of enthusiasm for the plot about Marie Antoinette and for the rumors that Puccini was making overtures to another librettist, Arturo Colautti.[68] The relations between Puccini and Illica deteriorated during the subsequent weeks to the point that on 25 February Puccini wrote to him in this vein: "I never expected such a letter as you wrote me! I would set you aside because you no longer enjoy my favor and confidence? Then why do I try to see you? Disappointments? *Bohème* and *Tosca* do not seem like disappointments to me." This falling out was caused by their lack of a subject to work on; it did not last very long.

On 7 March, a little more than a week after Puccini's letter, he sent Illica a copy of an Italian translation of John Luther Long's story, *Madame Butterfly*.[69] He apologized that the translation was only "so-so, but it will suffice to give you an idea of the work. In the play by Belasco there are much better things, above all the ending." Puccini's spirits had risen abruptly. The summer before Puccini, then forty-one, had written to Ricordi that his best years—"the last of my youth"—were being wasted. Now, speaking of *Butterfly*, he says, "I am completey taken with it!"

Although Puccini was aware of the differences between the original story of *Madame Butterfly* and the later play, Illica began working on the subject with only the story in hand; he did not see a translation of the play until June of that year. This sequence of events was to have important repercussions on the development of the opera and was to contribute something to the disaster of the

67. *Carteggi Pucciniani*, p. 205.
68. Colautti (1851-1914) wrote the librettos to Giordano's *Fedora* (1898) and Cilea's *Adriana Lecouvreur* (1902) and *Gloria* (1907).
69. Long (1861-1927) was a lawyer who lived in Philadelphia and wrote as an avocation. His story of *Madame Butterfly*, which first appeared in the *Century Magazine* (1897), was derived in part from a true incident told him by his sister, the wife of a missionary stationed in Nagasaki, and in part from Pierre Loti's *Madame Chrysanthème* (1887). Loti's tale had already been turned into a light opera by André Messager (1853-1919). It was first given at the opening of the Théâtre-Lyrique de la Renaissance, Paris, 30 January 1893.

opera's *première*. Unlike the heroine of the play, Butterfly does not die at the end of the story. When she learns she has been abandoned, she wounds herself but not fatally, Suzuki nurses her back to health, and when Pinkerton returns to the little house on the hill he finds it deserted. There are, besides, many incidents in the story that have no counterpart in the play.

Puccini's first grasp of the subject had quite a different emphasis from that he later gave it. He was enthusiastic about the plot at first for the opportunities it gave to stress the conflict beween Eastern and Western values and culture. He remembered that the role of Yamadori, Cho-Cho-San's Japanese suitor, had been acted in Western dress, and he thought this an improvement over the presentation of Yamadori in the tale because "we need the so-called Westernized element." This emphasis means that the original conception did not focus as completely on the figure of Madame Butterfly as it came to later. The result of all the many subsequent modifications of the text and score was to center attention more and more on the heroine.

Illica's first plan for the libretto was in three acts, but this arrangement was later altered.

> Act 1: Butterfly's house
> Act 2: the Consulate
> Act 3: Butterfly's house

The first two acts were to be derived primarily from the story; the third, from the play. The Consulate was located in the "European Concession," a setting that added variety to the stage picture and stressed the contrast between East and West. In April 1901 Illica writes to Ricordi that he has been going full sail: "In this first act there are even too many opportunities for music; however, I will leave them all in, and later it will be seen which to keep and which not, for all are beautiful." Illica's happy-go-lucky attitude about the structure and proportion spelled danger for the opera. A number of years would pass before enough of his "beautiful" moments were cut away to produce the first act we know today.

As with Illica, Giulio Ricordi's first introduction to the subject came through a reading of Long's story. Even though Puccini explained the differences between the story and the play, Ricordi was, as Puccini informed Illica, "a litle cold" to the idea of using *Madame*

Butterfly. Just how confused the participants were with the subject they were treating is illustrated by an incredible letter that Illica wrote to Ricordi sometime in April. This letter is Illica's reaction to the news that Ricordi has just acquired the rights to the Long-Belasco play. He protests that there is no need of Belasco's permission and even less to pay him for it! He is convinced that if Puccini had seen the play in an Italian theater, he would not have been nearly so impressed with it. Illica's confusion is obvious when he writes: "Now then, the moving last act is nothing other, basically, than the story and not Signor Belasco's play!"[70] Since the scene of Butterfly's hara-kiri occurs *only* in the play, Illica's mistake shows that in the month he had had the translation of the story in his hand, a month in which he had already carved one act of a libretto out of the story, he had neglected to read it to the end! As he had already developed his sketch for Act 1 out of the story and would have to follow the same procedure to make a sketch of the proposed Consulate scene, he blandly assumed that his last act could be evolved from the story as well. As we now know the libretto, both parts of Act 2 are a fairly faithful transcription of the play, certainly necessitating paying Belasco for the rights. But in April 1901 Illica had not yet read the play.

Ricordi's coolness toward the idea of using *Butterfly* was not allayed by some other comments in this letter from Illica: "Look . . . at the role of the tenor! Problems! We must think about that! Pinkerton is unsympathetic! He is presented . . . and must not be seen again! And his is the drama!" This last sentence provides another measure of Illica's confusion. It shows that he was thinking of the story; parts of it are told from Pinkerton's point of view, but in the play Pinkerton appears only briefly.

Puccini realized that Illica was experiencing problems, but he blamed them on the faulty translation of the story. Accordingly, he had an unnamed American woman make a new translation in order to develop some enthusiasm in Ricordi and to help solve some of Illica's "problems." Then early in June, almost three months after they had started on *Butterfly*, Puccini got hold of an Italian script of the play. This he read to Ricordi before he sent it on to Illica. With obvious relief Puccini reports to his librettist: "After the reading Signor Giulio was conquered completely. He told me he could not sleep because of the impression it made on him." With Ricordi

70. *Carteggi Pucciniani*, p. 211.

won over and the text of the play in hand, the project took on a brighter aspect.

The promise, however, continued brighter than the actuality. Puccini had to wait until October before he finally got possession of the libretto. To help him while the time until he could get down to composition, Puccini bought his first automobile in June 1901. He took to the then exotic means of transportation with great enthusiasm. In this, he was seconded by the example of Franchetti, an early convert and in 1900 president of the Club Italiano degli Automobolisti, and even more so by his friend and patron, the Marchese Ginori, who owned the first automobile imported into Italy. Puccini passed the six hottest weeks of the summer of 1901 at Cutigliano, a little community in the hills some twenty-two miles above Pistoia. Puccini enjoyed these times of *villeggiatura* as the seclusion and cool nights were favorable to his composing. For this purpose he had earlier acquired a villa at Chiatri, in the mountains above the pass of Quiesa, but it was so inaccessible and primitive that Elvira despised it. Later he would acquire still another villa, this one at Abetone, high up in the Apulian Alps, for the same purpose. The summer at Cutigliano was a frustrating time, however; Puccini had nothing to work on, and Elvira was ill and out of sorts.

Puccini's demands for some sign of a libretto to work on grew more desperate, until 1 October, when he wrote to Illica to acknowledge receiving the text of two acts at long last. "Fine, fine! I am very happy with your work, especially the first act." He has some reservations about the Consulate scene—especially that part based on the scene in the story where Kate Pinkerton sees Butterfly and, without knowing her identity, gushes over her and calls her a "plaything." He is also concerned about the intermezzo that is to connect the two parts of the last act. His description of it as *cupo-lento* (somber and slow) shows that he originally thought of it in terms very different from the work he actually composed. A month later, writing to Illica again, he makes another suggestion about the intermezzo, which shows that his ideas were becoming clearer: ". . . think about that intermezzo, so that I might use the chorus: we must find something good. Mysterious voices humming (for instance). I don't know what I want, but we need something, and you will find something, I am sure." This suggestion foreshadows the famous humming chorus that precedes the intermezzo.

Puccini was thinking ahead and planning, but he had not yet received the whole libretto. He was anxious for it, as he kept worrying about details and kept fiddling with piano sketches of ideas. The direction his mind was now taking is clear from another letter he wrote to Illica, this one on 10 January 1902: "At last I have embarked for Japan and I will do my best to re-create it. But more than articles on moral and material habits, I would like some notes of popular music for a clue. I have looked for it and found it, but it is poor and not much ("poca cosa")." Worrying about his new project, he still thinks about the welfare of his finished works. He writes to a friend in Pavia in March that he hopes "*Tosca* establishes itself and to shame the *superpubblico* of Milan that it can survive for some time yet." When *Madama Butterfly* was finally produced, Puccini had more than this *superpubblico's* "prudent reserve" to contend with!

Puccini still did not have the complete libretto by early June 1902. As Giacosa grew older and his health became more uncertain, he found Puccini's demands for changes ever more troublesome. Prompted by the impatient Puccini, Ricordi had demanded that Giacosa hurry up and finish his work. In answer Giascosa sent to Ricordi, on 20 May, a third-person account of his labors. Although he had finished Act 2 (still the Consulate scene) in February, Puccini had insisted on new changes for Act 1, besides wanting a large part of Act 2 to be rewritten; all this prevented Giacosa from completing Act 3 (the present two parts of Act 2). Protesting his own innocence, Giacosa laid the whole blame for the delay on Puccini.

The summer of 1902 was a trying one for Puccini at Torre del Lago. Always depressed when he had no work in hand, he had his troubles with Elvira, as well. Her disposition had not improved with time. Her position was difficult, a point that Giacomo well understood. Although she had lived with him for nearly twenty years, marriage was still impossible as her legal husband was still alive. Her social position was delicate, as she was either not received or chose not to go to many houses eagerly offering hospitality to Giacomo.[71] The passing years which had been kind to Giacomo's appearance had been hard on Elvira. At forty-two, she was a large, plain woman, undeniably plump and ill at ease in the world. In the light of her own irregular position, she feared the competition of younger

71. Although Elvira was often invited to La Piaggetta, the Ginori's villa just across the lake, she never set foot in it. The marchese's daughter told me that in her own home Elvira was a gracious and thoughtful hostess.

women, many of whom found Giacomo irresistible. There is no evidence that at this time Giacomo, whatever his diversions or however trying he found Elvira, ever thought of leaving her, although
seven years later there was to be a serious rupture. In 1902, however, their relationship was strained by Giacomo's passion for auto-
mobiling (a pastime that gave him from Elvira's point of view an
undesirable freedom of movement) and by the marriage of Elvira's
daughter Fosca and her removal to Milan. Undoubtedly Fosca's absence heightened the tension, and Puccini's letters to her reveal this.

Only at the end of August 1902 was Puccini able to lose himself
in work on *Butterfly*, but it was not until the middle of November
1902 that he finally received the completed libretto. Reading the
whole text, Puccini was struck by a basic problem in structure. On
16 November he wrote to Illica: "Do you know what I have discovered? That the scene at the consulate has brought me to disaster!
The opera must be in two acts. The first yours, and the other Belasco's play with all its details. I am absolutely convinced of this and
thus the work will produce a great impression. No entr'acte and
come to the end holding the public riveted for an hour and a half!
It's enormous, but it's the life of the opera. . . ." By giving up the
Consulate scene, which Puccini had come to see as basically irrele-
vant, he had moved away from his original idea of stressing the
interaction of East and West and come to focus on the central figure of Butterfly. His increasing involvement with the character of
Butterfly blinded him to the strain a second act of such outsize proportions would place upon an audience. Giacosa was alarmed by
this decision to play all of Act 2 without lowering the curtain and
strove to make Puccini reconsider his decision. Ricordi did his best
to mediate, but at first he was afraid the whole opera would be too
short to fill a full evening, and he looked askance at the prospect of
theaters giving it as a double-bill with *I Pagliacci!* Whatever Illica's
thoughts about the long second act, he came to approve of cutting
out the Consulate scene, assuring Ricordi of it in a letter written in
December 1902. Elsewhere in that letter he says: "I have reason to
believe that a little calm reigns round the famous Lago di Massaciuccoli! Let's wish them so . . . ."

One way or another, calm was not destined to prevail. In January 1903 Giacosa had become so apprehensive about Puccini's stub-
bornness on the question of Act 2 that he wanted to withdraw from
the project. This rebellion was barely put down, and Puccini was

dickering over some details in the final scene, when near-disaster struck. On 21 February Giacomo and Elvira motored from Milan to Torre del Lago for a few days. The evening of the 25th they were driven by Puccini's chauffeur over the Quiesa Pass to Lucca for dinner with Giacomo's old friend Alfredo Caselli. On their return up the narrow, sharply winding road, at a place called San Macario, on the Lucca side of the pass, the car left the road and plunged down a fifteen-foot embankment, coming to rest against a tree. Puccini was thrown out of the car; in fact, he was found beneath it, almost asphyxiated and with a compound fracture of the right leg. The others were not seriously hurt. Fortunately a doctor who lived nearby offered immediate assistance and put them up for the night. The next day Puccini was taken to La Piaggetta and from there across the lake by boat to Torre del Lago.

Puccini's convalescence was long and painful. Not until early June was he able to resume work on *Butterfly*. His leg had been improperly set and had to be rebroken, a painful experience that retarded his recovery, further delayed by the discovery that he was suffering from diabetes. In the meantime, because of the combination of pain and enforced idleness Puccini underwent a period of deep depression. From the depths he wrote to Illica on 13 May: "Addio tutto, addio Butterfly, addio vita mia!" At the end of May Ricordi became so alarmed by Puccini's slow recovery that he wrote a long paternal letter. Obviously believing that Puccini's health had been undermined by dissipation, Ricordi solemnly urged Giacomo to reform and to realize his extraordinary potentialities. "Puccini," he wrote, "who could have been the modern Rossini, that is truly *Imperator musicae*, has been in the way of becoming the unhappy Donizetti!"[72]

Starting back to work slowly at first, he finally completed the orchestration at the dangerously late date of 27 December 1903 at 11:10 in the evening. The delay in finishing the opera was dangerous because the *première* was scheduled to take place only a little more than a month and a half later. This fact, too, would contribute something to the coming fiasco. He had begun to orchestrate the opera on 29 November 1902, but because of the accident he did not complete Act 1 until 15 September 1903. Shortly before wind-

72. Suffering from venereal disease, Donizetti became paralyzed and was reduced to idiocy before his death on 8 April 1848. Ricordi's allusion to Donizetti in this context pointedly reveals the direction of his anxiety about Giacomo.

ing up the first act, Puccini wrote to Illica about his misgivings at having to score "all this eternal Act " and wondering, "Will it be too long?" At the end of September, Puccini went to Paris for the *première* of *Tosca* at the Opéra-Comique.[73] He was there a month, attending rehearsals at which Sardou made his presence much felt, consulting Parisian specialists about his recalcitrant leg, and in between working away on Act 2 of *Butterfly*.

When he returned to Italy he bought himself a new Lancia, but even this jaunty gesture could not bolster spirits tired by the exertions of the last months. On 24 November Puccini sent a letter to Illica that reveals his state of mind:

> . . . I am here alone and sad! If you could know my sufferings! I have much need of a friend, and I don't have any, or if there is someone who loves me, he doesn't understand me. I am of a temperament very different from most! Only I understand myself and I grieve; but my sorrow is continuous, it does not give me peace. Also work does not sustain me, and I work because I must. My life is a sea of sadness and I am stuck in it! . . .[74]

This dark mood has many causes: his physical condition, his ups and downs with Elvira, but most of all his work on the final pages of his score. With a man as sensitive to impressions as Puccini, the tragic plight of Butterfly could not fail to color his outlook. The one thing he seems not to have worried about unduly is the reception of his new opera by the *superpubblico* of Milan.

On 6 January 1904 Puccini arrived at Milan to foresee the preparations for the *première* of *Madama Butterfly* at La Scala. Three days before at Torre del Lago, Giacomo and Elvira had been quietly married, since Gemignani was now dead. While this move demonstrates Puccini's good faith toward Elvira and their eighteen-year-old son Antonio, who was legitimized by this marriage, it brought no sudden improvement to the relationship between Gia-

73. *Tosca* had its *première* at the Opéra-Comique on 13 October 1903, conducted by André Messager. It was sung by Claire Friché (Tosca), Léon Beyle (Cavaradossi), Hector Dufranne (Scarpia), and Gustave Huberdeau (Angelotti) in a French translation by Paul Ferrier. The audience was enthusiastic about the work; most of the critics were scathing.
  The thousandth *Tosca* at the Comique was performed 13 March 1948.
74. *Carteggi Pucciniani*, p. 248.

como and Elvira, who now had entered, in more senses than one, upon her difficult years.

Sometime around the middle of January the formal reading of the libretto took place upon the stage of La Scala, Giacosa intoning the lines to the assembled cast. Since Puccini had completed the score only two weeks earlier, the cast were given their parts in proof as they came off the press to learn bit by bit, Puccini being present to correct the parts. As a precaution to keep the loose scores from being lost, Ricordi gave orders that none of the music was to be taken from the opera house. While there was some practical justification for this order, Ricordi also liked to indulge in an air of secrecy by closing rehearsals to the public, as he had done more than a decade before at the time of the *première* of Verdi's *Falstaff*. Ricordi's scheme to build suspense rather backfired in the case of *Madama Butterfly*. The word got out that Puccini and his collaborators were being high-handed. The press resented being barred from rehearsals, including the traditionally "open" dress rehearsal. This state of affairs produced a climate of antagonism to the new opera before the public had heard a note of the score.

Within the opera house, however, optimism prevailed. The most cautious opinions were held by the manager, Giulio Gatti-Casazza. He had his doubts about the long second act and remembered calling "a meeting in my office. Present were Puccini, Giacosa, Illica, Ricordi, Campanini, and I. . . . I remember that Giacosa and I were of the opinion that it should be performed in three acts, but the others were for two acts. All of us, however, expected a success."[75]

The parts of Butterfly, Pinkerton, and the Consul Sharpless had been assigned to Rosina Storchio, Giovanni Zenatello, and Giuseppe de Luca. Storchio (1876-1945) had first come to Puccini's notice as Musetta in the Roman *première* of *La Bohème*. As early as April 1902 Puccini had selected Storchio for Butterfly, on the strength of having seen her in two such diverse parts as Donizetti's Linda and Weber's Euryanthe. Gatti-Casazza described her as one of the best-rounded and most perfect artists he had known in the theater. The tenor Zenatello had made his debut at La Scala the previous season in Berlioz's *Damnation de Faust*, but winning particular success as Riccardo in Verdi's *Un Ballo in Maschera*. Giuseppe de Luca (1876-1950) had been introduced to the La Scala audience on 10

75. Gatti-Casazza, p. 133.

December 1903 as Alberich in an Italian production of *Das Rhein-gold*. The conductor, Cleofonte Campanini (1860-1919), had been brought to La Scala at the opening of the season as a replacement for Arturo Toscanini, who had left in a huff the previous April when the audience had tried to insist on an encore. It is important to remember as we come to the story of the first performance of *Madama Butterfly* that these three singers and Campanini, too, were under normal circumstances in good favor with the public and press. All of them had participated in another *première*—Giordano's *Siberia*—earlier in this season and their performances had been much better received than the new opera. To Storchio Puccini wrote a letter on the morning of the *première* of *Butterfly* in which he said: "Your art is so true, delicate, and moving that certainly the public will be conquered by it."

The night of 17 February 1904 is a black mark on the proud history of La Scala. The fiasco had many causes. There were those offended by the air of secrecy and the closed rehearsals. The morning of the *première* Ricordi had issued the piano-vocal scores of the new opera, but they were all mysteriously bought up—some of them by people determined to find reminiscences of Puccini's earlier operas. Some of the fault was undeniably Puccini's: in its original form the first act was too diffuse and episodic; the second act, perilously long. If Puccini had been bruised by earlier contacts with the public at La Scala, he had not yet experienced its full capacity for cruelty. Ricordi was convinced the reception was planned and frankly says so in an unsigned article he wrote for his own publication *Musica e Musicisti* (March 1904): "The performance in the auditorium seemed just as carefully organized as that on the stage."

When Campanini raised his baton at 8:30, La Scala was crowded. An air of uneasy tension lasted until Butterfly's entrance, when murmurs of "*Bohème! Bohème!*" broke out. The offending passage contained the same sequence of notes in the same key (G-flat) as Mimì's phrase "Soli d'inverno" in the third act of *La Bohème*. (A hint of this allusion remains in the present score, but Puccini retouched this passage before the opera was given again.) After this outburst, a constant flow of wisecracks from the top balcony answered by demands for silence from Puccini's supporters kept the whole audience on edge, unable to lose themselves in the performance. The effect of the long love duet that closes Act 1 was lost because again the audience was outraged to detect again the sequence from *La Bohème*. When the curtain fell after Act 1, there was faint applause; the most vociferous clapping coming from Pietro Mascagni. The singers were called out twice, accompanied by Puccini, who still used a cane because of his injured leg. They were greeted with howls of scornful laughter. Carlo Gatti, who was present that night, remembers the corridors of La Scala during the intermission as filled with smug gloating over Puccini's discomfiture.[76]

Although during Act 2 there was some applause for the letter scene and the flower duet, everything else—*Un bel dì*, the intermezzo, the death scene, everything—was lost in recurring waves of shouting, laughter, and catcalls. Giuseppe de Luca told me in Rome in 1945 that many times the singers on stage could not hear the orchestra for the bedlam. The sadistic element of this demonstration revealed itself most cruelly at one point when a backstage draft caused Storchio's kimono to billow in front. Immediately there were cries: "Butterfly is pregnant! Ah, the little Toscanini!" (alluding thereby to a liaison that was common knowledge in Milan.)[77]

The intermezzo provided a particularly trying moment. Tito Ricordi, who was much interested in staging, had had the bright idea of stationing bird-whistles in various parts of the auditorium to simulate the birds of a Japanese dawn. What had been intended as a poetic bit of realism brought pandemonium. At the first whistle such a deafening variety of cackling and animal cries broke out that for a while La Scala became a lunatic aviary. According to Gatti-Casazza, the singers remained perfectly in character all through the performance, never giving the slightest indication they were performing before an unruly audience.

When the final curtain fell, there was general consternation backstage. Gatti-Casazza reports the opera finished to "absolutely glacial silence." He remembered, with irony, two episodes. One was Giacosa's very vocal complaints that the audience should show such little respect for his libretto; the other was the sudden appearance of Mascagni before the curtain, weeping and scolding the audience for its behavior. "Of course," Gatti-Casazza continues, "no one was

76. Carlo Gatti, *Il Teatro alla Scala* (Milan, 1964), I, 225.
77. Storchio was not, as Spike Hughes claims in his *Famous Puccini Operas* (New York, 1962), p. 112n, "noticeably bearing his [Toscanini's] child." Puccini would scarcely have risked his opera with a visibly pregnant Butterfly. Further, Storchio continued to sing at La Scala all the balance of this season and in the summer went to Buenos Aires, where she sang Butterfly with tremendous success. These public activities seem scarcely consistent with imminent motherhood.

moved by this great grief which, rightly or wrongly, was considered not very sincere."[78]

Puccini insisted on withdrawing his score. Deeply shaken, he firmly believed that with a few modifications *Butterfly* would prove its worth in another theater. At first Gatti-Casazza protested the withdrawal of the opera, a move that meant both a financial loss for La Scala and the trouble of rebuilding a season planned around numerous repetitions of *Butterfly*. Magnanimously Ricordi supported Puccini's position, although he had already printed scores of the La Scala version, and these plates were a loss. Puccini returned his fee of 20,000 lire to Ricordi.

There is no doubt the fiasco of *Butterfly* left scars on Puccini. Scars caused not only by the audience, but by some very destructive reviews that appeared the following day. One poisonous example bore the headline: "*Butterfly*, the diabetic opera, the result of an automobile accident." It would be unfair, however, to deny that some reviews, such as that by Giovanni Pozza in the *Corriere della sera*, expressed faith that retouched the opera would make its way. One result of this performance was that Puccini's already strained attitude toward La Scala and its public became quite aloof and remained so for nearly twenty years.[79]

The story of Puccini's revisions to *Madama Butterfly* is more complex than that of his changes to his other operas. Puccini loved this opera which had been so harshly treated at its birth, and he lavished particular care upon it. To discuss the revisions clearly, it seems advisable to deal with them chronologically.

78. Gatti-Casazza, pp. 134-5.
79. To examine the repertory of La Scala (published in vol. II of Gatti's *Il Teatro alla Scala*) is to be amazed at the relatively few productions of Puccini's operas there during his lifetime. In almost forty years—much of this a time when Puccini was the most popular living Italian composer—there were only sixteen productions of his works! Here is the list; the numbers in parentheses indicate the number of performances in each "edition."

1885 *Le Villi* (13)	1912 *La Fanciulla* (12)
1889 *Edgar* (3)	1916 *La Bohème* (9)
1894 *Manon Lescaut* (19)	1917 *Tosca* (8)
1897 *La Bohème* (16)	1922 *Il Trittico* (12)
1900 *Tosca* (12)	1922 *Manon Lescaut* (17)
1900 *La Bohème* (10)	1923 *La Bohème* (6)
1904 *Madama Butterfly* (1)	1923 *Manon Lescaut* (6)
1909 *Manon Lescaut* (8)	1924 *Gianni Schicchi* (2)

The second performance of *Madama Butterfly* at La Scala took place on 29 November 1925, the first anniversary of Puccini's death, with Toscanini conducting and Rosetta Pampanini (b.1900) as Butterfly.

Puccini made some changes in the opera before he brought it out again, a little more than three months after its initial fiasco, at Brescia, on 28 May 1904, where it won a resounding success. Campanini was again the conductor, joined by Zenatello and de Luca from the original cast; there was, however, a new Butterfly, Salomea Krusceniski (1872-1953). The revisions for Brescia were, however, neither the first nor the last Puccini made to the score of *Madama Butterfly*.

From the evidence that survived the bombing raids on Milan during World War II, the course of these revisions can be traced through the following stages:

1. Illica's first draft of Act 1 of the libretto is in the vault at Ricordi's.

2. The composer's autograph full-score, also in Ricordi's vault.

3. Ricordi printed the piano-vocal score of the La Scala *première*. As the opera was withdrawn the following day, this edition was small and copies of it are rare today. (The points of difference between this printed score and the autograph indicate changes made during rehearsals.)

4. The piano-vocal score of the Brescia version, which bears the copyright date of 1904, as does No. 3 above. (This score reveals the changes Puccini made between February and May 1904.)

5. Ricordi's piano-vocal score, copyright 1906. While this contains some further revisions, it differs markedly from No. 6 below.

6. Ricordi's piano-vocal score, copyright 1907. This is the opera as it is given today, with the single exception of two phrases for Butterfly in the entrance. These phrases had been altered to their present form by 1911.

To follow the course of these revisions sheds light on Puccini's craftsmanship and shows how he kept sharpening the focus on the central figure of Butterfly.

Illica's draft of the first act, written in a spidery hand, contains the main lines of Act 1 as we know it today. It begins with the scene between Pinkerton and Goro, followed by the arrival of Sharpless,[80] the entrance of Butterfly with her friends and relations, the

80. One little touch that did not find its way into the finished libretto illustrates Illica's way with local color. Shortly after Sharpless's arrival, he politely inquires after Pinkerton's mother and receives this reply. "E' là a Newport" (She's at Newport)!

marriage ceremony, the interruption by the Bonze, and the closing love duet. The problem with the sketch is that it contains much else besides. There is almost twice the number of words as in the present Act 1. This "extra" material is mostly taken up with the antics of the Japanese characters, and not just Butterfly's drunken Uncle Yakusidè. The unfortunate result of this "extra" material is to make the act choppy and episodic; worse, it continually interrupts and delays the establishment of Butterfly's character. The parts of Illica's sketch that show the closest resemblance to the present form are Butterfly's description of her visit to the mission and the love duet.

Illica's sketch clears up one minor mystery in the text of the opera. In the score as we know it today, Butterfly on more than one occasion refers to herself as *Madama F. B. Pinkerton*, although elsewhere it is clear that the naval lieutenant's name is Benjamin Franklin Pinkerton. Why this inconsistency in the order of the initials? All through Illica's sketch, Pinkerton's lines are indicated "F.B.P.," and the reason is found during the marriage ceremony when the Commissioner reads out the groom's full name: Sir Francis Blummy Pinkerton! This prepossessing name with its un-American title is all the more surprising as it appears in neither Long's original story nor the play. Illica's invention is, possibly, an effort at humor and at providing a name easy for Italians to pronounce.[81] Sir Francis Blummy Pinkerton remained in the text through the La Scala performance; this name was removed for Brescia. The initials F. B. are still there.

Puccini's autograph score and the printed score of the La Scala version (No. 3) differ only in a few details. In Act 1 Puccini added the chorus parts to Sharpless's *O amico fortunato*, and he changed five bars in the love duet so that the tenor would sing in unison with the soprano.[82] In Act 2 part 1 he omitted the stage direction that caused Sharpless on his arrival at Butterfly's house to remove his shoes. These small changes, like the others, are clearly designed to

81. At first Illica's consideration in matters of words easy for Italians to pronounce did not extend to changing the name of Pinkerton's ship, the *Connecticut*, surely a snaggle of consonants to give an Italian pause. By the time of the autograph score, however, the ship's name had been changed to that endearing compromise: the *Abramo Lincoln*.

82. The love duet gave Puccini much difficulty, as the many cancellations in the score testify. At one point Puccini pasted two pages together (a sure indication of suppressed material) and added a very typical ironic comment: "Il più bel pezzo dell' opera!" (The most beautiful part of the opera!)

strengthen a musical effect or to remove an awkward bit of stage business.

The Brescia score (No. 4) differs drastically from the La Scala version. The best known of these changes is the division of the two parts of Act 2 by an intermission, a change that required only slight modification. (Even though Puccini by so doing divided his opera into three acts, he insisted on retaining the designations: Act 2, part 1 and Act 2, part 2.) He added a four-bar coda to the humming chorus that ends Part 1 and removed a seven-bar transition in D-flat major connecting the humming chorus with the intermezzo that precedes Part 2. The new intermission necessitated another modification. At La Scala the intermezzo had been followed directly by Butterfly's lullaby, *Dormi amor mio*. For Brescia, he inserted seventeen bars of exposition to precede it.[83]

Another important alteration at Brescia was the addition of Pinkerton's *Addio, fiorito asil* in the final scene. The tenor's *romanza*—at times it becomes a duet with the baritone—replaces a dozen phrases of undistinguished declamation with a broadly effective cantilena. This substitution not only strengthened the score, but fleshed out the seriously deprived role of Pinkerton, making it a bit more attractive to leading tenors. It is not generally known, though, that *Addio fiorito asil* is not the only new material at this point. New also is everything between the trio for Suzuki, Pinkerton, and Sharpless[84] and Pinkerton's *romanza*.

If Puccini's insistence that Act 2 be played continuously at La Scala indicates a lapse of his unusually keen sense of what was effective in the theater, another change made for Brescia suppressed a further lapse. At La Scala, as she does now, Butterfly proudly produces her son, Trouble, showing him off to Sharpless, but instead of his being taken off again shortly after Sharpless's exit, as he is now, the child remained on stage all through the rest of the scene *and* the vigil, until Butterfly carries him off as she sings her lullaby. The La Scala arrangement meant that the child was kept on stage

83. The new material opening Act 2, part 2, begins with Suzuki's "Già il sole!" The first night at Brescia, Suzuki sang here "Già l'alba" (It's already dawn), but Puccini soon changed to the reference to sunlight because he wanted the scene played in stronger light. A minor point, perhaps, but one that clearly shows Puccini's attention to detail.

84. At La Scala this trio had been sung in G major, but as the climactic phrases lay uncomfortably high, Puccini lowered the passage a half tone. This change accounts for the anomaly of this melody being heard in the original key of G major at the entrance of Pinkerton and Sharpless and shortly after sung in G-flat.

THE BIG THREE

for the better part of an hour! The tot playing this part at La Scala had been so put off his stride by the unruly audience that Puccini wisely decided to remove so far as possible this source of "trouble." For Brescia, Puccini fixed the entrances and exits of the child as we know them today, but in doing so he had to make some musical changes. One of them is a major improvement. For Brescia, Puccini wrote Butterfly's *Trionfa il mio amor,* one of the great emotional climaxes of the score. Just after Pinkerton's ship has been sighted, Butterfly believing her faith is entirely vindicated sings an impressive phrase and the orchestra thunders out a melody from the love duet. At La Scala this passage had been quite different. After the ship has been recognized, Butterfly tells the child that his name is no longer *Dolore* (Trouble), but *Gioia* (Joy), and gives him an American flag to flourish, while the orchestra proclaims the opening bars of *The Star Spangled Banner.* This alteration serves to place Butterfly in sharper relief; before she had to share a big moment with the child, now she has it to herself.

The other changes between the La Scala and Brescia versions were mostly cuts. Puccini shortened the first act at four places, removing nearly ten minutes of music. It is significant that all the material cut from Act 1 comes after Butterfly's entrance and that very little of her part was taken out. The cuts in the rest of the score were less drastic, but it should be noted that when Puccini felt the action needed tightening, he did not hesitate to compress Butterfly's part, as when he excised two sizable chunks from the final scene.

All these changes for Brescia were sufficient to ensure the survival of the opera, but there was a modification of a different sort between this performance and the La Scala *première.* Rosina Storchio was a light lyric soprano, while at Brescia Puccini entrusted the role to Salomea Krusceniski, a dramatic soprano whose reputation was based on her interpretations of Aïda and Gioconda. In 1905, he gave his enthusiastic endorsement to the Butterfly of Emmy Destinn (1878-1930) when she created the role in London; Destinn was another notable Aïda and Gioconda. The prominence given these two dramatic sopranos suggests that Puccini later modified his original view of Butterfly as a sort of Japanese doll and came to stress more and more the tragic aspects of the role.[85]

85. Storchio was still singing Butterfly in 1919, but by then Puccini agreed that her interpretation was too brittle, her gestures too kittenish. When she came to the United States in 1920, "her strength and her resources were no longer those of the past" (Gatti-Casazza, p. 122).

The subsequent changes to *Madama Butterfly*, those revealed by the 1906 score and the present version, can be dealt with briefly. Although some of the padding of Act 1 had been cut after the La Scala version, still more of it was cut after Brescia. For instance, out went a passage of formal introduction of the Commissioner and the Official just before the marriage ceremony; out went a bit about one of Butterfly's cousins stealing sweets. The shrinking dimensions of Act 1, the progressive scrapping of Illica's inventions, emerges when the printed scores are compared: in the La Scala score Act 1 ran 196 pages; in the Brescia verson, 186 pages; in the present version, 168 pages. Two passages of Act 2, part 1, gave Puccini trouble. He cut twenty-seven measures from the flower duet, and he took out two passages, totaling about forty measures, from the scene of the preparation for the vigil. For 1906, he made one change in the final scene. At both La Scala and Brescia, Kate and Sharpless did not exit together, as they do now. Kate used to leave first, while Sharpless lingered to offer Butterfly money, which she refused. Puccini did not want this delay and arranged to have the two American figures depart together.

For 1907, Puccini cut four more passages from Act 1: a contrast that Butterfly draws between her two uncles, some more of the preliminaries to the marriage ceremony, Uncle Yakusidè's getting tipsy, and one passage from the love duet. These cuts may have become traditional by 1907, and Puccini may have quietly dropped them permanently by omitting them from the score. In Act 2, part 1, he reworked Butterfly's aria *Che tua madre dovrà*. The original words had described a fantasy of Butterfly's, how one day the Emperor would notice her child and give him an exalted position; now they were changed to stress Butterfly's conviction that she would rather die than return to her profession as a geisha. This is another example of the shift toward a more tragic and dramatic view of Butterfly. A purely practical addition was the nineteen measures of orchestral music inserted into the flower duet to allow for the stage business of decorating the house.

The most significant of these changes occur in the final scene. The role of Kate Pinkerton is curtailed drastically; some of her old lines are given to Sharpless, some of her passages have been given to Butterfly with a new vocal line. The device of presenting Butterfly as knowing intuitively the reason for Kate's presence effectively removes the motivation for many of Kate's former lines. Again, as

with so many of the changes over the three years since the first performance of *Butterfly*, these modifications increase the prominence
of Butterfly's role.[86]

The libretto of *Madama Butterfly* makes its effect when the audience's sympathies are solidly with the heroine. Surely one thing that
contributed to the fiasco of the *première* was the absence of any
opportunity for the audience to become emotionally involved in
Butterfly's fate. The action keeps Butterfly continuously on stage
from her entrance until the end of the opera, with the exception of
a few minutes near the beginning of the final scene. With this clear
and present focal point, the plot develops quite straightforwardly.
Each scene contributes to the whole, for the tragedy is inherent in
the characters of Butterfly and Pinkerton.

The final form of the libretto, as distinguished from the plot, is
one of the best Puccini ever set. Instead of the embarrassing pidgin
English Cho-Cho-San uses in both the story and the play, the liter-
ate and graceful Italian, coupled with Puccini's music, adds aesthetic
distance to increase Butterfly's stature as a dramatic figure. In contrast to the melodramatic outbursts found in *Tosca*, the lines here
are personal expressions, flavored with characteristic imagery.

One of the finest features of the text is the adroit treatment of
foreshadowing, particularly in the love duet. When he was composing *Tosca*, Puccini complained that Giacosa and Illica kept providing the same old stereotypes for the duet in Act 3; in the lengthy
duet in Act 1 of *Madama Butterfly* they created a major achievement of its kind. (It is less difficult, perhaps, to supply fresh words
for characters who do not know each other too well, or who have
rarely been alone together, than to present a convincing scene be-

86. Phonograph records afford some clues to the different versions of *Madama
Butterfly*. In Emmy Destinn's record of the death scene, the phrase "fior di giglio
e di rosa" is sung an octave lower than it appears in the score today. This phrase
was not changed until after 1906.

The 1906 version was used by the touring Savage Opera Company that introduced the opera to the United States; the singers of that troupe recorded a number of Butterfly excerpts for Columbia, circa 1907. The singers involved were
Renée Vivienne, Vernon Stiles, the mezzo Behnee, and the baritone Richards.

The recordings made by Farrar, Homer, Caruso, and Scotti are testimony to
the score as it was sung when it was introduced to the Metropolitan on 11 February 1907. Butterfly's entrance and the flower duet are vintage 1906; Farrar's
death scene is 1907. The oddest of these records is Farrar's *Sai cos'ebbe* (including
the aria *Che tua madre*). The aria is cut almost in half and uses some words from
the 1906 version and some of the present version, *plus* some which belong to
neither!

tween two people like Tosca and Cavaradossi whose affair is of long standing.) In any event, the contrasting approaches to love—Pinkerton, crass and eager; Butterfly, sincere and humble—are admirably set out. This contrast is established near the beginning as Butterfly adjusts her obi and combs her hair, while Pinkerton, watching her impatiently, describes her, not too flatteringly, as "squirrel" and "toy." When Pinkerton tries to tease a frank declaration of love from her, her answer is more revealing than she intends. She explains she does not speak words of love, "for fear of having to die for them." Later, she asks him to love her gently, explaining that "we are humble, silent people, used to little things, to caressing tenderness, yet deep as the sky, as the waves of the sea." Not only is this admirable and convincing in context, but it prepares us for the coming tragedy. Her sensitivity, shown by her occasional obliqueness, her inner strength, and her singleness of heart are movingly revealed.

On the whole, the librettists are more successful than one might expect with Pinkerton. If he is made totally crass, completely selfish, then Butterfly's devotion becomes incomprehensible. Pinkerton states his easy-going philosophy tersely in his Act 1 scene with Sharpless. There is bitter irony in Pinkerton's drinking a toast to a real marriage with a real American wife, just as Goro comes hurrying in to announce Butterfly's imminent arrival. Seeing this side of Pinkerton, we realize he is merely infatuated with Butterfly, but if we consider his words in the love duet as *she* hears them, then his ardent outbursts have a ring of sincerity. The plot does not, of course, contain the scene of Pinkerton's departure from Butterfly, but we get her side of it. She was convinced he smiled to conceal his deep feeling when he told her he would come back "when the robin makes his nest again." That Pinkerton is momentarily—if not like Butterfly, permanently—capable of real feeling comes across in his remorse as he learns the true nature of Butterfly's attachment to him. We come to see that Butterfly's tragedy is not just that she is Pinkerton's victim; rather, her faithfulness is an anomaly even in her own culture. Her attitude is incomprehensible to Goro and to Yamadori.

The consul, Sharpless, is an attractive figure. He is the *raisonneur*, who understands Pinkerton's motives and tries to warn him of probable consequences, just as he comes to understand Butterfly's rocklike loyalty and does his best to warn her. The importance of Sharpless does not lie in what he does or does not do, but rather in what he feels. He responds and is moved, at times to tears, by what he hears and sees. Thus, his role provides the audience with a point of view from which to behold and understand the tragedy.

The librettists have caught well the ritualistic side of Japanese life and made it a central part of the drama. The formality of address and manners gives an amusing touch to the introduction of the servants in Act 1 and to Butterfly's reception of Sharpless in Act 2, part 1. These rituals take on a deeper meaning when Butterfly puts on her bridal obi to await Pinkerton's return. The solemn preparations for Butterfly's suicide make the deed psychologically convincing—far more shattering in its effect than Tosca's impulsive leap from the battlements. These rituals impress us as a valid expression of character, not as empty formula.

Puccini's score for *Madama Butterfly* is a major achievement. Never before had he been master of such subtlety and refinement as a musical dramatist. His four years of adjusting the score completed, he had managed a concentration of effect upon a single tragic figure, such as he had never produced before. While there are those who do not find this opera exactly to their taste, yet those who find it possible to identify with the heroine's plight hold *Madama Butterfly* in special affection. Never before had Puccini composed a score that so snugly and evocatively fitted the dramatic action and expressed the moods of his characters.

After setting the highly charged drama of *Tosca*, Puccini returned to the economy and understatement characteristic of *La Bohème*. Those members of the first audience who screamed the title of the earlier opera were not merely complaining of a specific musical reminiscence, but in a sense acknowledging an affinity of approach, as in the interweaving of amusing, romantic, and tragic episodes. What chiefly distinguishes *Madama Butterfly* from *La Bohème* is Puccini's canny use of the exotic Japanese color that tinges much of the score.

Fundamentally, Puccini's way with local color, European or Oriental, has some common traits. He happens to use a lot more of it in *Madama Butterfly*, but just as he employed traditional tunes for the military tatoo at the end of Act 2 of *La Bohème* and for the *Te Deum* in *Tosca*, so he incorporated half a dozen real Japanese tunes into his score.[87] Although Puccini's reaction to Japanese music when he first encountered it during his research for *Madama Butterfly* was that it was poor, "poca cosa," he managed to assimilate it into his personal idiom with surprising success, without sacrificing its individual character and without being strapped by its limitations. These limitations consist of the scant range of most Japanese songs which rarely exceed an octave, the pentatonic character of the melodies, the regularity of the duple rhythmic patterns, and their native unharmonized condition.[88] Puccini's problem then was to absorb this unpromising material into the warp and woof of his own Italian style.

Puccini's accommodation of the native Japanese and pseudo-Japanese material—he uses both kinds—works something like this. He never gave a moment's thought to the use of such native Japanese instruments as the samisen and koto.[89] Few opera-house orchestras possess such instruments, and performers upon them are usually in short supply. Instead he combines the normal instruments of the orchestra to produce an exotic color, but one that blends satisfactorily with the rest of the scoring. For instance, right after the vocal climax of Butterfly's entrance, she and her companions make their obeisance to Pinkerton as this melody is played.

Puccini blends the harp (playing grace-note octaves), the piccolo, flute, and bells, all in unison, so that they sound like a little Japanese orchestra. For a bass line, the strings play a tremolo that imitates the

87. The sources of the Japanese tunes are discussed by Mosco Carner, *Puccini* (New York, 1958), pp. 367-8, and more fully by Juichi Miyazawa (using the most remarkable English!) in an article entitled "Some original japanese [sic] melodies in *Madama Butterfly*," printed in *Giacomo Puccini nel centenario della nascita* (Lucca, 1958), pp. 157-61.
88. Japanese vocal melodies when accompanied by an instrument tend to have a quasi-polyphonic rather than a purely harmonic relationship between the parts. The instrument leads and anticipates the voice in an altered form of the melody.
89. Puccini calls for "Japanese" bells in the scene of the marriage ceremony (Act 1).

melody, thereby preserving the characteristic homophonic texture of much Japanese music. Example 1 returns at two important points later in Act 1, but now its scoring is more Western in color and its harmony more traditional, as the dramatic situation demands. The first of these later appearances occurs as Butterfly describes her conversion at the mission, *Ieri son salita;* here the melody sounds in unison strings, accompanied by harp, flute, and clarinet figures and sustained chords for bassoon, clarinet, horns, and, later, muted trumpets. Here Example 1 sounds converted to Western musical practice. When it recurs at the end of the love duet, shimmering harmonies in the harp announce that the conversion is complete. Incidentally, the quiet endings to Act 1 and to Act 2, part 1, show that Puccini has broken his addiction to the Ponchielli-style peroration.

When Puccini wants to emphasize the Japanese character of a theme, he usually treats it as a single, unaccompanied melody. He does this for instance when Butterfly takes down her father's sword just before her suicide; there the cellos and basses thunder out the hara-kiri theme, which he freely adapted from an authentic Japanese tune.

2

But Puccini does not restrict this sort of treatment to his derivative Japanese melodies. He takes the broad theme, familiar from the first act, especially at Butterfly's words, "O quanti occhi fisi," and uses it in Japanese style. Near the end of the opera, when Butterfly kneels before the statue of Buddha, rescinding her conversion, this melody returns as a single line for the cellos playing on the D string.

3

The melancholy color and unstressed rhythm movingly convey Butterfly's shattered feelings at this moment. The only other sound in the orchestra is a continuing thudding ostinato for the timpani, which the audience hears not so much as music, but as the thudding of Butterfly's anguished heart.

Besides adapting native Japanese melodies and using his own material in a Japanese style, Puccini creates exotic effects by other means. When Goro ushers in the servants near the beginning of Act 1 to introduce them to Pinkerton, Puccini accompanies this action with a little theme descriptive of the scurrying, graceful movements, and the small-scale gestures of the Japanese people.

4

The scoring for harp, bassoon, and oboe in unison against a little staccato figure for the flute provides a note of delicate quaintness that contrasts admirably with the hearty, rhythmically aggressive lines of Pinkerton. In such a passage as Example 4, Puccini is not imitating Japanese-style music, rather he is like a painter creating the atmosphere of a genre scene.

The analogies to painting are irresistible in a score such as *Madama Butterfly*. Many moments seem like the musical equivalents of Japanese prints. There is the same emphasis on simplicity and clarity of line; for example one might cite the letter scene or the humming chorus of the vigil. The little fugato tune that opens the opera can almost be seen as a calligraphic line; its characteristic opening squiggle recurs at many points to emphasize the jocular talkativeness of the Japanese characters. The sense of deep space has its equivalent in the distant voices of the sailors heard in the prelude to the final scene.

Puccini was always highly susceptible to visual influences. He even pasted a drawing of a mother carrying a child in his autograph score at the point where Butterfly makes her triumphant appearance with Trouble to show him off to Sharpless. The strong pictorial sense that underlies the opening of the Barrière d'Enfer act in *La Bohème* and the description of the Roman dawn in *Tosca* is found at many points in *Madama Butterfly*. Besides the analogies to Japanese prints, comparisons might be made with the impressionists. For instance, the chorus that accompanies Butterfly's entrance sing a series of augmented triads that produces a splash of atmospheric color. Puccini had, further, been exposed to the musical impressionism of Debussy, having attended a performance of *Pelléas et Mélisande* at the Comique when he was in Paris during the autumn of 1903. Something of Debussy's manner, annealed to the personal idiom of Puccini, appears in such a phrase as this:

5

Much of the effect of this phrase comes from the use of a whole-tone progression in the vocal line accompanied by muted horns, but this does not explain the whole effect. Butterfly's words here form an impressionist image: "I believed I was dying, but it passes quickly as the clouds pass over the sea." The sense mirrors the rising and falling of the melodic contour and echoes the mournful color of the horns. In such a phrase as this, Puccini is both a poet and painter in tone.

So far this discussion of the score of *Madama Butterfly* may well give the impression that the opera is a concatenation of little effects. While it is true that Puccini's treatment of musical declamation has become more flexible and more richly characterized, yet the musical high points of the opera are, many of them, larger in proportion than the arias and duets of the earlier scores. For instance, the duet for Pinkerton and Sharpless in Act 1, *Amore o grillo*, is one hundred bars long, and the flower duet runs to more than one hundred and forty. The most extensive and varied of Puccini's efforts in this line so far is the love duet that concludes Act 1.

From the beginning of the scene, after the exit of the friends and relations with the Bonze, to the end of the act is almost two hundred and seventy measures. The variety and flexibility of treatment in this long scene is masterful. From Pinkerton's efforts to soothe Butterfly's tears at being rejected by her family, through her putting on her wedding obi, until Pinkerton finally carries her away with his own eagerness, the duet develops in a series of carefully regulated and contrasting episodes, although the whole effect is of a spontaneous development of passion.

Certain passages are particularly noteworthy.

6

This melody first heard in the muted violins has an impetuous sensuousness that describes Pinkerton's eagerness to arouse Butterfly. The orchestration gains richness and warmth, the leaping intervals become more insistent as Pinkerton's urgency grows. The key of A major recurs later in the duet, always associated with Pinkerton's persuasive wooing.

The presentation of Butterfly in this duet is more complex. Her love, her instinctive reserve, and her combined feelings of inferiority and gratitude to Pinkerton are vividly presented. The brief episode in which she begs to be loved a little, *Vogliatemi bene, un bene piccolino*, shows Puccini's sensitivity to her moods. Look for a moment at the two ways he sets her phrase "Vogliatemi bene":

7   7a

The repeated pitches of the first phrase, accompanied by the solo violin and strings, show her restraint, but later when the melody is repeated a minor third higher, the changing line has a heightened sincerity. From this moment, Butterfly's emotional intensity increases until she responds to Pinkerton's insistent demand that she be his with a cry of "Si, per la vita" (Yes, for all my life), words which take on a tragic significance.

The ecstatic conclusion of the love duet is a repetition, but not an absolutely exact one, of the music of Butterfly's entrance. The tessitura has been eased a bit by repeating it in F major instead of the original key of G-flat. Puccini's sense of how to modulate and postpone a climax can be seen in his rather unusual procedure of having the melody of Example 3 (in its original form) sung by the soprano and tenor in unison, but six bars later Butterfly sings it alone and *piano*. The last two bars of the vocal parts build again from *piano* to the climactic high C. The ebb and flow of this love duet is psychologically sound, and its effect anything but monotonous. Those who worry about Butterfly turning into a full-throated Italian soprano at this point are immune both to Pinkerton's persuasiveness and Butterfly's responsiveness to it.

Of all the operas Puccini had written so far, none showed the flexibility and nicety of balance that *Madama Butterfly* came to possess. It is not just an opera contrived of carefully calculated little effects, but a score that contains the most extended scenes that Puccini had undertaken so far. His management of these passages is so deftly varied that he evades monotony. A first-rate performance of the opera clearly reveals how supple Puccini's hand had become since the days of *Le Villi*.

3

SHARP ON THE HEELS OF SUCCESS

La Fanciulla del West, La Rondine,
and Il Trittico

After *Tosca* was completed, it took Puccini nearly a year to find the subject of *Madama Butterfly;* after *Butterfly*, it took him nearly three years to find the subject of *La Fanciulla*, and another three years were to go by before he finished it. Not that he didn't toy with and even seriously consider a number of other subjects in the meantime.

The Brescia resurrection of *Madama Butterfly* of May 1904 was still running successfully when Puccini began to write to Illica about the possibility of making a substantial opera out of Victor Hugo's *The Hunchback of Notre-Dame.*[1] The difficulties of making a clear, compact libretto out of that sprawling plot soon dissuaded Puccini from this idea. The emphasis on Puccini's next opera being a massive work came chiefly from Giulio Ricordi, who thought of *Butterfly* as a lightweight opera and who for a variety of reasons wanted to see Puccini, now at forty-five supposedly reaching artistic maturity, come up with a magnum opus.

Not wishing to arouse the notoriously touchy Illica, Puccini made quiet overtures to a Florentine dramatist, Valentino Soldani. Soldani proposed a medieval subject, the story of Margherita di Cortona. For some months Soldani would send material to Puccini, while

1. The subject Puccini was interested in was Hugo's *Notre-Dame de Paris*, and not, as Mosco Carner suggests, *Le Jongleur de Notre Dame.*

Puccini, who came increasingly to distrust both the subject and Soldani's imagination, sent back increasingly evasive requests for modifications. By early 1906 Puccini had completely disassociated himself from this proposal. Meanwhile, he kept making suggestions to Illica. Once his enthusiasm for Hugo had subsided, Puccini considered a series of three one-act operas derived from tales by Gorki, his enthusiasm fired not only by Gorki's artistry but by the challenge of writing a role for Chaliapin.[2] This foreshadowing of the idea of a "trittico" never got beyond conjecture, as Ricordi turned thumbs down on the notion, detailing the problems and expense of casting and producing three separate works as a triple bill. Ricordi also made clear his opposition to Puccini's passing fancy for composing either an *opera buffa* or an operetta. These last notions turned out to persist, but it was only after Giulio Ricordi's death in 1912 that Puccini composed *La Rondine* (originally conceived as an operetta) and *Gianni Schicchi* (an *opera buffa*), the latter opera being part of just such a triple bill as Ricordi had objected to in 1904.

Soon Puccini was writing to Illica about their old stand-by, Marie Antoinette. This scheme in various guises was to occupy them and strain their relationship over the next several years. When Puccini officially took up the subject of *La Fanciulla* in July 1907, he tried to soothe Illica's wounded feelings by going on record that *L'Austriaca* (The Austrian Woman), as the libretto was finally named, would be his next opera after *La Fanciulla*. It wasn't. The chief problem seems to have been that no matter how congenial the *idea* of the French queen's fate might be, when it came to putting together a coherent, viable plot the subject proved unwieldy and frustrating. Although Puccini definitely renounced this subject at least half a dozen times, it would turn up again when nothing better would suggest itself.

In February 1906 there was a concerted move, highly approved by Ricordi, to add to the ranks of Puccini's librettists Gabriele

2. Feodor Chaliapin (1873-1938) made his Italian debut—with his name Italianized as Scialiapin—at La Scala, 16 March 1901, singing the title role in Boito's *Mefistofele* (with Emma Carelli and Caruso). He returned to La Scala on 8 March 1904 to sing the devil in Gounod's *Faust* (with Storchio and Zenatello). Puccini was so impressed by the Russian basso on this second round of appearances (less than a month after the fiasco of *Butterfly* in the same theater!) that he considered him as the core of the Gorki project.

D'Annunzio.[3] In these years D'Annunzio's flamboyant extrava-
gances left him strapped for cash; libretto writing was a plausible
means of relieving financial pressures. Shortly before he and Puccini came into conjunction, D'Annunzio had just finished his first
job of this kind, adapting one of his plays to serve as the text of
Franchetti's *La Figlia di Jorio*. Although D'Annunzio's libretto was
praised, Franchetti's opera was no more than a *mezzo-fiasco*.[4] Since
this contretemps had not compromised D'Annunzio's reputation,
he welcomed the possibly lucrative opportunity to work with Puccini. In a few months he had prepared two libretti for Puccini's
inspection; one was *La Rosa di Cipro*, the other *Parasina*.[5] As soon
as Puccini saw these samples of the poet's work, he realized that
D'Annunzio's enameled style was not suited to his music, and, more
important, he understood that the poet's ego could not withstand
the rough and tumble methods he was accustomed to use to extract
a libretto fitted to his needs. In August 1906 they gave up the idea
of their collaboration without appreciable rancor.[6] In 1912 there
would be another futile round of negotiations between them.

Puccini's next idea for a subject embroiled him more seriously
than any of these previous proposals. Sometime prior to September
1906, Puccini had read Pierre Loüys's sensational novel *La Femme
et le pantin* (The Woman and the Puppet). Maurice Vaucaire, a
friend of Loüys, had made a workable dramatization of the novel,
a condition that much simplified the creation of a libretto. As soon

3. D'Annunzio (1863-1938), subtle poet, overwrought playwright, and flamboyant
patriot, had first occurred to Puccini as a possible collaborator as early as the summer of 1894, during the period before Puccini completely committed himself to *La
Bohème*.
  Besides his libretto to Franchetti's *La Figlia di Jorio* (29 March 1906) (which
nearly half a century later was set again by Ildebrando Pizzetti), D'Annunzio
wrote the texts to Mascagni's *Parasina* (1913) and Pizzetti's *Fedra* (1915). With
Tito Ricordi, he adapted his play *Francesca da Rimini* for Zandonai (1914) and
another play, *La Nave*, for Montemezzi (1918).
  D'Annunzio's French play, *Le Martyre de St. Sébastien* (1913) was supplied with
incidental music by Claude Debussy.
4. Franchetti's *La Figlia di Jorio* failed for two reasons primarily: Franchetti's
inadequate score, and a very inferior performance by Angelica Pandolfini (1871-
1939). After three performances the opera was withdrawn until Eugenia Burzio
(1879-1922) could learn the role of Mila, but even with her intense style the opera
only managed nine further performances.
5. By a strange coincidence, both the subjects of *La Rosa di Cipro* and *Parasina*
had been used by Donizetti, whose *Caterina Cornaro* appeared in 1844; his *Parasina* in 1833.
6. One reason for Ricordi's pushing D'Annunzio as Puccini's potential librettist
was the lengthy fatal illness of Giacosa, who finally died 2 September 1906.

as Puccini learned the rights to *La Femme et le pantin* were available, he enlisted Ricordi's enthusiastic support to the project. Ricordi's eagerness arose from his anxiety over Puccini's long idleness and from his hopes that such an opera would create a great splash as a sort of *Carmen-cum-Salome*. The plot of *Conchita* deals with a Spanish prostitute who reduces Matteo to a mere puppet by refusing to grant him the ultimate favor and who subsequently permits him to watch her consummate the sexual act with another man; this arouses Matteo to the point of giving her a brutal thrashing, treatment that causes Conchita to yield to Matteo and become, in turn, his abject slave. On 1 October 1906 Ricordi and Puccini signed a contract[7] for an opera on this unsavory subject, to be named *Conchita* after the heroine, the libretto to be prepared by Illica.

Within a month he had a scenario, incorporating his own and Illica's modifications of Vaucaire's dramatization, but by the time he got to Paris in November 1906 to assist at the Comique's *accouchement* of *Butterfly* his interest in the subject had declined. He was bothered by the unsympathetic, not to say repellent, character of the heroine. His desire to drop *Conchita* was strengthened by the strenuous objections both Loüys and Vaucaire made to the modified scenario for the libretto. Later, his resolution to give up the subject completely, no matter what the consequences, was buttressed by his observation of New York's reception to Strauss's *Salome* after its introduction to the Metropolitan on 22 January 1907. Puccini's *lucchesismo* was appalled at the idea of writing an opera that prudery might ban from lucrative theaters. When he finally made it public that he was renouncing the opera, this in April 1907, he had to pay an indemnity of 4000 lire, but he sincerely regarded himself as well out of it. Loüys's response to Puccini's rejection of *Conchita* was to threaten legal action. Although Puccini might give up *Conchita*, "the Spanish whore," as he came to call her, was destined to become an operatic character. Her debut in that guise occurred at the Teatro Dal Verme, Milan, on 14 October 1911, with music by Riccardo Zandonai, and the libretto jointly credited to Vaucaire and Carlo Zangarini.[8]

During these years of fruitless search for what was to become the

7. This contract is printed in Marek, pp. 56-7.
8. Most writers on this subject err in stating that it was Illica's libretto prepared for Puccini that Zandonai set. Since Illica lived until 1919 and since Ricordi's published Zandonai's opera, the absence of Illica's name from the libretto can only mean that it was substantially reworked by Zangarini, if not completely rewritten.

successor to *Madama Butterfly*, Puccini tried to mask his idleness by a restless round of traveling to supervise new productions of his operas, hoping to establish personally traditions for their perform-ance. Thus his motives for these trips were not entirely mercenary, although he was fully aware that his operas well prepared and cere-moniously launched brought in larger receipts and totted up a greater number of performances than when left to routine produc-tions. He knew too how carefully calculated were some of his ef-fects—the final moments of an act and the drawing of the curtain, for instance—effects that less than scrupulous adherence to his di-rections would cause to misfire. From the fiasco of the *Madama Butterfly première*, Puccini knew how much the success of this opera depended on careful preparation. His frequent modifications to the score were the result of close attention to numerous produc-tions in many theaters.

In October 1904 Puccini returned to London, where *Manon Les-caut* had been selected to open a gala six-weeks' autumn season at Covent Garden. The performance, with Caruso and Rina Giachetti[9] and conducted by Campanini, did much to increase Puccini's popu-larity in London, a city he became increasingly fond of in these years. The measure of Puccini's favor with the English is shown by the season's records: his was the lion's share—twelve performances of three operas—more than any other composer was given, even Verdi. It was during this visit to London that Puccini first met Sybil Seligman (1868-1935), his intimate friend for the rest of his life and the mother of Vincent, whose *Puccini among Friends* is a rec-ord of this friendship.

The following year a much more extensive trip took Giacomo and Elvira to Buenos Aires, where the Teatro de la Opera was giving what amounted to a special Puccini season: five operas, including the ill-fated *Edgar*. Puccini had to endure being fêted, an ordeal he never learned to enjoy; on the other hand he derived nothing but pleasure from hearing Storchio as Butterfly repeat her triumph of the previous season there. This South American jaunt caused Puccini to miss the introduction of *Butterfly* to England (Covent

9. Rina Giachetti was a soprano as was her sister Ada. Although Rina had the more notable career, to the extent that in London she became known as "the Ternina of the Italian season," Ada gained wider notoriety, as she was the mother of Caruso's two sons and was involved in a legal action that received wide pub-licity. Eugenio Gara, the editor of the invaluable *Carteggi Pucciniani*, occasionally makes the understandable slip of confusing the Giachetti sisters.

Garden, 10 July 1905). Whoever the Casa Ricordi sent in Puccini's place to direct the production did his work well, for the performance with Emmy Destinn, Caruso, and Scotti was a triumph with the public and all but a small segment of the press.[10]

Although Puccini missed this London *première*, he did attend its second production there that autumn, when the opera had, if anything, an even more fervent reception. In less than two months *Butterfly* was given eleven times.[11] From London Puccini went straight to Bologna, this was in late October 1905, for Toscanini was introducing *Butterfly* at the Teatro Comunale. For some reason Toscanini's conducting of the opera did not please Puccini. He wrote to Sybil Seligman, "I had to fight like anything at Bologna, but it was a real success."[12] Since Toscanini had first conducted *Butterfly* at Buenos Aires in July 1904, when the composer was not present, the Maestro had developed a reading of the score that may not have accorded with Puccini's views at certain points. In any event, Puccini was so conscious of his disagreement with Toscanini that he decided to forgo attending the first performance of *Butterfly* at Turin, where Toscanini was again conducting. These performances were given in January 1906.

Puccini was not the only one concerned with supervising the introduction of *Butterfly* outside Italy. In October 1906 Tito Ricordi went to the United States to officiate with both the *première* and the six-month coast-to-coast tour of the opera, sung in English by the Savage Opera Company.[13] This long sojourn was really a sort of temporary exile, as Tito's volatile temperament did not always make for peaceful relations with his father. In time Puccini would find life less than peaceful when it came to dealing with Tito, who succeeded to the management of the firm after Giulio Ricordi's death.

Of his numerous travels on behalf of his latest opera, none was more frustrating to Puccini than his trip to Paris in November 1906

10. Although I have been unable to determine precisely who took charge of *Butterfly* at its Covent Garden *première*, I would not be surprised if it were Tito Ricordi.

   Incidentally, this performance was conducted by Cleofonte Campanini and not by André Messager, as some sources state.

11. In the autumn of 1905 *Butterfly* was sung in London by Rina Giachetti, Gabrielle Lejeune (Suzuki), Zenatello, and Mario Sammarco (1868-1930) as Sharpless. Mugnone conducted.

12. Seligman, p. 69.

13. The U.S. *première* of *Butterfly* took place in Washington, D.C., on 15 October 1906. The English translation was the work of R. H. Elkin.

to see *Butterfly*'s baptism at the Opéra-Comique. A chief cause of his problems was the soprano Marguerite Carré (1880-1947), who as the wife of the director of the Opéra-Comique had exercised her perogatives to secure the role of Butterfly for the French *première* and in addition had grabbed the exclusive rights to the part for the next two years in all the principal theaters elsewhere in France.[14] If Mme Carré had been better suited to the role both in voice and in temperament, the situation would not have been so annoying, but Puccini found himself confronted with a tough-minded Frenchwoman secure in her position and insisting that those sections of the role that gave her difficulty be cut or simplified. Puccini knew there was no choice of replacing la Carré, and he could kick himself for compromising the future of his opera in a country that was an important source of income by allowing this property to fall into her unsympathetic hands.

The rehearsals progressed with a slowness that tried Puccini's patience, as the staging was in the hands of Albert Carré himself, who worked, in Puccini's words, with such "excessive meticulousness as to turn one's hair gray." The lengthy rehearsal period allowed Puccini time to sample the repertory of the Comique. He saw an opera based on another work by Pierre Loüys, *Aphrodite*, composed by Camille Erlanger; Puccini admired Carré's staging of this work, but thought the music "absolutely ugly—a horrifying tumult of sounds." On another occasion he saw *Pelléas* again and informed Ricordi "that it has extraordinary qualities of harmony and diaphanous orchestral effects, it is truly interesting, but it never transports you, never raises you up, it is always the same color, like the habit of a Franciscan."[15] It is odd to note that both these operas featured Mary Garden in two of her most famous creations, but Puccini was not sufficiently impressed by her to mention her name.

Besides the brittle ruthlessness of Mme Carré, Puccini had to contend with the hostility of André Messager. Messager was the chief conductor at the Comique and therefore the one who would normally introduce an important novelty, but he was also the composer

14. Mme Carré came by her ability to drive hard bargains for exclusive rights honestly. She was the daughter of Giraud, director of the theater in Nantes. To be quite fair, Carré was a shrewd actress, wise in the ways of the stage, if not exactly a warm impulsive nature. In roles which did not unduly tax her rather stiff white voice, she made her mark. Her debut at the Comique, in 1902 as Mimì, introduced her in a role in which she was admired.
15. Puccini's reactions to both *Aphrodite* and *Pelléas* appear in *Carteggi Pucciniani*, p. 334.

of *Madame Chrysanthème* (1893), an operetta about the relationship of a geisha and a French naval officer. Not surprisingly, Messager refused to conduct Puccini's score, which was assigned to the
relatively inexperienced hands of Franz Ruhlmann, who had come
to the Comique just a few months before. Undoubtedly Messager's
attitude was unsettling to Mme Carré, whose nerves were further
strained by what was for her the excessive challenge of her part. To
Puccini's further annoyance, the first performance kept being postponed, the last time because of the prima donna's indisposition. Yet
it would be a false assumption to suppose Puccini foresaw a disaster;
for although both he and Illica, who had joined him in December,
were put off by the atmosphere within the Comique, they were
sanguine about the opera's chances. When *Butterfly* was finally
given, on 28 December 1906, it was a hit with the public and a miss
with the critics, whose opinions seemed to count for little with the
regular patrons of the Comique.[16]

From Paris, Puccini made a hurried trip to Italy to gather his
things and sailed almost immediately for New York. He first arrived in the United States on 18 January 1907 at 6 p.m.; by eight
o'clock he was in the Metropolitan Opera House to see their first
Manon Lescaut. He was pleased. Heinrich Conried, then manager
of the Metropolitan, had arranged for Puccini's visit the previous
February. To celebrate having the composer *in situ* he had scheduled four of Puccini's operas, two of them—*Manon Lescaut* and
Madama Butterfly—new to the repertory. Caruso was singing in
all four, a nice sort of revenge for his having been passed over for
the privilege of creating Cavaradossi six years before. Although
Puccini's presence was designed to ensure the authenticity of all the
productions, his chief concern was with *Butterfly*.

In those days, as Puccini found to his dismay, the Metropolitan's
way with staging opera could be haphazard. The stage manager for
Butterfly was Eugène Dufriche, an experienced bass *comprimario*,
or singer of lesser roles, but scarcely the person to impose his will
on the *divi* of the company. Puccini discovered that Dufriche had
not even bothered to prepare the staging, since the composer would
be on hand. Puccini had to argue to wangle some extra rehearsals.

16. Besides Carré, the first French *Butterfly* was sung by Berthe Lamare (Sou-
zouki), Marguerite Bériza (Kate), Edmond Clément (Pinkerton), Jean Périer
(Sharpless), Fernand Francell (Yamadori), Gustave Huberdeau (le Bonze), and
Maurice Cazeneuve (Goro). The French translation was the work of Paul Ferrier.
By 1950 *Butterfly* had been sung over eight hundred times at the Comique.

He was ill at ease with the conductor, Arturo Vigna (1863-1927), whose control of the orchestra lacked authority. Puccini's attitude toward the prima donna, Geraldine Farrar (1882-1967), was quite reserved. Although Farrar was an American come home in glory after spectacular European triumphs, attributes that won her the combined honors of making her debut on the opening night and of singing the leading role in the most important novelty of the season,[17] Puccini thought her voice small for Butterfly in a theater of the Metropolitan's huge dimensions, and he was bothered by her lapses from pitch. In spite of these things, Puccini was hopeful the opera would succeed; its reception far surpassed his own more modest expectations, tempered as they were by his experiences at such operatic midwifery.[18]

Puccini remained in the United States for about two weeks after the Metropolitan's *prima* of *Butterfly*. In spite of the companionship of Elvira, he sought diversion with Scotti and Lina Cavalieri[19] and by attending the theater, as he would follow almost any lead in his search for a promising subject. Two of the plays he saw in New York were by Belasco: *Rose of the Rancho*, which had opened on Broadway the previous November, and the older *Girl of the Golden West*, first played in Pittsburgh in 1905. Puccini reported to Ricordi from New York that he had seen several plays set in the far

17. Although from one point of view, *Salome* might be called the most important novelty of the Met's 1906-07 season, in terms of immediate impact on the repertory that honor is claimed by *Butterfly*. Some insight to the importance of Farrar's place in the plans for that season may be gained if it is remembered she was offered and wisely turned down the role of Salome, which was sung by her more than worthy replacement, Olive Fremstad.

18. At the Metropolitan *première* of *Butterfly* the four principal roles were sung by Farrar, Homer, Caruso, and Scotti. The balance of the cast included Helen Mapleson (Kate), Josephine Jacoby (Mother), Estelle Sherman (Cousin), Katherine Moran (Aunt), Albert Reiss (Goro), Giovanni Paroli (Yamadori), Adolph Mühlmann (the Bonze), Arcangelo Rossi (Yakusidè), Bernard Bégué (the Commissioner), and Vittorio Navarini (the Registrar).

The presence in this cast list of the names of Butterfly's female relatives shows that the version of the opera introduced to the Metropolitan is not the final one. The Metropolitan continued to list the female relatives through the 1908-09 season; Yakusidè was listed through the season of 1935-36!

19. Cavalieri (1874-1944) was Puccini's companion at the Metropolitan's *première* of *Salome*, having sung an aria from *Mefistofele* during the concert that preceded Strauss's one-acter. Three days later Cavalieri pinch-hit for the indisposed Eames in *Tosca*. Cavalieri had never sung the role and appeared without orchestra or stage rehearsal, but she had the benefit of Puccini's advice. Malicious gossip of the day linked the beautiful Cavalieri and Giacomo, but what basis there was for this is impossible to tell.

West; he liked the ambience and thought the plays contained some promising scenes, but they left him with an over-all impression of contrivance and bad taste, of being old stuff. Although he was not aware of it the seed that would bear fruit as his next opera had been planted.

Sybil Seligman was probably the determining influence in Puccini's decision to make an opera from *The Girl of the Golden West*. While Puccini was in London in late May and June 1907, he discussed the play with her, and she became so interested in the idea that she volunteered to secure a copy of the play and to have a translation prepared for him. It should be remembered that in 1907 Puccini's English was very little better than it had been in 1900 when he saw the play *Madame Butterfly* in London; therefore, he had only a very general notion of the plot. That Sybil, whose judgment he trusted and who, of course, understood English, should hold a favorable view of *The Girl* carried a good deal of weight with Puccini.

As Puccini waited in Torre del Lago for the translation of *The Girl* to arrive, he was in a peculiarly receptive mood. He had lately paid a sizable sum to rid himself of *Conchita;* Marie Antoinette, of whom he began to think once more in a desultory way, could easily be laid aside still another time if something more promising came to hand. The first installment of the translation reached him on 8 July, the balance of the play a day or two later. By the 14th he had conceived how to combine the last two acts of Belasco's play into something very like the form we know as Act 3 of *La Fanciulla*. Immediately he wrote to George Maxwell, Ricordi's agent in New York, to inquire about Belasco's terms. He had already found a librettist, Carlo Zangarini,[20] who was a plausible choice, for besides being an experienced dramatist he was the son of an American woman, born in Colorado!

By the end of August Puccini had concluded agreements with Belasco and Zangarini. With increasing impatience Puccini waited for some sign of his new libretto, waited all through the rest of 1907. In December he attended Toscanini's new production of *Tosca* at La Scala and was delighted with it.[21] Finally, on 27 Janu-

---

20. Besides his work on *La Fanciulla* for Puccini and on *Conchita* for Zandonai, Zangarini collaborated on the librettos to Wolf-Ferrari's *I Gioielli della Madonna*, Zandonai's unsuccessful *Melenis* (1912), Gnecchi's *La Rosiera* (1927), and Ferrari-Trecate's *Le Astuzie di Bertoldo* (1934).
21. *Tosca* was given with Burzio (Tosca), Rinaldo Grassi (Cavaradossi), and Amato (Scarpia) on 29 December 1907.

ary 1908 he got part of Zangarini's work and was delighted with that, too. While waiting for the rest of the libretto, he took Elvira to Egypt in February 1908, a sightseeing tour to divert Elvira and improve her health. On their way, they stopped in Naples, where Giacomo heard Strauss conduct *Salome*.[22] The remains of the Pharaohs bored Puccini and left Elvira "apathetic." Puccini grew increasingly eager to start serious work on his new opera. In March they were in Rome for a gala of *Butterfly* and a banquet in Puccini's honor. By the beginning of April matters came to a head about the libretto of *La Fanciulla*, as Puccini still did not have the last act.

He insisted that Zangarini start working with a collaborator; Zangarini angrily insisted that he would go to court rather than have an unwanted collaborator forced upon him. It was not the quality of Zangarini's work that dissatisfied Puccini, but that he worked so slowly and that he could not make the small changes and revisions that Puccini was accustomed to demand. To get his way Puccini appealed to Ricordi, and in a few days he had his second librettist, Guelfo Civinini of Livorno.[23] Civinini reworked Zangarini's text for Acts 1 and 2 within the next month, and at long last in May 1908 Puccini could get down to work on *La Fanciulla*.

The work went slowly, but by June from his villa in Chiatri, Puccini could report to Ricordi that he was making "little steps." Part of his slowness in starting was caused by his not having the complete libretto in hand. Zangarini seems to have dropped out of the project almost completely with the arrival of Civinini. On 13 July, Civinini reported he was working on Act 3. But by the time it arrived, something else had happened to slow down Puccini's work. On 20 December he was forced to put it aside for eight months.

The tragic story that caused the interruption of *La Fanciulla* can be sketched only briefly here. In 1903 when Puccini was convalescing slowly at Torre del Lago from his automobile accident, a young local girl, Doria Manfredi, came to work as a maid in the Villa Puccini. Elvira's somewhat tempestuous ways had created a servant problem, but Doria was devoted and apparently impervious to her

22. The performance of *Salome* took place 1 February 1908 with Gemma Bellincioni in the title role. Here are Puccini's reactions, written to Fosca: "It was a success, but I don't believe anyone was convinced by it. Strauss conducted and, as was deserved, was respected and even acclaimed. La Bellincioni in spite of her vocal decline acted with art and danced with great effect (*Carteggi Pucciniani*, p. 364).

23. Civinini, according to Loewenberg's compendious *Annals of Opera*, wrote no other libretti than his share of the book for *La Fanciulla*.

mistress's temper. At some point after Giacomo's return from Chiatri in 1908, Elvira became obsessed that her husband was having an
affair with Doria. Although the girl insisted upon her innocence,
Elvira dismissed her. Firing Doria did not banish her, however, as
she lived in the village, and people talked about Elvira's actions.
Elvira called the girl foul names to her face or to anyone else within
earshot. The bitterness grew and raged more fiercely until the tormented girl took poison and after five days of agony died, 28 January 1909. Doria's outraged and vindictive family insisted on an
autopsy, which proved the girl still a virgin; whereupon they
brought legal action against Elvira, charging her with persecution
and defamation of character so severe as to cause an innocent girl's
suicide.

For his part, Giacomo had tried to befriend and help the girl,
knowing her to be unjustly accused, but when Elvira found out
about his efforts in Doria's behalf, she took it as clinching proof of
their guilt. Since he could not help the situation by staying and since
the peace he needed to be able to compose was gone, Giacomo went
to Rome, where he stayed at the Hotel Quirinale with his friends
Ciccio Tosti and his wife.[24] He needed their support, for after the
girl's death, the autopsy, and the instigation of legal action, the story
was spread over all the papers. Humiliated publicly and in deep despair, Giacomo believed his career was finished. He informed Elvira
he wanted a separation.

Certainly the hounded, but innocent figure of Doria arouses deep
sympathy. To view the tragedy from a distance and dispassionately,
one can, however, feel sorry for them all, even Elvira. She was
forty-eight and years of anxious jealousy suddenly flowed over ra-
tional bounds. She had had provocations aplenty in the past, and she
was unable to accept there was no provocation this time. What
made this affair unendurable in Elvira's eyes was her conviction it
was going on under her own roof. Until this time Giacomo had
managed to survive with Elvira. Pushed to it, he had frankly admitted his infidelities, but always insisted they were temporary and
somehow necessary to his creative spirit. Fundamentally, Elvira was
a very conventional woman, and her flouting of convention when
she left Gemignani for Giacomo had taken its toll. Now her need

24. F. Paolo Tosti (1846-1916) was a composer of hundreds of once-popular songs.
They are not all by any means of the order of the once ubiquitous *Good-bye;* some
such as *L'alba separa dalle luce l'ombra* are of real merit. Tosti and his wife Berthe
had known Puccini since he first came to Milan in the 1880's.

for conventionality had become fanatical. Although Giacomo knew that in the case of Doria he was innocent, he could not help but be aware that in some larger sense he shared in the responsibility for all that had happened. If atonement is achieved through suffering, both Giacomo and Elvira paid the price and dearly.

It has been suggested that this tragic interruption of work on *La Fanciulla* left its corrosive mark on the opera, that somehow the suffering and scandal diminished Puccini's creativity. Such a view is surely oversimple, based as it is upon the assumption that there must necessarily be a direct relationship between the events of an artist's life and his work. Once the details of the Doria scandal had been made public, they provided a convenient but inaccurate explanation for the disappointment felt by those critics who expected Puccini to keep on working the same vein he had mined so successfully in *Madama Butterfly* and its immediate predecessors. By neglecting to notice that Puccini was breaking new ground with an entirely different sort of plot and one with a more closely integrated musical investiture, they conspicuously underestimated both Puccini's growth as an artist and his achievement in *La Fanciulla*.

The tragic turmoil did interrupt Puccini's work on *La Fanciulla*, and it was not until legal involvement had been settled that he could get back to it. From Rome and the Tostis, Puccini had gone to other friends, to the seclusion of the Collecchioni's hunting preserve at Capalbio in the Tuscan Maremma, then to Torre del Lago, where he was joined by his son Tonio, who was much affected by his parents' problem, then to Milan, where he stayed in a hotel rather than in his apartment on the Via Verdi. In Milan he saw the Italian *première* of Strauss's *Elektra*, and it is not surprising considering all that Puccini had been going through that he found it "a horror." Elvira was sentenced in July. She was found guilty, given five months' imprisonment, fined, and made responsible for all costs. The case was appealed, but it was eventually settled out of court by Giacomo's paying a sizable sum to Doria's family. When this last indignity had been played out, Elvira rejoined her husband at Bagni di Lucca. From all accounts it was a subdued and chastened Elvira who came back to a visibly aged Giacomo.

For the artist, his creations have lives of their own. Soon Giacomo was able to lose himself in *La Fanciulla*. By September 1909 his sketches for Act 2 were well advanced, and two months later he was working on Act 3. The orchestration of the whole opera occupied him from January until 27 July 1910, about seven months, not that he worked on it consistently during that time; he finished Act 2 in early April and scored all of Act 3 during July after his return from a trip to Paris. These dates show the concentrated work he was capable of.

The plates for printing the opera were prepared as soon as Giacomo dispatched each act to Casa Ricordi. The printed parts were sent to New York. From there in late October 1910 Toscanini sent a telegram to Puccini to announce that the first reading of the score at the Metropolitan Opera House had gone most auspiciously. Accompanied by his son Tonio and by Tito Ricordi, Puccini sailed for New York on 9 November. At Giacomo's request, Elvira did not accompany him.

The *première* of Puccini's *La Fanciulla del West* was the first world *première* ever held at the Metropolitan. Nothing in that theater's subsequent history has matched the importance of this event. When Puccini arrived in New York on 17 November, he found his new opera well anticipated. There were reams of publicity; news-hungry reporters hounded his steps; Puccini was the man of the hour.

Within the Metropolitan all was anticipation. The rehearsals went swimmingly. David Belasco co-operated with the staging, helping to correct some of the unauthentic touches that had crept into the stage directions of Puccini's score. These rehearsals constituted some of the happiest hours of rapport between Puccini and Toscanini, all their past disagreements on artistic matters forgotten. Puccini had only one small reservation about his topflight cast: that Emmy Destinn as Minnie lacked vitality, but evidently this was corrected, for the critics remarked on her "great energy and sincerity." Finally, after two well-received open rehearsals before specially invited guests, the great night came on Saturday, 10 December 1910.[25] Outside the theater there was heavy snow and thick

25. The cast for the *première* of *La Fanciulla* included Emmy Destinn (Minnie), Enrico Caruso (Johnson), Pasquale Amato (Jack Rance), Marie Mattfeld (Wowkle), Albert Reiss (Nick), Adamo Didur (Ashby), Dinh Gilly (Sonora), Angelo Bada (Trin), Giulio Rossi (Sid), Vincenzo Reschiglian (Bello), Pietro Audisio (Harry), Glenn Hall (Joe), Antonio Pini-Corsi (Happy), Bernard Bégué (Larkens), Georges Bourgeois (Billy Jackrabbit), Andres de Segurola (Jake Wallace), Edoardo Missiano (José Castro) and Lamberto Billeri (the Postillion). Toscanini conducted.

One of the unexpected consequences of this *première*, unlike the flurry of recordings that followed the Met's mounting of *Madama Butterfly* is that not one

ice; inside, all was sparkling, brilliant, a triumph: a total of fifty-five curtain calls and the formal presentation of a wreath to Puccini.

The critical reception was rapturous, almost without reservation. Richard Aldrich in the *New York Times* the following day wrote a perceptive review. After lavishing high praise on the production, he mentions that "there is certainly far less of the clearly defined melodic luster, outline, point, and fluency, far less of what is tangibly thematic than there is in his earlier works . . . ," and he goes on to say that "the conclusion seems almost irresistible that all this is intentional; a part of the composer's scheme for the representation in music of this Western drama."[26] Aldrich had hit upon the difference in Puccini's new work that confronted early audiences of the opera, but the enthusiasm for *La Fanciulla* showed no early signs of abating.

The Metropolitan gave it nine times in New York that winter, also performing the score in Philadelphia and Brooklyn. The Chicago-Philadelphia Company introduced it in Chicago on 27 December 1910, repeating it four times before moving on to play it in Baltimore, Philadelphia (twice), and St. Louis.[27] But this was not all; the Boston Opera Company put on *La Fanciulla* on 17 January 1911; by the end of the season in late March that troupe had given the opera seven times.[28] Never before had so many American audiences been given the opportunity to see the newest opera by a leading composer so soon after its *première*.

The next important *première* of *La Fanciulla* took place at Covent Garden, its first performance in Europe. With Puccini in attendance, the event took place on 29 May 1911.[29] There was much

---

record of this music was issued by the artists of the first cast. Caruso, Destinn, and Amato were all under contract to Victor, but no, not one recording, not even Caruso's *Ch'ella mi creda*. What a fine souvenir that would have been!

26. This review in its entirety is reprinted in Richard Aldrich, *Concert Life in New York (1902-1923)* (New York, 1941), pp. 300-307.

27. The first Chicago cast included Carolina White (Minnie), Clotilde Bressler-Gianoli (Wowkle), Amadeo Bassi (Johnson), Maurice Renaud (Jack Rance), Francesco Daddi (Nick), Nazzareno de Angelis (Ashby), and Hector Dufranne (Sonora), with Campanini conducting.

28. For Boston the Western contingent included Carmen Melis (Minnie), Florencio Constantino (Johnson), Carlo Galeffi (Jack Rance), Carl Gantvort (Ashby), Luigi Cilla (Nick), Ramon Blanchart (Sonora), and Jose Mardones (Jake Wallace). Arnaldo Conti conducted. The Boston settings were used again at the Italian *première* at the Teatro Costanzi, Rome, in June 1911.

29. Of the leading singers of the New York *première* only Destinn as Minnie was on hand. Dinh Gilly (1877-1940), the Metropolitan's Sonora was promoted to Jack Rance on this occasion. In London there was no Caruso, only Amadeo Bassi (1874-1949) as Johnson, followed in some later performances by the American tenor Riccardo Martin (1874-1952). Campanini conducted.

of the preliminary excitement there had been in New York; there was considerable enthusiasm at the *première*, but a sense of letdown about the new opera appeared sooner in England than in the United States. Undeniably the Covent Garden production was inferior to the Metropolitan's. The staging lacked the richness of detail; the animating touch of Belasco was absent. Although Amadeo Bassi was a creditable tenor, he was no Caruso. Most sorely missed by those who had heard the New York performances was the presence of Toscanini. Although Campanini had the experience of conducting the opera in Chicago behind him, he was unable to reveal the complex sonorities of the score with Toscanini's persuasiveness and authority.

In Puccini's eyes the most important production of this opera after its world *première* was its introduction to Italy, for the true survival of the opera depended upon its ability to sustain itself in the many Italian theaters. The focal point of Puccini's hopes was Toscanini, who was to direct the performance at Rome's Teatro Costanzi on 12 June 1911.[30] Caruso was not available as he had fallen ill in February and could not resume his career until the autumn; again Bassi was the seasoned replacement. As before the audience was lavish with its applause for *La Fanciulla*, but the Italian critics seemed rather mystified by Puccini's new score.

In the publicity before the performance there had been a good deal of talk and speculation about Puccini's "second manner" and his "new career." The critics were somewhat disconcerted, therefore, to encounter some familiar features of the old Puccini. They praised the brilliance and originality of the orchestration and the skill with which Puccini evoked the California forest. One puzzled critic, Primo Levi, was put off by the apparent discrepancy between the grandiose elements in the score and the humble characters in their primitive setting.[31]

In relatively short order *La Fanciulla* was introduced to all the major operatic centers. A little more than a month after its Italian *première*, it was mounted in Buenos Aires, on 25 July 1911.[32] After the treatment that La Scala had accorded his last new opera, Puc-

---

30. The cast for the Italian *première* of *La Fanciulla* included Eugenia Burzio (Minnie), Bassi, and Amato.
31. Levi's review is printed in part in *Carteggi Pucciniani*, p. 391.
32. The opera was introduced to Buenos Aires by Adelina Agostinelli, Edoardo Ferrari-Fontana (1878-1936), and Titta Ruffo (1877-1953). Giuseppe Baroni conducted.

cini was in no hurry to bring *La Fanciulla* to Milan. It had been performed in many Italian theaters, as well as at Warsaw (in Polish), at Liverpool (in English), at Budapest (in Hungarian), at the Paris Opéra (in Italian), and at Marseilles (in French), before it was finally given at La Scala on 29 December 1912, where it ran for thirteen performances.[33] The following year the opera was introduced to Berlin and Vienna.

Outside Italy, *La Fanciulla* has had until lately a rather discouraging record. At the Metropolitan, for instance, its original momentum was expended after four seasons and twenty-two performances. At Covent Garden the record was even less impressive; it was dropped after two seasons and eight performances. The only proposed revival there, intended for Beecham's 1940 season, was prevented by the war. At the Metropolitan, *La Fanciulla* was dusted off in 1929 as a vehicle for Maria Jeritza, who had established a reputation as Minne in Vienna, but the mood of the Depression was not congenial to the opera's taking hold. In 1961, missing its fiftieth anniversary by one year, *La Fanciulla* was brought forward again and was received with surprising warmth by public and critics alike. Since then the score has shown real signs of establishing itself as a repertory piece. By an appropriate coincidence, *La Fanciulla* was the first opera performed in the new Metropolitan Opera House at Lincoln Center.[34]

The libretto of *La Fanciulla* was designed and supervised by Puccini himself, whom Zangarini later declared should be counted among the authors. Puccini's chief contribution was his proposal to combine the last two acts of Belasco's play into one highly effective scene. The idea of showing the manhunt for Johnson on-stage was Puccini's idea, as was the arrangement to follow it directly by the episode of Rance's insults and Minnie's arrival on horseback at the critical moment. His principal innovation was to move the final scene outdoors, instead of having it take place inside the Polka barroom as in the play. The setting of the giant redwoods and the looming Sierras in the distance adds much to the evocativeness of

33. At La Scala, the Minnie, Johnson, and Jack Rance were Tina Poli-Randaccio (1881?-1956), Giovanni Martinelli (b. 1885), and Carlo Galeffi (b. 1885), with Tullio Serafin (1878-1968) conducting.
34. A performance before students took place on 11 April 1966; it was an "acoustic test" of the new theater. Appearing on that occasion were Beverly Bower (Minnie), Gaetano Bardini (Johnson), Cesare Bardelli (Jack Rance), and Louis Sgarro (Jake Wallace).

the action. Puccini moved the schoolroom episode of Minnie's Bible lesson from Belasco's final act to the first act of the libretto, using the presentation of the idea of redemption as part of the exposition.

As an example of dramatic structure the libretto reads with a number of jolts; it seems crude and naïve, particularly if it is set beside the grace and poetry of the texts to *Bohème* and *Butterfly*. All too frequent are lines such as this, which Sheriff Rance addresses to Castro, the half-caste bandit: "Figlio di cane, mostraci la tua lurida faccia!" (You son of a bitch, show us your filthy face!) And then there is the business of Johnson's giving Minnie her first kiss; that strains credulity a bit! It is not hard to poke fun at the libretto of *La Fanciulla*, yet to do so is to miss the point.

Obviously, Puccini found something in this story that caught his imagination. His sense of the theater was too strong, his critical judgement too keen, to be taken in by a plot that offered nothing more than some exciting situations. A coherent, interesting plot was only one of the things he demanded of a libretto. Again and again in his letters to his various librettists he stresses his need of a dramatic idea that could release powerful and poetic emotions. The idea of redemption in this libretto is just such a catalyst. It enables Puccini to view his characters not just as puppets in a melodrama but as creatures in a myth. When the Italian critic Primo Levi objected to the discrepancy between the grandiose score and the humble characters, he did not grasp the point that Puccini intended his characters to be something more than just a barmaid and a badman and a sheriff.

After all, Puccini did not look at the California Gold Rush with an American's eyes. He regarded it half a century ago more as we do today, our eyes and ears conditioned by countless films. As the historical West receded, the milieu has become a mythical arena where virtue struggles against evil.

To make fun of Minnie's seemingly miraculously preserved innocence is to miss the point that she is intended quite simply as a miracle, a miracle in rough sordid surroundings. It is important to remember, too, that she feels herself compromised, if not corrupted, by her environment. She sees herself clearly as she tells Rance:

MINNIE: And I?
The owner of a saloon and gambling den,
I live on whisky and gold.
We're all the same!

And when she must, she cheats at poker, not just to save herself from Rance but to save Johnson's life. Her hysterical laughter at the end of Act 2 is not only an expression of relief at dangers avoided. Her laughter is tinged with a sense of irony. She knows she has cheated to save a man who had deceived her, a man she loves no matter what he has done. That Johnson speaks of Minnie's having "the face of an angel," is no empty rhetoric, but a part of the underlying symbolism.

Johnson is one of the more personable and virile of Puccini's heroes. Far more than just an amatory foil to Minnie, Johnson presents complexities of his own. Just as Minnie, with her $30 education, longs to be something other and better than she is, so does Johnson, with his dual existence as the reluctant bandit Ramerrez and in his assumed role as Johnson (the nice fellow from Sacramento). He is impulsive and he shows genuine sensitivity when he is moved by Minnie's description of herself as "a poor good-for-nothing" and when he begs she be spared the knowledge of his hanging. When Minnie discovers his true identity and reproaches him with it, his confession and his desire to escape his guilty past ring true.

The most original scene in the libretto is that between Minnie and Johnson at the end of Act 1. Here is anything but a conventional love duet. It is built upon irony: Johnson has come to rob the camp but stays to help Minnie guard it; and Minnie, while defending the gold, reveals her own defenselessness. All through the scene they address each other with the polite "voi" forms rather than using the more intimate "tu." This scene is psychologically sound because in it the mutual attraction that leads to love evolves naturally; it is not just one more tired example of the love-at-first-sight cliché.

Even Rance on close examination is more than a two-dimensional villain. In Act 1 he tells Minnie that he has never been loved, has never loved anyone until he met her, and the only thing that had stirred him before has been the desire for gold. But now he claims he would throw away all his treasure for just one kiss. Rance is a man of his word, though. After he has lost his poker game to Minnie he does not participate in the capture of Johnson, much as he would like to see him hanged. Johnson is turned over to the sheriff by Ashby, the Wells Fargo agent. Rance's obsessive love fits his gambler's nature; he cannot overcome the jealousy that consumes him.

And so we see him at the end of the opera, apart, huddled over his dwindling fire. The suffering and torment of Rance are as convincing as his cruelty and brutality.

The miners, too, are part of the myth. Wrenched from their homes by dreams of wealth, they are easy prey to homesickness. Living lives of backbreaking labor, relieved only by whisky and gambling, they find in Minnie the gentleness missing from their existence. They respond to her explanation of the Bible passage: "That means, boys, that there is no sinner in all the world to whom a path of redemption does not open," by letting Minnie persuade them to set Johnson free.

Vincent Seligman has suggested that the opera's happy ending—the first Puccini had attempted so far—has interfered with the opera's success. I cannot agree with this. It is true that if one approaches *La Fanciulla*, hoping it to be. another *Manon Lescaut, La Bohème, Tosca*, or *Madama Butterfly*, one may well be put off and disappointed by the lack of a tragic climax, but *La Fanciulla* belongs to a different order of fable. Its happy ending is not tacked on, but implicit in the values stressed by the story. The traditional ending of the hero's escape and departure is not any the less valid for being traditional. It is not a denial of fate but its postponement.

One might regard the plot of *La Fanciulla* as a myth, rather than a bit of misguided *verismo*, vintage 1849. The plot has some of the qualities of a gold nugget in its natural state. Undoubtedly its basic values are more clearly discernible today than they were fifty years ago. Irving Kolodin seems to be on the right track when he accounts for renewed interest in *La Fanciulla* "possibly because the 'West' no longer had realistic connotations and could be accepted in the same spirit of fantasy as any other operatic locale."[35] In 1911, Puccini had another explanation: "At a first hearing, the drama can get in the way of listening to the music, but at a second or third hearing the action is familiar and the surprises no longer have the same intensity; then the music can be heard. This always happens for operas with exciting librettos."[36] Today some good complete recordings of the opera allow us to approach the opera through the music without any distraction by the action.

La Fanciulla del West is the most ambitious score Puccini had composed so far. The opera has a prevailing vigor and large-scale

35. Irving Kolodin, *The Metropolitan Opera: 1883-1966* (New York, 1966), p. 224.
36. Letter of Puccini to Carlo Calusetti, dated 9 July 1911, printed in *Carteggi Pucciniani*, p. 392.

forthrightness that set it apart from his earlier work. In *La Fanciulla* Puccini calls for a larger orchestra than he had used before
and he employs it more inventively. His harmonic vocabulary has
become more astringent and varied.

Most biographies of Puccini concentrate on the operas he wrote
or thought of writing and conjecture about his private life, but few
of them put adequate stress on his continuing study of contemporary music, particularly during the years that separate *Madama Butterfly* from *La Fanciulla*. Understandably Puccini revealed little
about his detailed analytical study of scores. He was reluctant to
discuss his professional habits, for they might have been misinter-
preted by unfriendly critics. To listen to the thirty-four-bar prelude of *La Fanciulla* is to hear at once the results of Puccini's study
and to note how well he assimilated the techniques used by his
contemporaries.

The prelude opens with this exuberant sequence:

The upward sweep of the arpeggio and the augmented chords create right off a sense of bursting, restless energy and the crisp mountain air. We have come a long way from Tosca's Rome or Butterfly's Nagasaki. The sense of the outdoors in this prelude continues
with the contrast between the bright brass color of the opening sequence and the mellower woodwind sound in the second dynamic
theme:

Example 2 is heard frequently throughout the opera expressing the urgency of Minnie's love for Johnson (as when in Act 2 it accompanies their first embrace), but at its first appearance in the prelude it has always reminded me of the swaying branches of huge trees. Puccini has explained that he intended this prelude as a description of the primeval California forest, the musical counterpart of the scenic lantern-slides Belasco used as a visual overture to his play.

Puccini's score for *La Fanciulla* is more like "a play with music" than a conventional opera. Except for the love duet in Act 2 and Johnson's plea in Act 3, there are practically no passages that can be conveniently extracted from the score. Yet on close examination the opera is filled with brief sections that have melodic impetus, such as these three moments from Act 1—Rance's declaration to Minnie, her account of her childhood in Soledad, and her description of herself as a poor good-for-nothing. Such passages are really too brief and too dependent on their context to work satisfactorily as numbers on a recital program. In his review of the Metropolitan *première* Richard Aldrich commented on the scarcity of developed melodic passages, suggesting that this omission was intentional on Puccini's part.

Undoubtedly it was a decision that involved a certain risk of jeopardizing the opera's instant appeal to the public as well as a risk of financial loss. No small part of Puccini's income came from the sheet music royalties of excerpts from his operas, often transposed to alien keys and in surprising arrangements. (Have you ever heard Musetta's Waltz on an E-flat sarussophone?) When Puccini came to write *La Fanciulla* he found that the pace of the action did not allow time for extended formal arias. He was a shrewd enough musical dramatist to realize that full endings for arias destroyed smooth dramatic structure. Fond as he was of applause, he realized that ovations and cries of *bis!* were fatal to sustained tension. Almost all the critics of the early performances of this era mention the rare applause during the acts and the loud enthusiasm that did not break out until the curtain closed. Puccini's decision required real courage, and it involved his placing artistic considerations far above mere crowd-pleasing.

It is really irksome to see how many commentators on *La Fanciulla* bemoan the lack of arias and mutter about the "poor" quality of the melodies, as though this work were a *Tosca manquée*. There is an abundance of melody in this opera, but Puccini deliberately subordinates it to the revelation of character and the description of action. The person who listens just to voices during a performance will miss the main source of melodic interest—the orchestra. Puccini's experiments in the direction of unflagging musical characterization and description are frequently, if not everywhere, successful. The expository opening of Act 1 has its awkward transitions, and Puccini's tinkering with the act reveals he was aware of the problem. His experiments, nonetheless, are a clear indication of striking out in new directions, a sign that raises hopes for his future operas.

The orchestration of *La Fanciulla* supplies further evidence of Puccini's progress as a composer. He shows real imagination in obtaining color by his "voicing" of the instruments: sometimes he will give the top note of a chord to a bassoon, causing it to sound above the oboe, for instance (instead of the customary use of the oboe's line above the bassoon's). His combinations of orchestral tints are equally imaginative and evocative. To give a murky, brooding tone to the accompaniment of Rance's declaration to Minnie he adds the contra-bassoon to the string basses. For the Indian squaw's lullaby near the beginning of Act 2, he calls for an exotic-sounding juxtaposition of flute, bass clarinet, bassoon, muted trumpet, and harp, while four violins play an inverted pedal point. The little figure that introduces Minnie's Bible lesson employs the glinting combination of piccolo, glockenspiel, and celesta. The tremendously atmospheric opening to Act 3 is scored for an ostinato in the bass viola (specially tuned), while over it from time to time appears a sullen three-part fanfare, heard first in the bassoons, then the horns, and finally the trombones. Puccini's orchestral virtuosity shows up most strongly in the scene of the poker game at the end of Act 2. Starting off with an air of ominous intimacy, he builds tension up to an overwhelming climax. Solo strings and woodwinds are set off against their main sections, frequently divided, in a restlessly modulating melody that begins in and returns to F-sharp minor.

3

Later, a staccato bassoon figure is heard (twenty-seven measures in the score, played freely to suit the exigencies of the card game on-stage), which creates the tension to accompany the game itself, forming a foundation that allows the words (occasionally spoken) to emerge clearly. This figure grows louder as the game goes on, other instruments adding to its harrowing intensity. In this scene Puccini shows an almost-Straussian knack of knowing how to play directly on the nerves of the audience. Considering the remarkable and original grasp of orchestration of this score, it seems strange that it has not been cited in standard works on the subject.

Puccini's writing for the voice in *La Fanciulla* differs from much of his earlier practice. Certain aspects of Minnie's part make it seem like an anticipation of the role of the Princess Turandot. For instance, there is the demanding range—from B-flat below the staff to high C-sharp. The variety of expression is extremely broad, extending from tender unaccompanied passages (such as her description of how sometimes she curls up in her bearskin rug and sleeps by the fire) to her hysterical outburst at the close of Act 2. Much of Minnie's music is far less conjunct than that of his earlier heroines, as in her plea to the miners with its prominent use of intervals of the ninth:

4

an - che tu lo vor-ra - i, Joe...

The role of Minnie presents a rewarding challenge to a talented singing-actress.

The tenor role of Johnson is also heavy in its demands, heavier than the music of Puccini's earlier heroes (with the possible exception of Edgar). Not only must he be capable of such a big outburst as this:

5

(ver) - go - gnal Ahi - mè,   ahi - mè, ver-go - gna mi - a!

in his "confession" aria in Act 2, but there are many phrases, particularly in the long scene that ends Act 1, requiring considerable delicacy and restraint.

Puccini had strong convictions about the handling of the curtain at the ends of the acts of his operas, and in *La Fanciulla* his instructions are more explicit than usual. He maintained that "a curtain closed too soon or too late often means the failure of an opera." He used to say "the curtain should be like part of the music."[37]

The first act ends just after Johnson's departure. Minnie goes to extinguish the gas lamp, stops underneath it so the light is full on her face, as she repeats to herself Johnson's words that her face is like an angel's.

6 [38]

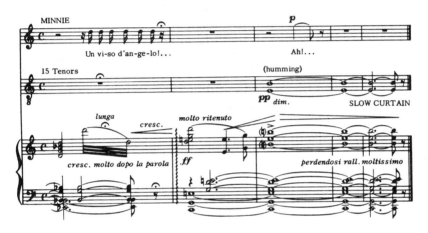

The *ff* theme here is that first heard at Minnie's entrance, but now instead of its original surge, it is suffused with a strong tinge of romantic melancholy. The curtain closes slowly during the ritard on the last bar.

In contrast, Act 2 has a fast curtain. Having lost the poker game, Rance exits rapidly but with dignity. Minnie bursts into hysterical laughter and then, after her last phrase, suddenly bursts into tears and embraces the head of Johnson, who has fainted from loss of blood and pitched forward on the table. The curtain is drawn quickly as the orchestra thuds out a sequence of E-flat minor chords.

The final curtain can be a most effective moment. As Minnie and

37. Ricci, pp. 13-14.
38. In Ricci, p. 159, appears a different vocal line for Minnie's phrase at the end of Act 1. I have no idea what might be Ricci's source for this variant. It is more exaggerated than the usual version of this phrase.

Johnson disappear from sight, their voices are heard from an ever-greater distance. The miners give way to their grief at Minnie's departure; Rance huddles in his cloak by the fire; only Billy Jackrabbit, the Indian, is unmoved, playing cards and smoking his pipe. The curtain closes very slowly over the final sustained chord (high strings *divisi*, the celesta, and a *ppp* for the bass drum). The conclusions to these three acts are a real measure of Puccini's ability to compose effective stage pictures, moments in which scene and sound seem indistinguishable.

The fascination that *La Fanciulla* holds lies not just in its musico-dramatic craftsmanship, but in its many anticipations of Puccini's later works. The use of the men's chorus, particularly in the nostalgic miners' song ("Old Dog Tray") reminds one of choruses in *Turandot*, particularly in the spacing of the parts and the treatment of the cadences. Also suggestive of *Turandot* is the way the shouting of the lynch mob looks forward to the outcries of the blood-thirsty populace of Peking. The despair of Johnson's description of his past life (*Or son sei mesi*, Act 2) foreshadows the tone of Luigi's "protest" aria in *Il Tabarro*.

La Fanciulla is an opera that has been too generally underestimated. As Puccini himself suggested, a second or a third exposure to it is necessary before one can really begin to know it. In my experience, repeated hearings only increase one's respect for *La Fanciulla del West*.

On the whole, the autograph full-score of *La Fanciulla* resembles closely the first edition of the opera published by Ricordi (copyright 1910), which differs at certain points from the present score. Briefly, these changes are mainly concerned with the following:

In Act 1, Puccini

1. just before the arrival of the postillion, removed a scene between Billy Jackrabbit (cadging drinks) and Minnie. This scene had become a traditional cut before it was quietly removed from the score.

2. removed a passage of thirty-four bars from the love scene, in which Minnie described in specific terms the miners' hard life.

3. at Johnson's words "No, Minnie, non piangete," added a chorus of fifteen off-stage tenors humming. Puccini instructs them "not to sound above the orchestra and to hum so that one can not distinguish they are a chorus."

In Act 2, he

1. added in 1922 sixteen bars to form a climax to the love duet. This passage with its difficult high C is almost universally cut to-day.[39] As music it is forgettable.

2. added a vocal climax to Johnson's "confession" aria—at No. 55. Here Puccini added three phrases to the vocal line.

In Act 3, he

1. to help the words and vocal line emerge, doubled some of the miners' parts.

2. added two repetitions to Minnie's cry at her entrance on horseback.

3. cut eight bars of Minnie's defiance of Rance—just before No. 33. Puccini ordered this cut for the Roman *première*.

4. considerably enlarged the choral and solo responses to Minnie's plea for Johnson's life, thereby making the miners' final capitulation come after more of a struggle.

There are other changes, but these mostly involve single phrases. Most of these alterations had been accomplished before 1915.

The autograph further shows one unusual feature in the order of composition. Puccini started working on Act 1 at what is indicated as No. 5 in the present scores. A month and a half later he added the thirty-four-bar prelude that precedes the curtain and further wrote another fifty measures, those accompanying the off-stage voices and the business of Nick the bartender's entering to light the lamps.

La Rondine

No sooner was *La Fanciulla* safely embarked on the impressive course of performances that introduced it to Italy than Puccini began to complain that he needed a new libretto. As happened after *Tosca* and again after *Butterfly*, he was to follow certain false leads before he could get down to work on what was to be his next opera; and, as before, he found it on one of his trips outside Italy to see one of his older works introduced to a new public.

Of his false leads, some were more ephemeral than others. For a

39. These sixteen bars were composed by Puccini in 1922 for a revival at the Teatro Costanzi, Rome, but as the singers balked at the extreme tessitura, they were not sung on that occasion. They were first performed in June 1923 at the Teatro Politeama, Viareggio, by Giulia Tess and Carmelo Alabiso.

while Puccini had the idea of converting a play by Gerhart Hauptmann (1862-1946), entitled *Hanneles Himmelfahrt* (The Assumption of Hannele Martern) (1892), into an opera. Hauptmann's
highly symbolic plot, replete with imaginary journeys, soon struck
Puccini as far too tenuous for the operatic stage.[40] Then he toyed
for some months with the idea of a Spanish comedy by the brothers
Álvarez Quintero, named *Anima Allegra*. This project first brought
Puccini into conjunction with Giuseppe Adami (1879-1946), a
dramatist and librettist and, later, a writer for films, who was to
play an important role in Puccini's future work. After Puccini's
death, Adami did Puccini the honor of publishing several collections
of their correspondence and a sympathetic biography. The most
memorable aspect of Puccini's brief involvement with *Anima Allegra* was the formation of a working relationship with Adami, for
the composer soon discarded the subject as lacking in appeal and
as deficient in dramatic intensity. Although *Anima Allegra* never
became the title of a Puccini opera, the libretto written by Adami
in conjunction with Luigi Motta was later set by Franco Vittadini
(1884-1948).[41]

Some former notions piqued Puccini's curiosity anew. As early as
1906, at Sybil Seligman's prompting, he had become interested in
Oscar Wilde's one-act melodrama, *A Florentine Tragedy*. That
prospect had not flourished long as Giulio Ricordi firmly used all
his influence to dissuade Puccini from the subject: Ricordi's antip-
athy to one-act operas had been only one cause; the other, his efforts to try to prevent Puccini's giving up *Conchita*. Giulio Ricordi
died 6 June 1912. Only a few weeks after that event Puccini started
thinking again about Wilde's play. In August 1912 he was urging
Illica to write a new act to introduce the action of Wilde's play;
exactly the same way Illica had written an introductory act for the
Belasco-Long one-act *Madame Butterfly* to convert it into a full
evening's fare. By October 1912 Puccini had lost interest in Oscar
Wilde.

By then the ground was being prepared for Puccini to renew

40. *Hanneles Himmelfahrt* was once thought of, but apparently not completed,
as an opera by Camille Erlanger (1863-1919); an opera based on this play by
Hauptmann and with the same name was composed by Paul Graener (1872-1944)
and had its first performances 17 February 1927 in Dresden and Breslau.
41. Vittadini's *Anima Allegra* had its *première* in Rome at the Costanzi, 15 April
1921, and a number of other productions followed. Bori introduced her Consuelo
(the "happy spirit" of the title) to New York on 14 February 1923.

contact with Gabriele D'Annunzio. As there had been in 1906, again there were cordial preambles, eager assurances, tense anticipation, followed by disillusionment. First, Puccini had hoped to get three one-act subjects from D'Annunzio. In 1904 Giulio Ricordi had scotched a proposed triple bill of Gorki subjects; this time D'Annunzio was not interested in this format, although the idea of a "trittico" would soon bear fruit from other sources. D'Annunzio's counter-proposal was one of the least suitable subjects ever made to Puccini—the Children's Crusade! D'Annunzio sketched the plot, and Puccini kept insisting there should be a strong love interest between a pair of precocious Crusaders. The suggestion must have offended D'Annunzio, for during the summer of 1913 Puccini called repeatedly on D'Annunzio in Paris, hoping to reach a compromise, but D'Annunzio was never at home. This time their relations broke on a more acrimonious note. By 1918 Puccini's opinion of D'Annunzio as a librettist was little short of scathing. "He always lacks the true, unadorned, simple human sense. Everything is always a paroxysm, an exaggeration, expressed in ultra-excessive terms."[42]

The most complicated of Puccini's unfruitful projects during these years was that involving Ouida's tale, *The Two Little Wooden Shoes* (1874). As early as 10 July 1911,[43] this subject had occurred to Puccini and he tried to find a copy of the Italian translation, entitled *Due zoccoletti* (1876). The idea lay fallow while he got and lost enthusiasm for other subjects, but it sprouted in 1913, when Puccini began to see D'Annunzio's crusading item as a lost cause. Puccini turned now to Illica, trying to enlist his interest in the Ouida plot, but his old librettist, although their working relations were of more than twenty years' standing, was not sufficiently interested. This overture and rebuff marked the end of Puccini's association with Illica; now he turned to a whole new circle of librettists.

But Illica's rebuff to the idea of *Due zoccoletti* did not diminish Puccini's interest. If Puccini's interest in the works of this highly

42. *Carteggi Pucciniani*, p. 470.
43. Many writers on Puccini use Adami's colorful account (in his *Il romanzo della vita di Giacomo Puccini* (Rome, 1944)) as their source for the events related to the affair of *Due zoccoletti*. Therefore they speak of Puccini's interest in this subject as dating from 1914. Puccini had, in reality, been thinking about it since July 1911, as the letter to Clausetti in *Carteggi Pucciniani* (p. 392) proves. When Puccinni first mentioned the subject to Adami in 1914, he made the idea sound like a new one rather than one that had been incubating for nearly three years.

sentimental English writer seems a bit unlikely, it can be explained by the circumstance that Ouida lived her last years at Massarosa, a little community on the north shore of Lago di Massaciuccoli, only a few miles from Torre del Lago. Impoverished and pretentious, Ouida was a notorious eccentric in the neighborhood. After her death in 1908 her memory was preserved—although perhaps not as she might have wished—by a number of crestfallen creditors.

It was not until 1914 that *Due zoccoletti* made the greatest clatter in the Puccini camp. First he turned to Adami to sound him out as a potential librettist, next he enlisted the Casa Ricordi's support, then he published an official announcement that he planned to write an opera based on the Ouida plot. At once the whole affair took a serious turn when there appeared, almost simultaneously, an announcement that *Due zoccoletti* would be made into an opera by— Pietro Mascagni![44] This apparent corroboration of Puccini's estimate of the subject served as a great incentive to him, bringing all his hunter's instincts into play. He pursued the subject through the legal marshes as though it were waterfowl.

As would be expected of a man of his practical experience, Puccini had made preliminary efforts to discover whether the rights to use the plot as basis for an opera were clear. The matter was cloudy indeed. Ouida had died intestate; the original publishers—Chatto & Windus—thought the copyright had expired; the Italian courts were addressed by Ouida's creditors. The upshot was a judgment that the prefect of Viareggio should adjudicate the matter. This dignitary was surreptitiously consulted by all the interested participants, and he finally decided that the only fair way to settle the affair would be by a public auction in behalf of the creditors, which was held in December 1914 at the Prefecture in Viareggio. Present were Puccini, Mascagni, Adami, Giovacchino Forzano (supposedly in the role of impartial literary expert, but he later wrote Mascagni's

---

44. On 18 August 1918 Mascagni wrote to Paladini a very ironical letter, commenting on the coincidences between the subjects used by Puccini and himself (the letter is printed in Paladini, p. 143):

". . . My friend Giacomo had scarcely received news that I was working with Carlo Lombardi [who was then preparing an operetta libretto for Mascagni entitled *Sì!*] and now a contract for an operetta by Puccini, publisher Ricordi, librettist Lombardi, has been drawn up. [This last was unfounded gossip.] It seems impossible! I wrote *Iris* . . . and I found between my feet another little Japanese girl. I set *Lodoletta* in flight . . . and I saw another bird in the air. [Here Mascagni alludes to the meaning of *lodoletta*—little lark—and of *rondine*—swallow.] I am thinking of an operetta . . . and I see another staring me in the face. I can't believe this is still a matter of coincidence. Enough! I have one hope: my operetta has as its title a simple *Sì!*: let's hope the other is called *No!*"

libretto on the subject), Dr. Gino Cantù (as Ricordi's official representative), and all the creditors. Cantù made the winning bid of 4000 lire and officially bestowed the rights thus purchased on Puccini. But now that Puccini had his quarry, he lost interest in it. And so Mascagni's announcement, not Puccini's, turned out to be the accurate one, for at the Teatro Costanzi on 30 April 1917 was the world *première* of *Lodoletta*—as Mascagni's libretto of *Due zoccoletti* was named.[45]

As during other years of fruitless subject-hunting, Puccini kept up a keen interest in his existing operas. In October 1911 he went to Liverpool, where *La Fanciulla* was produced in English.[46] This company used a special "reduced" version, made under Puccini's supervision, that called for a smaller orchestra. Puccini was back in Milan by 14 October 1911 to see the *prima* of Zandonai's *Conchita*, an attention revealing his interest extended even to subjects he had discarded. In April 1912 he was off to Monte Carlo again for *La Fanciulla*.[47] The opera won twenty-two curtain calls and earned Puccini the support of the famous Monte Carlo impresario Raoul Gunsbourg (1859-1955), the man who would provide the launching site for *La Rondine*. In August 1912 he went to Bayreuth for *Parsifal*, a further indication of Puccini's timely concern with works by other composers.[48] This Bayreuth junket was a source of embarrassment to Puccini. Cosima Wagner, learning that Puccini was in the audience, asked to have him introduced to her, but as Giacomo's lady companion was not Elvira he maintained his incognito and thus lost an opportunity to meet the formidable chatelaine of Bayreuth. Further productions of *La Fanciulla* took Puccini to Marseilles in November 1912, to Berlin in March 1913, and to Vienna in October of that year. The trail of *La Rondine* begins in Vienna.

Even before Puccini dropped *Due zoccoletti* as an idea, he had

45. Mascagni's *Lodoletta* is often described, especially by Puccini's biographers, in slighting terms. The score contains some very effective moments, particularly the arias recorded by Gigli and Toti dal Monte.
46. The Liverpool cast was headed by soprano Jeanne Brola, tenor John Coates, and baritone Clarence Whitehill (1871-1932).
47. Poli-Randaccio, Martinelli, and Domenico Viglione-Borghese (1877-1957) sang *Fanciulla* at Monte Carlo. Viglione-Borghese was so successful as Jack Rance that Puccini always referred to him as "il mio sceriffo."
48. The Bayreuth production of *Parsifal* was of the moment during 1912, because on midnight 31 December 1913, Bayreuth's exclusive rights to the score expired, and it was slated for many performances early in 1914. Puccini's reaction to the opera was highly favorable, but he believed its atmosphere was so special it would not succeed outside Bayreuth. In this case Puccini was a poor prophet—for instance, when *Parsifal* was staged in Milan (January 1914) it was given twenty-seven times that season!

enmeshed himself in the tangle that produced *La Rondine*. Whenever Puccini was traveling he enjoyed sampling theatrical wares.
One night in the third week of October 1913 his desire to sample
led him to the Karltheater, the headquarters of Viennese operetta,
then in its hey-day. During the performance Puccini was approached by the directors, Harry Berté and a certain Herr Eisenschütz, who offered Puccini a large sum and advantageous property
rights to compose an operetta for them. At first Puccini refused, but
the more he thought about 200,000 *kronen* and property rights the
more intrigued he became. He wrote to his good friend Baron Angelo Eisner Eisenhof[49] to check the proposal out. Puccini had
known Eisner since November 1892 and had come to rely on Eisner's fluent Italian to compensate for his own poor German.

On 11 November 1913 Puccini wrote to Eisner that he was satisfied with the 200,000 *kronen*, but that he wanted to reserve to Ricordi the rights in Italy, France, Belgium, England, and North
America, leaving everything else to Berté and Eisenschütz. The
operetta text was to be supplied from Vienna in German; Puccini
would arrange to have it translated into Italian and compose his
music to the Italian version; then this Italian translation would be
retranslated into German for performance! So eager were these
Viennese entrepreneurs to grab up a Puccini work they agreed, the
final contract depending on Puccini's accepting a proposed libretto.
Barely a month later he received a text that struck him as trite, and
he flatly rejected it as lacking developed characters, originality, and,
worst of all, any interest whatever. Along with his turning down
the libretto, he writes to Eisner on 14 December 1913, "I will never
write an operetta: a comic opera, yes." Puccini means by this he
will not write isolated musical numbers to be interspersed with
spoken dialogue, the traditional format of the operetta, but rather
a complete score, in which everything is sung. That this is his meaning is clear from the next words of this letter to Eisner: "A comic
opera, yes: like *Rosenkavalier*, but more diverting and more organic."[50] (The mention of *Rosenkavalier* may seem far-fetched
here vis-à-vis *La Rondine*, but it makes it undeniably clear that Puccini is thinking of a regular opera form, like that of his earlier
works.)

49. Eisner's services to the cause of Italian opera were not confined to Puccini. He
was a principal promoter of the Donizetti centenary observances in Bergamo
(1897), exhibiting his collection of manuscripts and letters.
50. *Carteggi Pucciniani*, p. 417.

Since Adami in his biography of Puccini gives the impression that the conversion of *La Rondine* from an operetta to a comic opera did not take place until the summer of 1914, when Puccini had already begun to compose the score, many people have assumed that the transformation took place then, with resulting damage to the opera, making it a sort of hybrid. Adami was writing nearly thirty years after the events, and as Puccini's letters show the decision against an operetta format had been made before the libretto of *La Rondine* even appeared. The abolishment of the prose passages from the German libretto and the whole change of emphasis occurred, therefore, as Adami began to work on the Italian version of the text.

The second libretto for Puccini's perusal did not arrive from Vienna until March 1914. The second effort was the work of Alfred Willner (1859-1929) and a certain Heinz Reichert.[51] Puccini accepted this libretto on the strength of its first act alone and concluded his contract for the work about 2 March 1914. In his letter to Eisner announcing these developments, Puccini again reaffirms in the strongest terms his intention not to write an operetta.[52]

Not until the end of May 1914 did Puccini receive the whole German text. At once he started to feel misgivings about it, wishing it had some individuality, a touch of the grotesque, a little originality at least. Nevertheless he got down to composing the opera, having then at hand the first act of Adami's Italian text. Among other things, he and Adami had already agreed that the role for the maid Lisette should be designed for a coloratura-soubrette and to be a part prominent enough to require a leading singer. The work progressed fitfully, what with all the furore over *Due zoccoletti* and tempting offers from the Viennese publisher Herzmansky for that project to distract Puccini, but by Christmas Day 1914 he could write to Eisner to announce that he had completed the first two acts of *La Rondine*. He goes on to inquire: "Tell me, given the present frightful state of things due to this horrible war, what will happen to this opera?"[53]

---

51. Willner was an experienced librettist, having written three texts for Karl Goldmark: *Das Heimchen am Herd* (1896) based on Dickens; *Berlichingen Götz* (1902) derived from Goethe; and *Ein Wintermärchen* (1908), after Shakespeare. Willner also contributed to the books of such operettas as Johann Strauss's *Die Göttin der Vernunft*, Fall's *Die Dollarprinzessin*, and Lehár's *Der Graf von Luxemburg* and *Eva*.

Of Reichert's other activities as a librettist, beyond his contribution to the original German text for *La Rondine*, I can find no trace.

52. *Carteggi Pucciniani*, p. 422.

53. Ibid., p. 430.

It should be remembered that although World War I began in August 1914, Italy preserved its neutrality for a while, but when Austria-Hungary refused to accede to Italy's demands for the Trentino, Italy finally declared war on Austria-Hungary on 23 May 1915. As the relationship between Italy and Austria deteriorated, Puccini began to find himself in an uncomfortable position, under contract to nationals of a country soon to become his nation's active enemy. Since Puccini's behavior and motives during the early years of the war have come under considerable criticism, it might be well to consider them here for a moment. While on the one hand Puccini as both man and artist was Italian to the marrow and proud of his *italianità;* on the other he was at home in the world at large, a habitué and a well-known figure in London, Paris, New York, Berlin, and Vienna. There is another even more fundamental root to Puccini's orientation. For him, home was not Italy, but quite specifically Torre del Lago—his retreat where he could compose and hunt and relax with his old cronies and feel himself at one with the basic aspects of life in his native Lucca. Even Milan, where he maintained an apartment, was not another home but a center from which to manage his career, the center of the spokes that stretched to opera houses around the world. In a period of high nationalistic fervor, it is small wonder that a *lucchese,* who deep inside himself could regard even Lombardy as a "foreign" place, should feel himself disoriented. Puccini was not *a Homo politicus;* his letters, which survive by the hundreds, reveal no real interest in party or national affairs. As a creative artist, who never conducted his works in public, as a man who found himself profoundly ill-at-ease and tongue-tied if he had to talk at a public function, he had really no way but his music to express his feelings as an Italian. His inability to make the grandly defiant gesture, the sort of thing that came so naturally to a Toscanini, left Puccini vulnerable to criticism.

In February 1915, hoping to preserve his own neutrality, which was still Italy's official position at that time, Puccini found, as Italy would, that neutrality has its cost. He was attacked ferociously from France, in the form of an open letter by Léon Daudet, for not having signed a formal protest by leading intellectuals around the world against the German bombardment of Rheims. Puccini replied with a dignified statement explaining that he had not been asked in time to sign the letter protesting the bombardment and affirming his stand as an Italian. Undoubtedly, this event shook Puccini. Until then, having prospered under the orientation of the Triple Alliance, his feelings were not particularly anti-German, but as the war progressed he became deeply concerned with the fate of the Italian troops, particularly since his son Tonio was in uniform. Puccini was perfectly aware that underlying the indignation of Daudet's attack was a resentment common among French intellectuals against the prominent place occupied by Puccini's operas in the repertory of the Comique. Puccini also saw his operas boycotted in Germany. During the war, Puccini lived quietly without suffering the deprivations felt by many Italians and completed four operas.

To go back to *La Rondine*, the first of the operas Puccini completed during the war, he finished it about the middle of October 1915. Even before this time, Puccini was seriously bothered by his Viennese contract and by its stipulation that the *première* of the opera would be in Vienna. In the spring of 1915 he made overtures to be released from it, but they were fruitless. In early September 1915, he went to Interlaken, Switzerland, and on this neutral soil he met Harry Berté, one of the impresarios of the Karltheater. Puccini managed to gain some easement of the terms of the contract for *La Rondine;* not a total release, but what amounted to fifty per cent of the rights, and these he was free to negotiate with an Italian publisher. For instance, Puccini thus was free to sell the performance rights in Italy, but the Viennese publishers retained those for a number of countries, including Austria, Germany, and the United States. Most important for his immediate peace of mind, Puccini obtained the right to arrange for the *première* of *La Rondine*. Considering the uncertainties of the war, this was an important advantage. Puccini tried to enter into an agreement with Ricordi for the partial rights he now held in his newest opera, but as that firm was accustomed to dealing with Puccini for exclusive and unrestricted rights, his attempts to negotiate with them were repeatedly rebuffed.

Puccini's difficulties with Tito Ricordi have been exaggerated by Puccini's biographers, eager to add "interest" to their books. It is true that Puccini found Tito's ways high-handed, irresponsible, and frequently annoying, and on occasion he was really affronted by them. But whatever his disagreements with Tito on a purely personal basis, his basic loyalty to the firm, of which Tito happened to be the head, did not waver. Probably with some hyperbole, Puccini said that he offered *La Rondine* to the Casa Ricordi "a 100 times."

Their refusal to take up the offer was due to the special terms of the offered contract and not meant as a criticism of the work itself. Not until after repeated approaches to Ricordi proved futile did the name of Sonzogno enter the picture (in October 1916), and the contract with Casa Sonzogno was not signed until some time between 10 December 1916 and 11 January 1917.[54] Before that contract was signed, Puccini wrote and signed an important statement to Tito Ricordi, dated 3 December 1916:

> Dear Tito,
>   In this private letter I declare to you that as long as the directorship of Casa Ricordi shall be entrusted to you, I will be happy to grant to the firm the first option in acquiring any of my future work whatever.[55]

So much for Puccini's difficulties with Casa Ricordi!

In December 1916 Puccini started negotiations with Raoul Gunsbourg for the first performance of *La Rondine*, and they were speedily and amicably completed. Monte Carlo, far from the war in miles and atmosphere, continued to present spring seasons of opera uninterrupted by the pressures that drastically diminished activities in many theaters during those years. It was there on 27 March 1917 that *La Rondine* was first produced.[56]

The well-chosen cast was liberally applauded: five calls after the first act, eight after the second, and eight after the third. The critics were enchanted, and the reviews are sprinkled with such words as "exquisite" and "delicious." During the short season, the work was repeated twice, on 1 April and again on the 8th. Puccini, who came with Elvira and Fosca, stayed for the first two performances and was delighted with them.

The subsequent career of *La Rondine* has only very rarely matched its auspicious beginning. The prima donna, Gilda della

---

54. In a letter to Vandini (10 December 1916) "Until now I have not concluded negotiations with Sonzogno" (*Carteggi Pucciniani*, p. 447). In another letter to Vandini (11 January 1917) "Then I have made arrangements with Sonzogno for *La Rondine* and it will be given at Monte Carlo in March" (*Carteggi Pucciniani*, p. 449).
55. *Carteggi Pucciniani*, p. 447.
56. The *prima* of *La Rondine* was sung by Gilda della Rizza (Magda), Ines Maria Ferraris (Lisette), Tito Schipa (Ruggero), the tenor Francesco Dominici (Prunier), Gustave Huberdeau (Rambaldo), Langee (Yvette), Andree Moreau (Bianca), and Jean-Francisque Delmas (Gobin). Gino Marinuzzi conducted.

Rizza, and the conductor, Gino Marinuzzi, went from Monte Carlo to Buenos Aires, where the opera on 24 May 1917 had its second round of performances: a total of seven that season.[57] Its first Italian performance took place on 5 June 1917 in Bologna. The reviews were disappointing, even worse after the inept performance that introduced the work to Milan at the Dal Verme on 7 October 1917.[58] In the aftermath of this producion Puccini was moved to write: "The critics? The worst of the useless races on the earth." Yet the opera had received a total of sixteen curtain calls and there had been an ovation for Puccini by the audience. Once again, the public did not agree with the critics.

Vienna, which was to have seen its initial flight, did not see *La Rondine* until it was put on at the Volkstheater, 9 October 1920. Not even the conducting of Felix Weingartner was able to salvage a weak, poorly staged performance.

In spite of Puccini's urging and his efforts to get Sybil Seligman to persuade various managers, *La Rondine* was not put on at Covent Garden or at any other London theater. In this connection it is well to remember that after the war Covent Garden did not reopen until 1919, and by then Puccini was more interested in trying to urge the management to produce *Il Trittico*.

Puccini turned his considerable powers of persuasion on Gatti-Casazza, then the manager of the Metropolitan. To this purpose Puccini addressed a letter dated 12 August 1921 to Gatti:

> . . . About *La Rondine*, do you know that the third version is ready? Now I believe that libretto is also in good shape. It is the sort of opera that performed with *chic* and with a good choice of singers and with finesse of staging can not fail. Modesty apart, for me it is perhaps my best music. . . .[59]

Gatti did not get around to staging *La Rondine* until after Puccini's death, but, to judge from accounts of the production, the composer would have been delighted with Bori's Magda and Gigli's fluent singing as Ruggero. The Metropolitan *première* took place as a

57. Besides della Rizza again as Magda, the Teatro Colón production of *La Rondine* was sung by Nera Marmora (Lisette), Charles Hackett (Ruggero), Guiseppe Nessi (Prunier), and Cesare Melocchi (Rambaldo).
58. At the Teatro Dal Verme, *La Rondine* was sung by Maria Farneti (Magda), Toti dal Monte (Lisette), Gennaro Barra (Ruggero), Francesco Dominici (Prunier), and Giuseppe Tisci-Rubini (Rambaldo).
59. This letter is in the Archives of the Metropolitan Opera House, New York.

matinee, 10 March 1928.[60] When the Depression curtailed the Metropolitan's seasons, the opera was dropped from the repertory after ten performances. It returned, again with Bori, for three performances during the winter of 1936, the last of these, on 21 March, was the last complete opera she sang in New York.

La Rondine appeared for the first time at La Scala on 24 January 1940 with Mafalda Favero as Magda. In 1961 it made quite a success in Philadelphia, so much so that the Act 2 ensemble had to be repeated, then Magda was sung by Licia Albanese.[61]

The libretto of *La Rondine* is an old-fashioned confection, liberally laced with sentiment. It reads like the plot of an early Garbo movie. It resembles one, too, in that it needs an early Garbo to put it over. The role of Magda requires an experienced actress of great charm and eye-riveting magnetism, one who can beguile an audience into falling in love with her and into taking her rather incredible renunciation seriously. Without a potent singing-actress, Magda seems like an incredibly sentimental tart. A bore, in other words.

The plot is pure escapism from the harsh world of the 1914-18 war back to the palmy days of the Second Empire. This milieu of the demi-monde is rarely realized with Gallic clarity or touched with redeeming pinches of self-satire, but with Italianate flamboyance and ready emotionalism.

The most original feature of the libretto is the pair of subsidiary lovers—Magda's maid, Lisette, and the poet, Prunier. Good timing and a light touch are essential to these roles. Prunier has eccentric tastes, prides himself on them, in fact. He dabbles in clairvoyance and palm-reading, and he is fond of talking of himself as being born for great adventures with the likes of Galatea, Berenice, Francesca, and Salome. Instead, and in spite of all his protests, he is attracted to Lisette and her outspoken ways. He likes to take her out when her work is done and she is wearing her mistress's clothes. He enjoys dominating Lisette, even to the extent of taking her away and trying to palm her off as a chanteuse, whose repertory is confined to

60. Besides Bori and Gigli, the Metropolitan's first production of *La Rondine* was sung by Editha Fleischer (Lisette), Armand Tokatyan (Prunier), Pavel Ludikar (Rambaldo), and was conducted by Bellezza. The settings for this production, by Joseph Urban, were excellent.

   The 1935 revival was conducted by Panizza, and Bori was joined by Nino Martini (Ruggero), Fleischer again as Lisette, Marek Windheim (Prunier), and Louis D'Angelo (Rambaldo).

61. The Philadelphia performance took place 24 February 1961, with Giuseppe Bamboschek conducting.

Prunier's songs. Lisette's career lasts only one night; indeed it is such a fiasco that she comes straight back to Magda and re-enters her service. As soon as Lisette is wearing her white apron again, Prunier cannot resist asking her what time she gets off work. Adami has handled much of their dialogue with considerable skill.

Not so much can be said of his treatment of the plot structure he inherited from Willner and Reichert. Even though Adami's hands were freed by the agreement of September 1915 and he could revise the plot at will, he has been guilty of considerable clumsiness. The exposition of Act 1 is all talk and no action, a rather artificial discussion of ideas and attitudes. The scant opportunities for much action come late in Act 1, a situation that challenges the resourcefulness of a stage director.

Adami's greatest failure is the feeble character of his "hero," Ruggero Lastouc. Ruggero first appears for about three minutes more than halfway through Act 1 and is given one sentence of dialogue. In Act 2, the scene of his encounter and subsequent infatuation with Magda, he is not established clearly as a person, only as a *jeune premier*. He has greater opportunities in the last act, but even here he is shown to grave disadvantage. Unlike the famous renunciation scene in Act 2 of *La Traviata*, where the elder Germont persuades Violetta to leave Alfredo, Adami has written the renunciation scene in *La Rondine* for the heroine and her lover. Further, we are asked to accept the fact that Ruggero, who has seen Magda's salon and who has picked her up at a dance hall, has not the slightest inkling that she is other than snow-white until Magda tells him so. Inexperience and naïveté can be encountered in real people, and these traits can form a splendid basis for the development of an interesting character. Adami fumbled his opportunity.

The weakness of Ruggero's character is the basic flaw in the plot of *La Rondine*. This shortcoming is more damaging to the work than a number of rather far-fetched incidents, such as Lisette's failure to recognize her own mistress at Bullier. That scene, at least, affords a chance for some amusing by-play. Nevertheless, if one can overlook the deficiencies of the plot and suppress the temptation to carp at them, one can find real pleasure in a well-acted performance of *La Rondine* that has a genuinely beguiling Magda heading the cast. As Puccini wrote to Sybil Seligman when he was trying to get the opera produced: "It will go well in London because it's a melodious score and the subject is a moral one. . . ."[62]

62. Seligman, p. 275.

Listening to a performance of *La Rondine*, one recognizes at once the hand of Puccini. There are the characteristic melodies full of feeling, the familiar rhythmic ebullience, the sweetly astringent harmonies, and the enormously skillful orchestration. Much of the score is far superior to the libretto.

The opera is full of dance music of various kinds, not a very surprising conclusion about a work that was originally thought of as an operetta. The prelude opens with a dance rhythm in duple meter, rather like a one-step:

1

When Lisette and Magda's trio of friends give Ruggero advice about where to spend his first night in Paris, they give it in an ingratiating polka. Puccini uses considerable skill at achieving rhythmic variety in this brief passage.

2

The most frequently encountered dance rhythm is the waltz, but Puccini's waltzes seem more Gallic than Viennese. Several of these are associated with Magda, particularly in her Act 1 aria, *Ore dolci e divine*, with its nostalgic evocation of a past escapade.

3

Early in this aria, Puccini adapts a waltz pattern to a less conspicuous rhythm, giving the impression of the dance tune remembered but not felt.

4

The big waltz tune of the score has plenty of lilt and a bona fide musical hall atmosphere. It is heard extensively throughout Act 2. In the last act, the waltzes are only used as nostalgic reminiscence.

Puccini's orchestration for *La Rondine* is a model of taste and elegant effect. He uses a smaller orchestra than for *La Fanciulla:* pairs of winds, four horns, treble brasses, harp, glockenspiel, celesta, timpani, bass drum and cymbals, triangle, snare drum, and strings. Near the beginning of Act 1, Magda's three friends—Yvette, Bianca, and Suzy—sing rather affected words to the theme associated with romance:

5

But Puccini's intention that the theme itself, as opposed to the words sung to it, should be heard as sincere and evocative is shown by his shimmering scoring: strings *divisi*, flute, clarinets, muted bassoon, and the harp vibrating the bass notes.

Another example of Puccini's skill at blending instrumental colors occurs a little later as Prunier begins his poem. Prunier sits at the piano on stage and starts to play; first we hear the piano alone and then woodwinds are added which blunt the precussive quality of piano, and at the refrain, Puccini scores for a solo violin, celesta, and harp harmonics. Then when Magda takes over for the second verse, the illusion of the piano being played has been established even though the orchestra has taken over; for Magda's verse, the scoring is warmer, all strings *divisi*.

In *La Rondine* Puccini's harmonic practice is bold. The figure

associated with the poet Prunier involves a piquant juxtaposition of
keys.

6

Later in Act 1, when Lisette bursts in to announce that Ruggero
has been waiting downstairs for hours, her breathless bustling is
characterized by an astringent bit of bitonality, the sequence of F,
G, A, pitted against F-sharp, G-sharp, A-sharp, the upper part rising through a sequence of unrelated keys, until suddenly just before
she begins to sing, the passage abruptly modulates into E-flat.

   Two passages in the score are real highlights. One is the miniature
love duet for Prunier and Lisette. How different from *La Bohème*,
Butterfly, and *Fanciulla* is the dramaturgy that gives this moment to
a love scene for the subsidiary pair. It is based on a little theme introduced by solo oboe and bassoon in octaves.

7

As so often happens in Puccini's treatment of melody, he states it
twice and then repeats it a minor third higher, now doubling the
voice with muted violins. Prunier's mocking self-deprecation is indicated by a little figure for two flutes playing at the interval of the
major seventh. This deft little episode with its aura of furtive romance has no counterpart in any other Puccini score.

   The love scene for Magda and Ruggero is full of melodic interest.
As she sits down at Ruggero's table, her first lines, cast in Puccini's
supple substitute for recitative, are accompanied by Magda's personal motive—introduced in Act 1 when Prunier told her fortune

and likened her to a swallow (*rondine*). Soon Ruggero is comparing Magda favorably with the girls back home at Montaubon. This
episode, a brief solo in 2/4 dance rhythm, leads into an ingratiating
melody suggesting Magda's sentimental and expansive mood.

8

As they start to dance, their voices join in an anticipation of the big
waltz theme, but here Puccini writes it as a slow 4/4—one beat corresponding to one bar of the waltz.

9

The culmination of the scene occurs in a big quartet with chorus,
the four lovers now joining in a toast. The melody is one of those
broad diatonic themes that has the stamp of Puccini on it. The melody is first sung by Ruggero, and as the other voices enter, the
phrases are ingeniously overlapped.

10

A particularly effective vocal effect occurs in this quartet after a
climactic phrase ending on a top B-flat: the solo voice of Magda,
singing the sequence top C, B-flat, G, leads into the resumption of
the ensemble. Later this effect is twice repeated, but then other
voices double Magda's lead-in line. The vocal and instrumental parts,
(especially those of the cellos and horns) show Puccini's mastery of
ensemble complexity. In every performance of *La Rondine* I have
seen, this quartet has stopped the show.

The score of *La Rondine* contains many pages that reward close examination. Puccini's hand had rarely been more canny. I can only agree with Mosco Carner's judgment of this delectable score; speaking of Puccini's pungent use of harmony and his "sophisticated and exquisitely subtle" orchestration, he concludes, *"La Rondine* surpasses any operetta known to me in craftsmanship and attention to detail."[63]

I doubt whether *La Rondine* will ever establish itself permanently in the repertory. It deserves, however, an occasional revival, but only when a singing-actress capable of meeting the challenge of Magda is available. Audiences who go to *La Rondine* expecting it to be another *Bohème* or *Butterfly* are bound to be disappointed, but those who are willing to let *La Rondine* be its delicate and old-fashioned self will find much to enjoy.

The alterations of *La Rondine* are not without interest. I have not seen the autograph score, but the Library of Congress has a printed full-score, bearing a note that it was received 27 October 1917. This score, deposited at the Library of Congress to establish the copyright in the United States, is the first version of the score, as it was performed at Monte Carlo in March 1917.[64]

The second version was initiated during the summer of 1918. On 5 July Puccini wrote to his publisher Renzo Sonzogno:

> I need the entire full-score of *Rondine*. I have made some valuable accomodations and valid little changes in the first act; Prunier baritone, Lisette raised tessitura, Rambaldo more conspicuous, Ruggero less stupid, and Magda finishes the first act singing effectively. For the second act we will see what is to be done. At least we must change the *mise en scène*, that is, the scenario. As for the third act, there are real problems. It is a great reef [*scoglio*] because the subject is the great enemy. I am looking for Adami from day to day. . . .[65]

This letter deserves comment because nearly all the writers on this subject say that Prunier was originally a baritone role. It was not. The first Prunier was Francesco Dominici, a tenor whose other

63. Mosco Carner, *Puccini: A Critical Biography* (New York, 1959), p. 400.
64. Maestro Tenaglia kindly lent me his copy of the first edition of the piano-vocal score of *La Rondine* (Sonzogno, 1917). As an appendix, it contains the Act 2 quartet transposed down a whole tone—i.e. in D-flat major.
65. *Carteggi Pucciniani*, p. 462.

parts included such roles Dr. Cajus in *Falstaff* and Monostatos in *The Magic Flute*. The confusion arises either from a misunderstanding of Puccini's intent in the letter quoted above, where he is clearly talking about *projected* changes, or else it stems from confusion between Francesco Dominici the tenor and a bass named Ernesto Dominici, who was active in the 1930's.

Ten days after this letter to Sonzogno proposing alterations in *La Rondine*, Puccini wrote again to report that he and Adami were seeing eye to eye about the changes. For one thing, they wanted to alter the period of the action from the crinolines of 1860 to modern dress. On 8 August he writes again to announce that he has added a *romanza* for the tenor to the first act; further he is planning to transpose some of the music at the ends of Act 1 and 2. On 17 September he reports that he is still struggling over the revisions. Then he put by his work on *La Rondine* for some months as he was busy with the first performances of the *Trittico*. The following year, on 21 August 1919 he informs Sonzogno that the problem of Act 3 seems well resolved. It was this second edition of *La Rondine* which was performed at the Volkstheater in Vienna (October 1920) and which produced little impression. Even though Puccini blamed the heaviness of the singers and the awkward staging, he recognized that this second version was not as effective as the original.

On Christmas Day 1920 he writes to his friend Riccardo Schnabl that he is thinking of reworking *La Rondine* once more. He plans to revert to the original version of Acts 1 and 2; that is, Prunier a tenor once more, no *romanza* for the tenor, and the soprano speaking the final words at the end of Act 1. He has new ideas about Act 3, however; planning to open it

> . . . with a prelude for the woman's voice off-stage (it is nothing else than the first scene of the act, but played with the curtain down); certainly with improvements and some vocal effect it can go well, especially since the first scene was a bit sluggish. Rambaldo will enter, and after the departure of tenor, angry and violent, she remains alone, etc, abandoned, etc. etc.[66]

This letter is interesting because Puccini made none of these changes in Act 3. The curtain rises immediately, Rambaldo does not appear

66. Ibid., p. 499.

at all in Act 3, it is Magda who exits at the end, leaving Ruggero alone on stage, his face in his hands. In effect then, the so-called third version of *La Rondine* is substantially the same as the first, save for a few changes in the text.

Il Trittico

The idea of creating a full evening's entertainment with several short operas had occurred to Puccini as early as 1904. Giulio Ricordi had been sternly opposed to the idea then, not merely because of the production and casting problems it raised, and not just because he could foresee Puccini's multiple bill being dismantled and parts of it being played in conjunction with operas published by some publishing house other than Ricordi, but chiefly because then he was doing everything in his power to force Puccini to write a full-length work of major proportions. The notion of a triple bill, however, continued to appeal to Puccini on a variety of grounds. Following the success of *Cavalleria Rusticana*, one-act operas were much in vogue.[67] An evening of short works would provide the opportunities for contrast that always appealed to Puccini. Further, he believed that acceptable short libretti would be easier to find than full-length ones. Then, Puccini realized the importance of doing something "original" to attract public interest, and no modern Italian composer had written a complete mixed bill designed to be performed as a unit. With all these reasons present to him, Puccini kept an eye out for likely one-act subjects.

Either during his visit to Paris in the summer of 1912 or during November of that same year, Puccini saw a play entitled *Le Houppelande* (The Cloak) by Didier Gold at the Théâtre Marigny. He was sufficiently impressed by it to inquire after the rights. On 9 February 1913 he describes it to Illica. "The subject is *apache* in all its meanings, almost, and even without the almost, Grand Guignol. But it makes no difference. It pleases me and strikes me as highly effective. But this red stain needs something different to

67. Something of the vogue for one-act operas in the early 1890's can be seen from this partial list: Brüll's *Gringoire* (1892), Mugnone's *Il Birichino* (1892), Coronaro's *Festa a Marina* (1893), Boezi's *Don Paez* (1893), Rachmaninov's *Aleko* (1893), Schjelderup's *Sonntagmorgen* (1893), Forster's *Die Rose von Pontvedra* (1893), Umlauft's *Evanthia* (1893), Hummel's *Mara* (1893), Raimann's *Arden Enok* (1894), and Massenet's *Le Portrait de Manon* (1894).

contrast with it: and it is this that I am looking for: something that
will have some elevation to it and an opportunity to write music
that will take wing. . . ."[68] This, Puccini's first mention of the subject that was to become *Il Tabarro*, precedes the proposals that led
to *La Rondine* by nearly a year, and it antedates as well Puccini's
great push to acquire *Due zoccoletti*.

It was not only the press of other projects that kept Puccini from
jumping right into his *apache* subject. From the start, he realized he
needed one or two contrasting works to go with it. When he wrote
to Illica in February 1913 to sound him out on other brief subjects,
his inquiry proved fruitless, as by this time the relationship between
Puccini and the uncertain-tempered Illica was broken irrevocably.[69]
During the summer of 1913 Puccini thought he saw some prospects
for rounding out his triple bill. One was a comedy by Tristan Bernard (1866-1947); the other, an "elevated" trifle by D'Annunzio.
Nothing came of these ideas. Bernard's plot, a satire about African
natives exhibiting white missionaries in a cage, did not long appeal
to Puccini. D'Annunzio disappeared from active consideration after
Puccini and he had their falling out. Without companion pieces *Il
Tabarro* remained some time in limbo, even though Puccini had
gone to the trouble of having Adami prepare a libretto based on
Gold's play.

Puccini's original intention had been to compose *Due zoccoletti*
when he completed *La Rondine*, but when that score was finished,
he still did not have the whole text for the Ouida subject, which
Puccini was coming to distrust. (Sometime in 1916, he definitely
gave up the notion of ever writing *Due zoccoletti*.) And so with
La Rondine out of the way and the Ouida subject in suspension, for
want of anything else, even though he had not yet found the companion pieces, Puccini started work on *Il Tabarro* in October 1915.[70]

Puccini did not feel completely satisfied with the original text
supplied him by Adami. He thought the dialogue lacked the requi-
site toughness and earthiness. He consulted the *livornese* dramatist

68. *Carteggi Pucciniani*, p. 410.
69. I do not know the precise reason for the break between Illica and Puccini. The
letter of 9 February 1913 is the last one to Illica printed in the *Carteggi Pucciniani*, except one Gara conjectures as of February 1915, at the time of the tohu-bohu
over Puccini's public reply to Léon Daudet's open letter. In this letter Puccini reproaches Illica with being "very unjust toward your old companion" (p. 434). If
there are further letters after February 1913 they were possibly destroyed to prevent publication or suppressed by a discreet editor.
70. *Carteggi Pucciniani*, p. 439.

Dario Niccodemi (1874-1934)—who had spent many years in Paris —to help him get the Italian equivalent of the bargemen's *argot*. As he worked on the music of *Il Tabarro* and felt it was going well, Puccini regretted that the subject was only a one-acter. In September 1916, Puccini amicably negotiated a contract with Tito Ricordi for *Il Tabarro*, applying some of the funds he had already received from the voided contract for *Due zoccoletti* against the new work. This transaction took place concurrently with Puccini's efforts to get Casa Ricordi to accept the 50 per cent interest available of *La Rondine*—further evidence that Puccini never seriously considered a permanent break with his old publishers.

Puccini composed *Il Tabarro* in rather unusual order. He finished his sketches from the beginning of the work through the second duet for Giorgetta and Luigi, but since the rest of the libretto took time to put in shape (Adami having put many futile hours into *Due zoccoletti*), he began on 21 April 1916 to orchestrate the opening of the opera. He worked rapidly, for on 2 May 1916 he informed Adami that he had orchestrated all his sketches and he was eagerly waiting for the rest of the text. The concluding sections of the opera were written without great difficulty, and he signed the close of his autograph full-score on 25 November 1916. He finished *Il Tabarro* without having a glimmer of where the companion pieces were to come from.

For a while he had hoped for a two-act subject from Didier Gold, the author of the play *Il Tabarro* is based on, but when Puccini saw Gold's other drama he knew it would not do. He even toyed for a while with having *Il Tabarro* produced as a double bill with *Le Villi* in Rome, but this plan fell through.[71] Growing increasingly anxious for the future of this opera, which he knew was of uncommon value, Puccini made all sorts of overtures to potential librettists, anxious to find the missing sections of his triple bill.

The desired material came from Giovacchino Forzano.[72] In January 1917, Forzano showed Puccini a sketch for a one-act opera set

71. The focal point of the proposed Roman production of *Il Tabarro*, discussed during the winter of 1916-17, was the baritone Ruffo, who would have been splendid for the role of the murderous Michele. But in January 1917 Ruffo was called into the army, and the project went up in smoke.
72. Forzano (b. 1883), besides supplying the libretti of *Suor Angelica* and *Gianni Schicchi* and of Mascagni's *Lodoletta*, later wrote the books to Mascagni's *Il Piccolo Marat* (1921), Leoncavallo's *Edipo Re* (1920), Wolf-Ferrari's *Sly* (1927), and Giordano's *Il Re* (1929). Forzano was also an accomplished stage director, notably during Toscanini's years at La Scala 1921-29), where he was responsible for staging the world *premières* of Boito's *Nerone* (1924) and Puccini's *Turandot* (1926).

in a convent, a work for an all-female cast. Puccini was delighted with this sketch, which came to be called *Suor Angelica*, finding in it just the sort of "elevation" he had been looking for. On 3 March 1917 Forzano wrote to Tito Ricordi from Viareggio, where he had gone to read the completed libretto of *Suor Angelica* to Puccini, that the composer was very satisfied with it, so much so that he had started to compose the first scene. Forzano goes on to report: "I have also finished a brief sketch of *Gianni Schicchi*. You know the Maestro's opinion of this subject, which truly comes off rich in interest and with uncommon humor. . . ."[73.] Thus, for Puccini to have found his second subject was also to have found his third. The long search for three varied subjects to make up his triptych was over at last. On 23 June 1917 Puccini had in his possession the completed libretto to *Gianni Schicchi*, and Forzano wrote to Tito Ricordi that Puccini's response to it "has surpassed my expectation."

The composition of the two remaining operas of the *Trittico* went along without notable difficulties. The words sung by the angelic choir during the miracle scene at the end of *Suor Angelica* were provided by Puccini's old friend, Don Pietro Panichelli, who had supplied Puccini with some Latin phrases for the first act of *Tosca* nearly two decades earlier. The priest found the words praising the Virgin that were put into the final scene of *Suor Angelica* in his breviary. Puccini's autographs give us the dates he started to score the concluding parts of the *Trittico: Suor Angelica*—25 July 1917 (Puccini's name day); *Gianni Schicchi*—3 February 1918.[74]

By the end of June 1918 Puccini had either finished *Schicchi* or was near enough to finishing it that he could plan when and where *Il Trittico* would be introduced. The privilege of the world *première* "on Earth" (sic!) was obtained by the Metropolitan for a fee of $7000 and a guarantee that it would be held before 31 December 1918.[75] The Italian *première* would be held at the Teatro Costanzi, shortly thereafter.

in the same evening, or $200 if just one of the *trittico* were given by itself. This
73. *Carteggi Pucciniani*, p. 451.
74. Puccini wrote the autograph full-scores of the *Trittico* in pencil. All his earlier scores are in ink. Whether this was convenience which made corrections easier or whether it was an expedient forced on Puccini by wartime conditions I do not know. In any event, it suited him because he used pencil for the full-score of *Turandot*, too.
75. The terms for the Metropolitan's agreement are preserved among the records in their archives. Besides the $7000 for the world *première*, the Metropolitan guaranteed five performances. There was also this provision: the royalties would be $400 if all three operas were given in one performance, $300 if only two were given

The next few months were busy ones. Besides beginning his revisions to *La Rondine*, Puccini concerned himself closely with the preparations of the sketches for the sets of the *Trittico* and with the correction of proof for the new scores. There was reason for haste as the conductor for Metropolitan *première*, Roberto Moranzoni, had hazarded crossing the Atlantic in wartime to consult with Puccini and to take back to New York with him the sketches for the sets and the musical scores. Moranzoni sailed for America in September 1918. Puccini did not go to New York for the *première*, deterred not only by the difficulties of traveling in those days but by his commitment to supervise personally the Roman *première*, scheduled for 11 January 1919.

On 26 October 1918 Gatti-Casazza and Moranzoni cabled Puccini that the orchestral read-through of the scores had gone most promisingly. On 12 December Gatti wired Puccini to announce that the dress rehearsal, held before a few specially invited guests, had produced a most favorable impression for the works as a whole and that the reaction to *Schicchi* was enthusiastic. Two days later on 14 December the operas were given their public baptism.[76]

---

in the same evening, or $200 if just one of the *Trittico* were given by itself. This condition shows that the possibility of the triple bill's being dismembered, a condition that Puccini always protested vehemently, was considered even before the operas had been given at all.

For the sake of comparison, here are the royalties paid by the Metropolitan for performances of Puccini's other operas during this same season of 1918-19 (five performances guaranteed):

Madama Butterfly—$400 each
La Bohème—$400 each
Tosca—$400 each
Manon Lescaut—$350 each

In this one season the Metropolitan was prepared to pay Ricordi's $16,400 for performing rights!

76. The casts for the world *première* of *Il Trittico* are as follows:

Il Tabarro—Claudia Muzio (Giorgetta), Alice Gentle (La Frugola), Giulio Crimi (Luigi), Luigi Montesanto (Michele), Angelo Bada (Tinca), Adamo Didur (Talpa), Pietro Audisio (Song-Peddler), and Marie Tiffany and Albert Reiss (the Two Lovers).

Suor Angelica—Geraldine Farrar (Angelica), Flora Perini (the Princess), Rita Fornia (the Abbess), Marie Sundelius (the Sister Monitress), Cecil Arden (Mistress of the Novices), Mary Ellis (Genovieffa), Marguerite Belleri (Osmina), Marie Mattfeld (Dolcina), Kitty Beale and Minnie Egener (Two Aspirants), Leonora Sparkes (Nursing Sister), and Phyllis White (Novice).

Gianni Schicchi—Florence Easton (Lauretta), Kathleen Howard (Zita), Marie Tiffany (Nella), Marie Sundelius (La Ciesca); Giuseppe de Luca (Gianni Schicchi), Giulio Crimi (Rinuccio), Angelo Bada (Gherardo), Paolo Ananian (Betto), Adamo Didur (Simone), Louis D'Angelo (Marco), Pompilio Malatesta (Spineloccio), Andres de Segurola (Ser Amantio di Nicolao), Vincenzo Reschiglian (Pinellino), and Carl Schlegel Guccio).

The following morning Gatti sent still another cable to Puccini.

> MOST HAPPY TO ANNOUNCE THE COMPLETE AUTHENTIC SUC-
> CESS OF THE TRITTICO STOP AT THE END OF EACH OPERA LONG
> VERY SINCERE DEMONSTRATIONS MORE THAN FORTY WARM CUR-
> TAIN CALLS ALTOGETHER STOP IN SPITE OF PUBLIC NOTICE FOR-
> BIDDING ENCORES BY INSISTENCE LAURETTA'S ARIA WAS RE-
> PEATED STOP PRINCIPAL STRENGTH MORANZONI MAGNIFICENT
> STOP FARRAR MUZIO EASTON DELUCA MONTESANTO DIDUR IN-
> COMPARABLE SINGERS AND ACTORS STOP DAILY PRESS CONFIRMS
> SUCCESS EXPRESSING ITSELF VERY FAVORABLY ON WORTH OF THE
> OPERAS ENTHUSIASTICALLY FOR SCHICCHI STOP[77]

Turning to the New York critics, one detects a shade less enthusiasm and a greater diversity of opinion than Gatti's cable suggests. Although most of the reviews stated a preference for *Gianni Schicchi*, John H. Raferty of the *Morning Telegraph* opted for *Il Tabarro*. James Gibbons Huneker, writing in the Sunday *New York Times* was particularly impressed with *Il Tabarro*, stating his belief that opera would become popular. The greatest agreement was on the point that *Suor Angelica* seemed inferior to the other two.

I have talked to people who saw the original Metropolitan production of the *Trittico*. The things that stand out in these accounts are: the powerful impression produced by Muzio's acting (and her spine-chilling scream) in the melodramatic conclusion of *Il Tabarro*, the lack of effect produced by Farrar as Angelica,[78] the insinuating rascality of de Luca's masterly Schicchi, and the obstreperous behavior of the claque protesting the house rule against encores. The Metropolitan kept the triple bill intact for two consecutive seasons, the three works being given a total of ten times, the last time together on 1 March 1920.[79] *Il Tabarro* has been revived once at the Metropolitan—for three performances in 1945-46 with Albanese as Giorgetta. *Gianni Schicchi* has been given in more

---

77. Carbon copies of Gatti's cables are preserved in the Metropolitan Archives.
78. Farrar had had an operation on her throat some months previously, and she was not in good vocal estate. At this stage of her career, after her time in Hollywood, the lack of inhibitions of a music hall artist like Zazà was more congenial to Farrar than the role of a nun.
79. A significant change in cast for the Metropolitan's second season of *Il Trittico* was the substitution of Pasquale Amato for Montesanto as Michele in *Il Tabarro*. In the ordinary course of events Amato would have created the role, but ill health prevented his appearing with the Metropolitan in 1918-19.

than a dozen seasons, most often as a curtain-raiser for *Salome*. *Suor Angelica* has never been revived at the theater where it had its world *première*.

The Roman *première* attracted considerable attention both for the fact that it introduced an evening's worth of new Puccini music and for the interest of the *trittico* form. Since the war was now over, there was some effort to create a gala atmosphere, and the royal family was present in force. Rather naturally, Puccini put more emphasis on this Roman production than on the New York one, as he took great pains with the staging and interpretation.[80] The critics, as in New York, were divided in their estimate of the relative value of the three operas. *Gianni Schicchi* won the most consistent praise; *Suor Angelica* won some very favorable notices; but *Il Tabarro*, with few exceptions, was regarded as the weakest of the three. In Rome, as in New York, the production was retained for a second season.

The next important production of *Il Trittico* was that at the Teatro Colón in Buenos Aires, where the three operas made their appearance on 25 June 1919, conducted by Tullio Serafin.[81] They were given a total of six times that season, and that was the end of their corporate existence in the Argentine. *Suor Angelica* returned in conjunction with *Gianni Schicchi* for two more performances in 1922, thanks to the presence of Gilda della Rizza. By itself, *Gianni Schicchi* appeared in three other seasons. The pattern established in New York of the triple-bill's coming apart at the seams, while *Gianni Schicchi* showed the greatest vitality, was repeated. (These statements about the performance history of these operas in Buenos Aires only apply to the years up to 1933.)[82]

Marinuzzi, who had directed the Roman performances, was again on hand to introduce the triple bill to Chicago on 6 December

80. The Roman *première* of *Il Trittico* was conducted by Gino Marinuzzi (1882–1945). The principal singers for *Il Tabarro* were Maria Labia as Giorgetta, Edward Johnson (using the stage name of Edoardo di Giovanni) as Luigi, and Carlo Galeffi as Michele; for *Suor Angelica*—Gilda della Rizza (Angelica) and Matilde Blanco Sadun (the Princess); for *Gianni Schicchi*—della Rizza (Lauretta), Johnson (Rinuccio), and Galeffi (Schicchi).
81. At Buenos Aires the leading roles in the triple bill were sung in *Il Tabarro* by Maria Labia; Rinaldo Grassi, and Domenico Viglione-Borghese; in *Suor Angelica* by Ester Mazzoleni and Matilde Blanco Sadun; in *Gianni Schicchi* by Raymonde Vecart and Vanni Marcoux.
In 1920 *Schicchi* was given alone, conducted by Serafin, the cast headed by Anna Sassone-Soster, Carlo Galeffi, and Francesco Merli.
82. See Ernesto de la Guardia and Roberto Herrera, *El arte lirico en el Teatro Colón: 1908-1933* (Buenos Aires, 1933).

1919.[83] Because he had worked under Puccini's supervision and because Johnson and Galeffi were singing the same roles they had in Rome, the auguries for *Il Trittico* were favorable. The results were less so: three performances in that season and no more of either *Il Tabarro* or *Suor Angelica*. To London, where Puccini went the following summer to lend his assistance to the production, the situation was even more disheartening. In spite of Puccini's fulminations, *Suor Angelica* (even with della Rizza) was separated from its partners and dropped after the second performance. *Gianni Schicchi* was given six times, and *Il Tabarro* seven. Gaetano Bavagnoli was the conductor in London.[84] Next Puccini betook himself to Vienna for the first performances of his one-acters there, on 20 October 1920. The operas were sung in German. Puccini was fascinated by Jeritza's animal spirits as Giorgetta in *Il Tabarro* and moved by Lotte Lehmann's very touching Angelica. For a while at least, *Suor Angelica* held its own better in Vienna than it had elsewhere.

Il Trittico was not introduced to La Scala until 29 January 1922.[85] At the time of this production Puccini was very put out that Toscanini refused to conduct the performance; the assignment was given to Ettore Panizza. Although Puccini had known since the time of the Roman *première* that Toscanini disapproved of the triple bill on artistic grounds, Puccini cannot be blamed for hoping that his operas would have their La Scala *première* under the most auspicious circumstances possible. Toscanini's refusal rankled with Puccini, and it was not until the following season at the time of the anniversary *Manon Lescaut* that they were reconciled.

At La Scala *Il Trittico* was given seven times in the spring of 1922, but the following year only *Gianni Schicchi* was brought back, and then just for two performances. Although the reception of *Il Trittico* at La Scala resembled those it received in other theaters, the story has a different ending. In the thirteen years following the *première*, the works languished; *Gianni Schicchi* appeared three

83. In Chicago the *Trittico* casts were headed by: for *Il Tabarro*—Edward Johnson and Galeffi; for *Suor Angelica*—Rosa Raisa and Cyrena Van Gordon; for *Gianni Schicchi*—Evelyn Herbert, Johnson, and Galeffi.
84. The first cast for the triple bill in London featured for *Il Tabarro* Ida Quaiatti, Thomas Burke, and Dinh Gilly; for *Suor Angelica* della Rizza and Jacqueline Royer; for *Gianni Schicchi* della Rizza, Thomas Burke, and Ernesto Badini.
85. At La Scala *Il Trittico* was introduced by Augusta Concato, Filippo Piccaluga, Galeffi for *Il Tabarro*; Maria Carena and Elvira Casazza for *Suor Angelica;* and Mafalda de Voltri, Luigi Marini, and Galeffi for *Schicchi*.

times without its companion works, and *Il Tabarro* once, alone. In 1935 the complete *Trittico* was revived, and then during the next fifteen years there were five more "editions" with the triple bill intact.

The adherence to Puccini's original design of giving the three operas together is more widely followed today than it used to be. While occasionally certain theaters still give the operas out of their intended context, the notion is now more generally held that the works appear to better advantage in conjunction than when given separately. For instance, in the United States, the whole triptych has been performed recently in San Francisco and by the New York City Opera Company.

The three operas all deal in their various ways with death. In *Il Tabarro*, Michele murders Luigi, commiting a brutal *crime passionel*. In *Suor Angelica*, the nun's suicide is the impulsive act of one who has suffered a cruel blow that was inflicted as brutally as possible. Dying, Angelica realizes she has committed a mortal sin and cries out for salvation. In *Gianni Schicchi*, old Buoso has died from natural causes before the story begins; the plot revolves around Schicchi's enactment of the dying man and playing a trick to make possible the marriage of Lauretta and Rinuccio.

Or, to put it another way, if these three operas present diverse views of death, each contains its varied affirmation of life. In *Il Tabarro*, Luigi and Giorgetta speak nostalgically of the crowded, bustling life of their suburb, Belleville. They both hope to escape the dreary life on the barge and go to another place where they can feel more intensely alive. Michele tries to persuade Giorgetta to resume her life as his wife. While *Il Tabarro* deals with sensual life, *Suor Angelica* is concerned more with spiritual life. The sisters present a picture of the lenity of convent existence, but in contrast we see the intensity of Angelica's love for the child she was forced to abandon. In *Gianni Schicchi*, the final emphasis on the young lovers and their future affords the strongest possible contrast with the grief and torment of the barge-master and his wife and of Angelica. Audiences have increasingly found that the three operas played in the order Puccini conceived make a coherent total impression.

The libretto of *Il Tabarro* has a tautness and economy that is truly impressive. Everything that occurs is clearly motivated by character. Giorgetta's affair with Luigi stems from her dissatisfaction with the drabness of her existence, from her inability to accept the death of her child, from her aroused need of a younger man.[86] We understand that Michele murders Luigi because he loves his wife so deeply that he cannot tolerate the thought of her relationship with another man. Luigi is a young man of intense feelings: resentful of his miserable working conditions, passionately in love, and intensely jealous.

The clarity of motivation is not reserved just to the major characters. There is the stevedore Il Tinca—his name means the tench, a fish related to the carp—who drinks to avoid thinking about his sluttish wife. (In Gold's play, he goes off to murder her; in the opera he goes off to get drunk.) There is Il Talpa—the mole—who only wants to rest after an exhausting day's work. There is Talpa's wife La Frugola—the rummager—who collects junk and dreams of the day they can have a little shack in the country, where her husband can laze in the sun and her tabby Caporale can lie at her feet. Each of these characters in his own way complements the central conflict. Nowhere is this more apparent than when we think of Frugola's description of waiting in their little shack for death "that cures every ill," or of Michele's statement, made after he has worked himself into a murderous jealous rage, that peace can be found only in death.

In *Il Tabarro* even the walk-on characters are related to the core of the plot, forming an oblique commentary upon it. The seller of sheet-music sings a little ballad about how those who live for love will die for love. Just before Michele begins his monologue, two lovers cross the stage happily planning a rendezvous for the following night. The libretto of *Il Tabarro* has neither loose ends nor padding.

In contrast to the libretto of *Il Tabarro*, that of *Suor Angelica* is considerably looser in structure. The exposition consists of a series of vignettes that establishes a picture of convent life. These scenes with their seemingly random sequence provide the necessary contrast for the main plot. The looseness of structure is confirmed by Puccini's cuts and changes, for he hoped to tighten up the opening. For instance, there is the episode of the Nursing Sister who comes to Angelica to tell her that one of the sisters has been stung by

86. In the score for *Il Tabarro* the ages of the characters are specified: Giorgetta is twenty-five, Luigi twenty, Michele fifty.

wasps and to ask for a remedy. In some productions this scene was cut, but Puccini later came to feel it was important in that it established the fact of Angelica's skill as a herbalist, an important point since she later commits suicide by drinking a decoction of plant poison.

The gentle, rather meandering opening comes into focus with the central episode of the interview between Angelica and her granitic aunt, the Princess. Without having seen the naïve, good-heartedness of the mild sisters, the relentless cruelty of Angelica's aunt would seem less monstrous, less pathological. Scenes between contrasting types of women are a staple in operatic plots. The scene between the formidable Princess and the tortured nun, frantic for news of her child, is one of the most powerful confrontations in Puccini's operas.

In contrast to this gripping scene, the conclusion of the opera seems weak, but here the fault does not lie in the libretto. Granted the context, granted the situation, something extraordinary must happen at this point. If the final scene is thought of not as an event but as a vision seen by the dying Angelica, then we can accept the ingredients of the vision—Madonna, angels, the child that moves toward Angelica—as psychologically valid in terms of her experience, training, and aspiration. Although there are many resemblances between the plot of Suor Angelica and that of Le Jongleur de Notre-Dame[87]—the cast being restricted to a single sex, the details of monastic life, the general atmosphere of religious naïveté—the miracle that closes Massenet's opera differs from the conclusion of Suor Angelica because the vision is seen not by the dying Jean (who has nothing to repent) but by the monks who have come into the chapel to watch in horror his juggling before the Virgin's statue. Granted that the miracle in Suor Angelica may be psychologically valid for Angelica herself, many people who see the opera, particularly in England and the United States, are put off by it. There are two reasons for this not uncommon feeling of disappointment: first, a feeling of embarrassment at the sentimental explicitness of the stage-picture; and second, and more important, a justifiable reaction that Puccini's music at this moment lacks precisely the "elevation" that he was so fond of talking about.

87. Puccini may well have been familiar with Massenet's opera from seeing it at the Opéra-Comique, it having been first given there on 10 May 1904 (the world premiere was at Monte Carlo in 1902). Or he may have seen it in Milan, where it was first given at the Teatro Lirico, 18 October 1905 (in Italian).

The libretto of *Gianni Schicchi* is tart and vivid. Who cannot help laughing at old Zita who exclaims after learning that Buoso's prize bequests have gone to the monks: "Who would ever have said that when Buoso went to the cemetery that he would be the cause of real tears!" The greed of the relatives, a trait that Puccini knew at firsthand, is mercilessly exposed and forms a sharp contrast with Schicchi's trickery, which has its altruistic side as the bequests he makes to himself are ultimately intended to provide Lauretta with a dowry so she can marry Rinuccio. To offset the atmosphere of avarice and chicanery, Forzano has provided brief touches of two antidotes: the vivid sense of Florence in the springtime of the Renaissance and the youthful romance of Lauretta and Rinuccio.

Undoubtedly *Gianni Schicchi* stood out from its fellows at the first performances because it was the most immediately accessible, its humor obvious even to those who understand little Italian. The humor is stylized by the classic device of repeating certain lines until they become comic refrains. For instance, the relatives several times appeal to Simone for counsel as he is the eldest and, as some always add, he was the *podestà* (mayor) of Fucecchio; when Schicchi seems unwilling at first to co-operate, three times the lovers despair that they will not be married on the first of May; and then there is Schicchi's repeated reminder of the peculiarly Florentine punishment for those who falsify wills: the amputation of the right hand and, worse, banishment from Florence—*Addio Firenze!* The motifs established by repetition help the audience follow the action more closely than they usually do in operatic works.

The libretti of these three operas—allowing that the looser structure of *Suor Angelica* sets it a bit behind its tauter companions—are among the best that Puccini set to music. Not only is each of them effective in its own way, but they work together. The comic relief provided by *Gianni Schicchi* is strong because it is preceded by *Il Tabarro* and *Suor Angelica*.

Some critics who like to distinguish "periods" in composers' careers claim that with *Il Tabarro* begins the period of Puccini's classic or mature style. Others who prefer to see an artist's output in terms of cycles are apt to say that Puccini, after the apprentice-work of *Le Villi* and *Edgar*, reached an early climax with The Big Three, which were followed by a slump, by a falling off of his creative energy, and that somehow and surprisingly he found his

true path only at the very end of his career with *Turandot*. I find
both these descriptions of Puccini's career inadequate, because both
fail to stress the central fact of Puccini's music—the dynamic consistency of his style.

Puccini's style is *dynamic* because although his idiosyncracies and
interests remain relatively constant, he continually develops his resources and expressive range. Just as he became more polished and
worldly as he grew older, while remaining the same rather retiring
person who was truly at ease only with old friends, so is there a
core of consistency to his music. To test the truth of this assertion,
all one has to do is to listen to a minute from any of his operas, early
or late, to be able to identify it as by Puccini.

The score of *Il Tabarro* is a major achievement; some even claim
it to be the least flawed of all Puccini's operas. In mood it sometimes
suggests the vigorous expression of *La Fanciulla*, but without the
occasional diffuseness that weakens some parts of that score. It resembles *La Fanciulla*, too, in its almost palpable atmosphere, but one
feels Puccini could present more vividly a Parisian stevedore than
a miner of the American Far West.

As Puccini was undoubtedly influenced by Japanese art in his
score of *Madama Butterfly*, so did the French impressionists leave
a strong imprint on the evocative prelude to *Il Tabarro*. The intensely pictorial impression that Puccini hoped to achieve is confirmed by his direction that the curtain rise even before the prelude
begins. In the failing light of evening on the bank of the river, its
waters steadily flowing to the sea, the scene is suggested by this
·figure:

1

The prevailing grayish tone is suggested by the muted strings and
their parallel harmonies, but softened by a solo flute (in its lower
octave that Puccini exploits with frequent effect), solo clarinet, and

solo bass clarinet. The triplet figures accompanying the melody are played only by the string basses. As the melody continues, the other solo woodwinds fall silent, and a solo bassoon doubles the violins and solo cello. As the opening phrase is repeated, the violins are silent, the solo flute and cello, harmonized by chords of fourths played by muted horns and violas, soften the mood. From the distance is heard the whistle of a tug-boat, and later an automobile horn. A scrutiny of this passage shows how Puccini carefully tinted each shifting contour of the restless, sinuous melody. So much fun has been made of the youthful Puccini's enthusiasm for doubling his melodies at climactic moments by a whole arsenal of instruments that his mature mastery and frequent reticence of orchestral writing in *Il Tabarro* can come as a revelation.

Although the prevailing triplet movement of the rhythm is maintained almost without interruption throughout the opening episode, Puccini avoids real monotony, while creating that impression, by shifting the meter, by altering the rhythmic accompaniment, and by modifying the orchestral color almost from measure to measure.

Puccini's fondness for specific detail is shown by other more directly musical touches than just his inclusion of boat whistles and automobile horns. When the hurdy-gurdy man starts to play his waltz his instrument's failings in matters of pitch are imitated by the melody being given two flutes playing major sevenths rather than true octaves and by having the oom-pah-pah (bass clarinet and chords for two clarinets) played in an alien key. When Luigi starts to dance with Giorgetta the animal attraction flickering between them is suggested by a chromatic string figure:

Luigi and Giorgetta's relationship has already been clarified for the audience, even though there has yet been no direct verbal allusion to it. It is developed further by their "Belleville" duet, with its rather self-conscious exuberance, and at the same time a kind of nervous restraint, as they are not alone, but just carried away by their conversation with La Frugola and Il Talpa. Only later when they are alone do their feelings emerge unmasked. Their stealthiness, their tight-wound nerves are suggested by a *marcato* C-sharp minor melody over an insistent ostinato:

3

This duet has a clear form. The middle section in the relative major is dominated by a surging theme descriptive of Luigi's passion.

4

Then the melody of Example 3 recurs, followed by a concluding section, climaxed by one of the most demanding vocal passages Puccini ever wrote.

5

The baritone role of Michele is one of Puccini's most powerful creations. Somewhat in the tradition of Scarpia and Jack Rance, he differs from them in that he is capable of a real, although somewhat obsessive, tenderness. In his duet with Giorgetta, dominated by a gently insistent melody, the ambivalence of his feelings is subtly revealed. Particularly so in the phrase, on reiterated D, when he reminds her how she used to rock their baby's cradle.

Michele's great monologue, *Nulla! Silenzio!*, is the climax of the score. Instead of being merely a description of a fixed state of mind or feeling as with many of Puccini's arias, it shows us Michele wrestling first with the problem of Giorgetta's behavior, then with the question of the identity of her lover, and finally with his powerfully excited anticipation of strangling his rival. During this monologue, he is transformed before our eyes from a suspicious husband into a revengeful murderer.

The monologue begins in C minor with a motive already established as referring to Michele's cloak (the *tabarro* of the title), and by association to Michele's protective love for Giorgetta in the early days of their marriage.

6

The rigidity of this figure is consistent with the obsessive side of Michele's nature. It begins *mf* but suddenly grows softer, suggesting Michele's intent listening for the footsteps of Giorgetta's lover. The low strings, the bass clarinet, and bassoon sound ominous. At the ninth bar occurs a descending scale passage that suggests a man sinking into the depths of jealousy.[88]

7

The A-natural, which occurs prominently and unexpectedly—in the descending C minor scale the note would normally be A-flat—reinforces our sense of Michele's strange self-hypnotized state. As Michele's mind ceaselessly probes, his restlessness is suggested by

88. In the first version of Michele's monologue, much less effective than the present one, Example 7 recurred more frequently, marking the periods of the monologue. This first version, sung by Robert Merrill, may be heard on the Decca-London complete recording, as an appendix at the end of Side 2. There is also an old H.M.V. recording by Dinh Gilly.

shifts of orchestral color. A figure in thirds, suggestive of Michele stalking his prey, is played by the bassoons, then by the muted horns, and repeated by the muted trumpets. As his anger grows, the orchestral fabric thickens. After a chromatic rush, the violins and cellos in contrary motion, the figure of Example 6 is played by the full brass over a propulsive string figure. At the final climactic phrase, the chords of Example 7 recur, their harmony brutalized by the addition of stinging seconds.

The opera closes with a full force peroration, consisting of Example 6 followed directly by Example 7. The cadence of Example 7 (A-G) is obsessively repeated three times. The cloak has become a shroud.

Seen as a whole, *Il Tabarro*, for all the brutality of its subject, proves on examination to be a work of real refinement. The melodic lines in the orchestra have a length and fluency uncommon in Puccini's earlier operas. For a work that moves as spontaneously and irresistibly as the river by which the action is laid, *Il Tabarro* contains a surprising number of formal patterns: the strophic songs of La Frugola and the Song Vendor, the antiphonal passage for the passing lovers, the ternary form of Michele's monologue, the even more elaborate structure of Giorgetta and Luigi's second duet. The mastery apparent in *Il Tabarro* is the logical extension of Puccini's previous accomplishments.

On the whole, *Suor Angelica* marks a lower level of achievement, but its two great episodes—Angelica's scene with the Princess and her aria, *Senza mamma*—as well as a number of interesting lesser ones can carry the score, especially when it is presented in its intended context: an effective contrast to a shocking melodrama. The stage picture of the Romanesque chapel and cloister, the cypress trees, the convent cemetery in the background, afford a strong contrast to the setting of *Il Tabarro*.[89] The opera opens quietly: first bells chime, then their melody is repeated by strings and celesta. The subdued sound and clearly diatonic motion of the music provide an aural contrast with *Il Tabarro*. The prevailing quietness is

89. For the scene between Angelica and the Princess, Puccini proposed to Gatti-Casazza that the scene be changed from the cloister to a *parlatorio*, and then, after the Princess's exit, changed back to the cloister. This proposal was not carried out at the Metropolitan *première*, but Puccini's letter suggesting it is in the Metropolitan Archives. This idea was tried out in rehearsal for the Italian *première*, but it was rejected before the first performance.

maintained perilously long for an audience whose nerves have been stretched by Seine-side violence.

The vignettes of the opening episodes contain many felicitous touches: realistic details such as a piccolo's birdsong and the flute and oboe imitation of the bleating lamb; the effective scoring of brief orchestral prelude to the "recreation" episode, with its gentle melody played by the first desks of the violin and cello sections doubled by a muted horn. The first climax of the score comes at the conclusion of Angelica's little aria about human wishes, and it is all the more noticeable because it is the first moment of passionate emphasis after a full five minutes of restrained and docile understatement. The phrase is thematically important:

It emphasizes Angelica's words "La morta è vita bella" (Death is life made beautiful), an idea that reveals the hysteria latent in Angelica's nature and helps make credible the ensuing action. This phrase is the first moment in the opera that separates Angelica from the other nuns in the audience's attention. (We should remember that there is nothing about Angelica's costume to single her out.) It is the first moment of music louder than *mf* in the score so far. Example 1 recurs only once later in the score, but at the climactic moment when Angelica drinks the poison.

Just before the Abbess tells Angelica that the Princess has arrived a striking theme uncoils in the strings:

The first bar is in C-sharp minor, followed abruptly in the second by a C minor chord for four muted horns. The fateful presence of the Princess is anticipated even before she is seen. After her entrance Puccini suggests Example 2 without repeating it by the simplest and strongest means. The harsh old woman's first sung phrase is unaccompanied except for her last note (D) which clashes with the C minor chord for the horns. He compresses the whole motive into a single chord, establishing at once the Princess's inflexible character. This scene is full of dramatic touches expressed musically. For instance, after Angelica has reproached her aunt with being inexorable, the old woman protests, her composure broken for the first time. The Princess's outrage is described by a vigorous chromatic theme, but when she finishes her outburst, this theme is compressed into a sequence of jarring chords, scored for strings, bassoons, and clarinet.

3

One can picture the Princess's chest heaving indignantly as she tries to regain her self-control.

When Angelica can no longer restrain herself from inquiring about her son, a phrase that dominates much of the rest of the score is introduced:

4

The piano score only indicates the pattern of this obsessive melody and thudding ostinato bass. The melody is doubled by the violins and violas, the oboe and two clarinets, the bass line given to the lower strings and the bassoons, with a chord for the horns stressing the first beat of every measure. Two flutes play a counter-melody from time to time that clashes with the principal theme. Angelica's anxiety is suggested by the abrupt alterations from *Allegro moderato, ma agitato* to *Andante sostenuto*, the tempo switching six times in ten measures!

Angelica's aria *Senza mamma* follows directly after the Princess's exit. The opening phrases are accompanied very lightly, quiet strings and a harp chord *pp* to punctuate the ends of the phrases, which allows the touching words to project clearly. The repeated patterns in the vocal lines suggest Angelica's fixation. The second part of the aria, which Puccini did not add to the score until shortly before the Roman *première*, is based on the principal melody of the intermezzo.

5

O - ra che sei un   an - ge - lo del cie - lo,   o - ra tu puoi ve - der - la

The striking thing about this aria is its inwardness; there is no big climax, indeed it ends *pianissimo* on a high A supported by augmented harmony. Instead of cutting loose at this point, as he might have been tempted to do in his younger days, Puccini has achieved the power of restraint.

For the scene of the miracle, Puccini supplements the orchestra with a whole phalanx of instruments off-stage—including two pianos, an organ, three trumpets and cymbals. A little of the restraint of *Senza mamma* might have been an advantage, because all these forces—the organ doubling the woodwinds, the pianos much of the time in unison—have the effect of crossing each other out. In this episode the lack of clear rhythmic contrast and the absence of clearly diverging line in the melodies Puccini combines fail to produce the truly soaring effect he obviously hoped to achieve. The traditions of writing church music that Puccini absorbed at Lucca during the 1870's were all very well for the introduction to this opera, but they betray him at the end. The musically ineffective miracle brings what has been up to this point an interesting, and occasionally arresting, opera to a disillusioning conclusion.

Although *Gianni Schicchi* is Puccini's only comic opera, its style is related to the scenes of comic relief in *La Bohème*. The sense of high spirits is the same, but the humor has become mordant and less obvious. Unlike Puccini's other operas, *Gianni Schicchi* is true ensemble opera. The score moves like quicksilver, fitting each shift of the plot, each comic inflection, to attain a delicate balance between words, action, and music.

Puccini's ability to create an individual note and atmosphere for his operas right from the first measure is particularly apparent in *Gianni Schicchi*. After a brief flourish to establish the pace of comic bustle, Puccini introduces the note of the hypocritical grief of the relatives:

1

The pattern of the slurred descending second has been a traditional way of expressing grief in Italian operas since before the days of the *Miserere* from Verdi's *Il Trovatore*. Puccini uses that interval here, but he presents it in rapid pairs which gives the effect of unctuous sniffling rather than heartfelt grief. The true character represented by this interval shows up, with magnificent irony, as the relatives enthusiastically agree to Schicchi's proposal to impersonate the late Buoso:

2

The scherzo that accompanies the relatives' frantic search for the will sets off these mock-grieving seconds against scurrying flourishes and staccato passages for the violins and flutes. As Rinuccio announces he has found the will, an important theme appears:

3

Although the significance of Example 3 is not immediately made clear, it forms the basis of the love music for Rinuccio and Lauretta. At this rather vigorous introduction it is scored for violins, flutes, English horn, and trumpet. It recurs at the final love duet in Puccini's favorite key of G-flat, richly harmonized in the strings and woodwinds, with shimmering harp arpeggios and broken chords on the celesta. The only other music that approaches this vein in the score is Lauretta's familiar *Oh! mio babbino caro*, but it is more restrained. The regular rhythm and balanced phrases might make this aria seem a little trite, but it is exquisitely written for the voice and the form (three units of four phrases each) is neatly varied.

One of the most beguiling moments in the score is the trio of the women flattering Schicchi:

This a moment of delicious parody. The melody is melting, the harmonies ravishing, the accompaniment of solo woodwinds exquisite. The exaggerations are subtle: little glissandi on the harp, the phrases for Nella that smack a little of the Rhinemaidens, the intricate interplay of the parts, and the cloying chromatics of the phrase where they greet him as their "savior." This trio is the highpoint of the score.

The character of Schicchi himself is not too well favored in his music. True, he has a *buffo* aria, *In testa la cappellina!* (On his head a night-cap) but the accompaniment is dominated by a staccato chromatic figure appropriate to a parlando style. Even though the aria has a big high G in its climatic phrase, it is not the sort of aria to tempt a singer to program it on a recital. His little song of farewell to Florence becomes a sort of motif:

This scrap of melody, which looks forward to the idiom of Ping, Pang, and Pong in *Turandot*, is arresting, but the situation (he is reminding the relatives of the penalty for tampering with wills) lends itself to overdoing. The vocal line is doubled by the cellos, and each pair of phrases is punctuated by a little fanfare for two muted trumpets playing in thirds. After Schicchi has sung Example 5, seven of the relatives sing it in unison. The first phrase is repeated by Schicchi during his dictation of the will as a threat to the relations when they start to protest his bequests to himself. Although Gianni has the last word in the score, it gives him no chance as a singer because the lines are spoken. It is a traditional witty epilogue ending with an invitation for applause.

The merits of Puccini's score to *Gianni Schicchi* are many. The pace is unrelenting; the points are made with wit and brevity. Much of the orchestration has a clarity and easy naturalness that belies its underlying sophistication. It is difficult to think of any opera where the music fits the action more closely or comments on it with such tart humor. If the score has an apparent weakness, it is that it seems a little thin when it is heard apart from a full stage performance. And one might well wish that the title role had one vocal moment that could compete with the tenor's aria or Lauretta's music. These are, however, minor reservations. Granted its one-act frame, *Gianni Schicchi* must rank as one of the great comic operas.

The autographs of three scores of *Il Trittico* are in the archives of Casa Ricordi. They tell only part of the story of the changes and revisions that were made in these works.

The chief difference in the autograph of *Il Tabarro* is the presence of the abandoned original version of Michele's monologue. It makes much greater use of Examples 6 and 7 (*Il Tabarro*) than does the present arrangement. The words, however, are entirely different and far less effective than those in the present monologue. Michele addresses the river that continues to flow unceasingly even though there are corpses in its depths, and ends asking the river to give him death. The original monologue shows Michele contemplating suicide, then lighting his match (which Luigi believes is his agreed signal from Giorgetta), and Luigi's arrival culminates in the murder. The present arrangement, which was apparently first sung at La Scala in 1922, is infinitely superior; it shows Michele brooding about Giorgetta's lover and planning to murder him. According to Maestro Tenaglia, however, there are really more than two versions, for Puccini made some modifications in the first version before discarding it for the present one.[90]

There are several changes in *Suor Angelica*. Originally, the second part of *Senza mamma*, the section that introduces the melody of the intermezzo at the words "Ora che sei un angelo del cielo," was not in the score, but was added for the Roman *première* at the Teatro Costanzi. The new ending of the aria entailed dropping out a few bars following its original shorter version.

The autograph and the first printed edition of the opera—that of all three operas in a single volume—contain the so-called aria of the flowers, which followed directly after the intermezzo. In this aria Angelica greets the flowers as friends and asks them to yield the poison that will soothe her grief. The aria (*andante*) is eighty measures long, accompanied by repeated modal arpeggios.[91]

The elimination of the aria went against the grain with Puccini. At the Roman *première* the conductor Marinuzzi cut it at rehearsal. Puccini ordered it back, but Marinuzzi thought it slowed down the opera. Puccini compromised by altering the first two lines of the aria and by shortening the orchestral but not the vocal part. Apparently the last time the aria of the flowers was sung in a performance was at the La Scala *première*. It was cut in the repetitions that season, and Puccini made the cut permanent.

The autograph of *Gianni Schicchi* shows a few minor changes. Originally Puccini wanted the relatives to whisper hoarsely the *Requiem aeternam* at the rise of the curtain, but this is crossed out. Rinuccio's aria to Florence was originally in A major. Puccini wanted it raised half a tone,[92] indicating the transposition was to begin thirty-nine bars before the aria and to run some twenty bars after its close. The trio for the women is shorter and has a different ending in the autograph. Puccini also changed a phrase or two in the final love duet.

Considering the length and relative complexity of these three operas, the small number of changes Puccini made in them is surprising.

90. The autograph of the present version of Michele's monologue is bound in with the rest of the autograph of *Il Tabarro*.
91. See Fedele d'Amico "Una ignorata pagina 'malipieriana' di *Suor Angelica*," *Rassegna Musicale Curci*, XIX (March 1966), 7-13. D'Amico points out a resemblance between Angelica's aria of the flowers and the first of Malipiero's *Sette canzoni*. This article also gives an interesting account of the vicissitudes of Puccini's aria before it was eliminated permanently from the score.
92. See *Carteggi Pucciniani*, p. 481. On 2 March 1919 Puccini requested Maestro Tenaglia to see to this transposition.

4

UNTASTED TRIUMPH

Turandot

Puccini was sixty when *Il Trittico* was introduced at the Teatro Costanzi in Rome. Stretching behind him was a record of success in the opera house that none of his contemporaries could match. The operas he had written during the last decade, although they had not found the eager acceptance that had greeted the Big Three, were nonetheless alive and in demand by a number of theaters. Stretching ahead of him now was the familiar problem of finding the right subject for his next opera. At sixty, Puccini embarked on the search, but not with his old youthful eagerness. And, as before, he had other things than operas on his mind.

When Puccini was in Rome in December 1918 and January 1919 to stage *Il Trittico*, he was approached by Prince Prospero Colonna, then the mayor of Rome, with an invitation to write a hymn to Rome to commemorate the victorious conclusion of World War I. Don Prospero promised to provide an appropriate ode, the work of Fausto Salvatori. Not being fond of writing isolated pieces of music, Puccini demurred, but under the circumstances he could not refuse gracefully. In due course he received an ode from Salvatori, but, finding it deficient in the popular character he felt it should have, he asked to be excused. So eager was Prince Colonna to sponsor this work by Puccini that he had Salvatori send a second ode. As this poem was more satisfactory, Puccini made his

initial sketches on 28 March 1919 and completed the composition a
few days later on 2 April.[1]

The first performance of the "Inno a Roma" was scheduled to
take place outdoors in the Piazza di Siena, Rome, on 21 April 1919,
but was postponed because of a severe storm. The work was finally
introduced six weeks later in the old Parioli stadium on 2 June, conducted by the famous bandmaster Vesella, who had arranged Puccini's orchestration for his band. The hymn was greeted with tremendous enthusiasm. But after this auspicious introduction nothing
more was heard of the work, which Puccini had composed in a
style that could be performed by school children, until 1923, when
it was published by Sonzogno. During the Fascist regime "Inno a
Roma" acquired a rather dubious popularity, and as these connotations still cling to the work today, it gathers dust. Since Puccini
composed it a good three years before the March to Rome, neglect
of the piece on these grounds is not justified.

For Puccini, writing the "Inno a Roma" was no substitute for
composing an opera. As 1919 took its course, Puccini was still looking for the right subject. On 14 October, he writes to Carlo Paladini[2] that he wants "the Torre and a good libretto." The Torre he
mentions here is not Torre del Lago, but the Torre della Tagliata,
an old Spanish tower on the promontory of Ansedonia in the Maremma. It is significant at this time that Puccini mentions the tower
first and the libretto second. Puccini suffered from a peculiarly
lucchese disease, the *mal della pietra*. He had what almost amounted
to a compulsion to acquire houses. Besides his villa at Torre del
Lago, he had acquired the title to his birthplace in Lucca on the Via
del Poggio, and over the years he had accumulated the house in the
mountains above Chiatri as well as a summer house at Abetone.

His relationship with the Torre della Tagliata is worth mention-

1. See Urbano Barberini, "Puccini e l' 'Inno a Roma'," *Strenna dei Romanisti*
(Rome, 1965).
2. Paladini (1861-1922) was a journalist and professor of English, born at Lucca,
and a boyhood friend of Puccini's. In 1903 Paladini published one of the first
biographical studies of the composer to appear, later included in Paladini's *I primi
passi di Giacomo Puccini*, published in *Giornalino della domenica*, 12 December
1920.
Paladini and Puccini had a serious misunderstanding in 1904, partly because of
an interview about *Butterfly* that Paladini published without Puccini's approval and
partly because of Paladini's ironic comments about the fiasco of that opera, comments duly recounted to Puccini. In 1918, their former friendship was resumed
because of a spirited defense of the *pineta* of Viareggio written by Paladini. Their
friendship continued until Paladini's death, 10 July 1922. Puccini was one of the
pallbearers at Paladini's funeral.

ing as it reveals something of Puccini's frame of mind during these crucial years. For almost thirty years Puccini had been a devotee of hunting in the Maremma,[3] and he had a natural desire to acquire his own base of operations there. From the outside at least, the Torre della Tagliata was picturesque enough, but it lacked such niceties as a passable access road and drinking water. After considerable trouble he managed to lease it from the government in the latter part of October 1919. In his new enthusiasm he ordered extensive remodeling. During the hunting seasons of 1919 and 1920 he got there only occasionally. On 28 December 1920, Puccini informs Paladini: "This year the Maremma has bored me, disillusioned me. I am not at all happy! My nerves are still stretched, but better. . . ."[4] Two weeks later he is considering selling the tower. He initiates several negotiations to sell his lease, but they all fall through. Next he embarked on a second set of alterations to the tower. In December 1921 he returned for ten days, but this miserable stay finally convinced him that the Torre della Tagliata was both impractical and uncomfortable, and he promptly disposed of it. Puccini's irresolution and frayed nerves are an indication that he had lost his youthful resilience. As he came to channel his creative energy into amazingly intensive bouts with *Turandot*, his nerves and his health suffered.

Another concern of Puccini's during these years is also symptomatic of his frame of mind. Puccini had set his heart on being named a Senator of the Kingdom of Italy. He was eager for this title not because of any political ambitions, but he wanted the public recognition of his accomplishments as an Italian. Although there was the example of Verdi, who had been elected to the Senate in 1861, Puccini was more stirred to set in motion the necessary wheels to secure this honor by the example of Pietro Mascagni, who was busily engaged in trying to gain it for himself. Puccini the man was unassuming as a private citizen, but Puccini the artist had an uneasy *amour-propre*. Those critics, such as Torrefranco and Pizzetti,[5]

3. Today the Tuscan Maremma is very different from the place Puccini knew. Before the land had been drained, cleared, and put under cultivation, it was one of the least civilized regions of Italy, a refuge for many species of game—and for outlaws.
4. Paladini, p. 117.
5. Fausto Torrefranco, *Giacomo Puccini e l'opera internazionale* (Milan, 1912) and Ildebrando Pizzetti, "Giacomo Puccini," *Musicisti contemporanei* (Milan, 1914). Pizzetti's article had first appeared in periodical form about four years earlier. It attacks Puccini as a purveyor of "bourgeois" art.

who championed the music of the younger generation regarded Puccini as the symbol of the commercial and bourgeois spirit in music; they lumped him with the *verismo* school, so sadly out of fashion, and excoriated him. Their running attacks got under Puccini's skin. He believed he had been true to himself as an artist; he had not been oblivious to new trends in music; and he had never regarded himself as one of the *veristi*.

If Puccini's wish to be named Senator seems like a foolish desire for self-gratification, it is important to remember that his desire was colored by the impression the public would receive if Mascagni were given the honor before he was. Puccini had a genuine pride in his accomplishments, and his contribution as a sort of cultural ambassador for Italy was very considerable. Finally the whole question of Puccini as Senator was resolved in May 1924, when his nomination was officially announced. It is very typical of Puccini, who had been humorless about the matter before he received the honor, that he afterward made a joke of his title, sometimes calling himself *Suonatore* (Musician) instead of Senatore.

Although these several concerns involved his time and attention, Puccini was still a composer of operas, and he needed to get down to his own work. His straightforward attitude toward his métier is revealed in a letter he wrote to Paladini on 26 November 1920.

> . . . How I admire you for the patience you have, you who were born already a bit of a professor. Think what I would have done had I not guessed my lucky lottery number was writing operas! I was good for nothing else. Teaching? What? Or since I don't know anything—Playing the organ? Yes, with that facile hand for re-arranging![6] A bandmaster? I would have wound up playing a drum slung across my belly with what authority I possess. By now I would be broken by poverty and grief—and especially the latter with that morbid sensitivity that has always dominated me.[7]

For all the complexities and contradictions of Puccini's character, he never lost a streak of natural humility, but this he would only expose to those who had been his friends from the years before his success. And Puccini's self-estimate is perfectly accurate: the thing he was best fitted to do was to write operas.

6. This is an ironical allusion to the charge frequently levelled against Puccini that his scores were full of warmed-over recollections of his earlier works.
7. Paladini, pp. 150-51.

As he began to cast around for a subject to provide the successor to *Il Trittico*, Puccini put his lines out. In August 1919 he wrote to Paladini that he would be pleased to find a little subject about Lucca.[8] It is singularly fitting that someone who felt the strong ties Puccini did for his particular corner of Italy should want to celebrate it. When no little *lucchese* subject appeared, Puccini arranged with Adami to work with Renato Simoni[9] to see what they might come up with. When the publisher Sonzogno, who hoped to snare a second Puccini score, wrote to the composer to inquire about his new projects, Puccini replied that he was looking for a subject dealing with "a great grief."

On 18 December 1919 he wrote to Gatti-Casazza in New York and mentioned his desire for a new subject. By a strange coincidence, that very afternoon of 18 December Geraldine Farrar had made up a party consisting of George Maxwell (Ricordi's agent in New York), the conductor Roberto Moranzoni, and Gatti-Casazza, to go to the Belasco Theater to see Belasco's play *The Son-Daughter* which Farrar judged to be tailor-made for Puccini. The group was sufficiently impressed with what they saw for Maxwell to secure an option on the play and send a copy of it to Puccini. Gatti wrote the composer urging him to consider the subject seriously and to plan for the opera to have its introduction to the world at the Metropolitan.[10] Obviously Puccini was unimpressed by *The Son-Daughter*, for no more is heard of it as a subject for him. The most interesting aspect about this proposal, considering that Puccini was soon to settle on the subject of *Turandot*, is that Belasco's play was also a Chinese subject.

When Adami and Simoni brought Puccini their first proposal, they read him an original drama laid in the suburbs of London about 1830. Puccini liked their first act, but the rest of it left him cold. It is not precisely clear from the account in Adami's biography of Puccini whether it was the refusal of the English subject

8. Ibid., p. 117.

9. Renato Simoni (1875–1952) was a dramatist and served as drama critic for the *Corriere della sera* and as editor of *Lettura*, succeeding to this last post on the death of Giacosa. By 1919 Simoni had already had some experience as a writer of libretti having been connected with Cilea's *Ritorno dell' Amore* and Giordano's *Madame Sans-Gêne*.

   After his work on *Turandot*, Simoni wrote the libretto to Rocca's *Il Dibuk* and revised the text to Paisiello's *Nina*.

10. A carbon copy of Gatti-Casazza's letter is in the Archives of the Metropolitan Opera House.

or of some later proposal that led by chance to the subject of Puccini's next opera.[11] In the middle of March 1920 Puccini had come to Milan to consult with Adami and Simoni before going to Rome to see the second production there of *Il Trittico*.[12] Discouraged, Puccini and his collaborators were casting around for a plausible idea when a sudden turn in the conversation produced the idea of Gozzi[13] and his *Turandotte*.[14] Adami remembered that at home he had a copy of Maffei's translation of Schiller's adaptation of Gozzi's original play. There was just time enough to fetch it so Puccini could read it on the train to Rome.

On 18 March 1920 Puccini sent his impressions of the work to Simoni. The number of acts would have to be simplified; it would take work to make the action move rapidly and effectively; above all, it would be necessary "to exalt the amorous passion of Turandot, who for such a long time has suffocated beneath the ashes of her great pride." It is striking indeed that one of the first comments Puccini should have written about the opera dealt with the very point that proved its greatest stumbling block, that crucial scene which he did not live to complete. In the same letter Puccini reports that he had talked to a woman who had seen Max Reinhardt's production of Vollmöller's version of *Turandotte* (with incidental music by Busoni[15]), which had capitalized on a tiny heroine surrounded by tall men and large furnishings. He disapproved of this approach because he held that "*Turandotte* is the most normal and

11. Adami, *Il romanzo della vita di Giacomo Puccini*, p. 223 ff.

12. On 18 March 1920 Puccini reported to Simoni the success of *Il Trittico*'s second Roman production. On this occasion, Angelica's aria of the flowers was omitted.

13. Carlo Gozzi (1720-1806) was a Venetian dramatist, whose fairy-tale *fiabe* have proven a rich mine for operas. Such varied works as Prokofiev's *Love of the Three Oranges*, Wagner's *Die Feen*, and Casella's *La Donna Serpente* were derived from Gozzi.

Turandotte (1762) has appealed to many composers, among them the twenty-three-year old Weber, who wrote an overture and six pices of incidental music to Schiller's adaptation of the original Gozzi text. Operas on the subject have been written by Blumenroeder (1810), Karl Reissiger (1835), J. Hoven (1839), Hermann Lovenskjold (1854), Antonio Bazzini (1854), who was one of Puccini's masters at the Milan Conservatory, and Ferrucio Busoni (1917).

14. The Gozzi's title is *Turandotte*, indicating that the final "t" of Puccini's title should be pronounced.

15. Feruccio Busoni (1866-1924) wrote incidental music for Reinhardt's production of Gozzi's play at the Deutschestheater, Berlin (1911). Later Busoni enlarged his incidental music to form a two-act opera, written to his own libretto. Busoni's *Turandot* was first given in Zurich on 11 May 1917, as part of a double bill with his *Arlecchino*, also having its first performance.

human play of all of Gozzi's dramas."[16] His reaction to the subject was to ask Simoni and Adami to prepare a libretto; then he would come to a definite decision whether to proceed with *Turandot*.

In the middle of May 1920, shortly before Puccini went to London to see *Il Trittico* launched there, he received the first act of their libretto. He was delighted with their work and urged them to prepare the second act and, if necessary, a third act. But to hedge his bets, Puccini was encouraging the preparation of another libretto. This prospect was the work of Giovacchino Forzano and entitled *Sly*. It was rather freely derived from the "induction" to *The Taming of the Shrew*. Puccini was not convinced by Forzano's first act and told him his final decision would depend upon the second. By the middle of July, Puccini knew that *Sly* would not do. Forzano salvaged his work, however, first turning it into a stage play and later back into a libretto for Wolf-Ferrari.[17]

About the same time Puccini quietly decided to forgo *Sly*,[18] he received a draft of Acts 2 and 3 of *Turandot*. He was dismayed by what he read; all the promise of the first act seemed dissipated. In a state of considerable agitation he invited Adami and Simoni to meet him at Bagni di Lucca. Puccini always preferred a face-to-face discussion of problems with his librettists to a cumbersome and time-consuming exchange of letters.

That summer of 1920 Puccini had decided to go to Bagni di Lucca for a number of reasons. He had old associations with the place, having played the piano at the casino as a boy. It appealed to him now as an old-fashioned, rather stodgy resort. In the aftermath of the war, he found his native Italy a not very congenial place. He was bothered by the social unrest; he was upset by the political uncertainty of those days; he detested the parvenu types that appeared almost everywhere; he missed the old leisurely values of the world he had grown up in and hoped to rediscover them at Bagni di Lucca. Another cogent reason for his going there was the presence of Baron Fassini, an authority on China.[19]

Simoni and Adami arrived at Bagni di Lucca on 3 August and stayed several days. It was a fruitful meeting, and they quickly

16. *Carteggi Pucciniani*, p. 490.
17. Wolf-Ferrari's *Sly* had its first performance at La Scala, 29 December 1927. Pertile sang Sly; Panizza conducted.
18. It is clear from a letter published in Paladini, pp. 153-54, that as late as January 1921, Puccini did not want to make a public renunciation of Forzano's *Sly*.
19. Adami, *Il romanzo della vita di Giacomo Puccini*, p. 229.

agreed on steps for revising the libretto. One can only deduce the tenor of their discusison from clues in their subsequent letters. Apparently it was at Bagni di Lucca that the character we now know as Liù began to develop. On 28 August Puccini writes to Simoni: "Give me news of *Turandot*. Adami has written to me that he is working. Have you considered well the new conception of the little woman (*piccola donna*)?"[20] For all his growing involvement with his subject, Puccini is still informing his friends that he has not yet definitely decided to compose *Turandot*. He wants to see a new version of Act 1.

By September 1920 his interest in the subject has grown. He writes to Adami that he is anxious about the libretto; idleness is making him restless. He further reports that he has started making notes of musical ideas, harmony, and tempi. In November he comes back from Vienna, where *La Rondine* went badly and *Il Trittico* well, feeling rather melancholy. He lets Adami know that *Turandot* may prove impossible to finish because he is too far from his librettists when he needs them. He concludes this letter by urging Adami to "work as if you were working for a young man of thirty, and I shall do my best; and if I do not succeed it will be my fault!"[21]

Sometime in December Puccini sent to Simoni a very interesting outline for revising the libretto of Act 2. This document proves that what Puccini here calls Act 2 is the counterpart of the present Act 3, although it includes a number of unfamiliar details. He begins by urging Simoni to be rapid and to stop only when lyricism demands it, and continues:

> entrance of Turandot, nervous;
> *Nessun dorma*—Peking, romanza for the tenor;
> Temptations: *drink, women*, no banquet. The masks are the ones who offer them to him and they are the protagonists of the scene.
> Invitation *to tell his name* to save their lives. Calaf: *No, I lose Turandot.* Invitation to flee—*no*—then a little plot aside and a threat of death. *No incubi.* Turandot arrives—*duet shorter—torture shorter.* The three announce their hearts are broken—*I have lost her*, my heart, why are you beating? Liù says she wants to remain, to tempt Turandot to pity. *Darkness*—Scene in a room with draperies, slaves and Liù.

20. *Carteggi Pucciniani*, p. 495.
21. Adami, *Letters*, p. 270.

Turandot on the point of jealousy. *Not a long scene.*
Darkness.
Final scene: large white palace—*Pegonie,* all already present
including the Emperor in their places. *Rising sun.* Calaf:
farewell to the world, to love, to life. His name? I don't
know, *terse.*
Big love phrase with modern kiss and all present start to sing
lustily![22]

These rather cryptic notes by Puccini seem confusing at first
glance. The act was to have been in three scenes. The first of these
is not unlike the present opening of Act 3, but with two significant
differences: Turandot enters at the beginning of the act, where now
she arrives two-thirds of the way through; there is no mention of
Liù's death; indeed, she is very much alive at the end of the scene.
The proposed second scene, inside the palace, is between Liù and
Turandot, and something—apparently Liù—arouses Turandot's jealousy. Of this motivation, fortunately, nothing was retained and the
scene was dropped. The final scene resembles in some respects the
present final scene. But what is all this about Calaf's farewell to the
world, to love, to life, which sounds a little like the "hymn" Illica
wrote for Cavaradossi in the last act of *Tosca?* Apparently, Calaf
has revealed his name and has been condemned to death. But when
Turandot is asked to reveal his name, she is to reply with a terse
"I don't know." Thereby she saves Calaf's life, proving that she has
learned to love, and the scene ends with a joyous finale. If all this
was to be Act 2, what was there left for Act 3? At this stage of the
game, nothing. Because Puccini had started to hold out for casting
the opera into two massive acts.

Throughout the early part of December, Puccini's anxiety to
have some material to work on kept growing. Finally, on 22 December 1920, Adami delivered the revised form of Act 1 to Puccini
at Torre della Tagliata. Adami remembered this as a difficult encounter with Puccini, who promptly made all sorts of drastic suggestions for changing Act 1. To judge from Puccini's letters written
the following month, his meeting with Adami had been worthwhile.
In January 1921 Puccini wrote to his friend Vandini in Rome that
Turandot would be spectacular, and yet have some emotion in it.
"In fact, I am very pleased with it."[23] About this time he had another

22. *Carteggi Pucciniani,* p. 496.
23. Ibid., p. 501.

and eminently satisfactory conference with Adami and Simoni in Milan.

At last, near the end of January 1921, Puccini was able to begin sketching and composing in earnest. He reports that he is working ten to twelve hours a day. That this Act 1 he was working on is not exactly the opening act we know becomes clear from some comments in his letters. On 30 April 1921, to Adami, he wrote: "I am at the masks and in a little while I come to the riddles. I think I have made great strides. What about Act II? Act III?"[24] This letter would seem to indicate that he was working on an Act 1 that consisted of two scenes: the first, a shortened version of the present Act 1; the second, a shortened version of the present Act 2, scene 2. When he inquires about Act 3, this is probably an indication that the librettists, who opposed Puccini's idea of two huge acts, wanted to set the final scene (Calaf's near-execution) as a short concluding act.

Other excerpts from Puccini's letters of that spring and summer make these points even more sharply. On 7 June, he writes again to Adami: "I am working like a Roman slave. It is terribly difficult, but I am getting on. I am finishing the masks (frightfully good). But I have already done the music for the ghosts and the two songs of Calaf and Liù."[25] When he speaks of the masks, he is referring to their first appearance, not to their intermezzo scene that opens Act 2. That scene had not yet been conceived. From this letter of 7 June we can see that Puccini is approaching the end of the present Act 1. Then on 20 June: "I am at the riddles now."[26] And on 17 July: "Soon I will need the second act."[27] These last two excerpts side by side leave no question that the riddles took place in the then Act 1.

By the middle of September he has reverted to his idea that *Turandot* should be in a two-act form. He tries to persuade Simoni that the third act is unnecessary; he thinks there is a real danger of diluting the action too much between the enigmas and the final scene; he wants to compress some events and eliminate others to arrive more rapidly at a scene "where love explodes." He writes to Adami as well to try and win him over to the two-act format. This letter to Adami shows that the notion of Turandot's jealousy has

24. Adami, *Letters*, p. 272.
25. Ibid., p. 274.
26. Ibid., p. 275.
27. *Carteggi Pucciniani*, p. 511.

been discarded. For a middle scene in his big Act 2, he suggests
something played before a drop-curtain: "a hymn to the risen victory? or else a dance, and add an epilogue with Liù, slaves, and
Turandot?"[28]

All this insistence on two acts led to some hard feelings between
Puccini and his librettists during the autumn of 1921. Not that Puccini was ever other than considerate and polite with Adami and
Simoni, or they with him, but the letters of this period convey a
real sense of the frustration that comes from pulling in different
directions. Although he found their periods of silence rather un-
nerving, Puccini continued to send suggestions. On 26 December
1921 he writes to Adami that he thinks Act 1 should end with the
striking of the great gong. This suggestion may be more of a concession, for it means that if Act 1 ends at this point, then the riddles
will occur in Act 2. From this time on, Puccini never reverts to his
idea of completing the opera in two big acts.

This letter of 26 December 1921 was written from Puccini's new
villa in Viareggio, where he composed most of *Turandot*. He had
been forced to move away from Torre del Lago because during the
war a peat-processing factory had been established there as an emer-
gency measure to cope with the fuel shortage. Puccini detested the
ever-expanding factory, the increasing work force, the noisome
chemical odors that destroyed the tranquility of the old Torre del
Lago he loved better than any other place in the world. Puccini
tried every means of persuasion he could muster to combat the factory, but his protests were in vain. The government's *force-majeure*
in the matter of the factory and his own *mal della pietra* combined
to persuade him to purchase and most elaborately remodel a villa
at what was then the northern edge of Viareggio, facing the *pineta*.
He kept his house in Torre del Lago, using it as a base for an occasional day's hunting, but Viareggio assumed the status of a permanent residence.

In his new villa and waiting for the libretto to crystallize, Puccini
began to orchestrate Act 1 of *Turandot* on 21 March 1922 at 11
P.M. For this opera, he had provided himself with specially large
music paper with the title *Turandot* printed at the top and his mon-
ogram at the bottom. Not long before he undertook this work, he
had started to sketch ideas for the intermezzo scene for Ping, Pang,
and Pong (Act 2, scene 1), which had lately been decided upon.

28. Adami, *Letters*, p. 276.

The orchestration of Act 1 he had finished, all but one little passage that needed words, by 3 November 1922, and on the 22nd he sent the completed act to Milan in the safe-keeping of Tonio. In December he tackled the intermezzo scene again, but complained that he still did not have it right.

All this time he worked on the orchestration of Act 1, there were other things, some having to do with other parts of *Turandot* and some having nothing at all to do with it, that occupied Puccini's attention. One was Rose Ader, a soprano in whom Puccini became interested, apparently in 1920 or 1921. She had been singing in Vienna, but Puccini persuaded her that she would have more of a career if she learned her roles—Violetta, Gilda, etc.—in Italian, and he tried to use his influence to get her engagements. In April 1922 he wrote to Gatti-Casazza, asking him to engage her: Gatti's reply, dated 19 June, is tactful: "I have been to Vienna. I have seen Signorina Rosa Ader and I must tell you there is no possibility for her at the Metropolitan . . . she belongs to that category of artist that is not lacking in America and which we are obliged to favor for obvious reasons of local politics . . . ."[29]

In June 1922 Puccini received the balance of the revised text of *Turandot*. He assured the Casa Ricordi that he was completely satisfied with it. In the latter part of August he and his family and some friends went on a motor trip to Germany and Austria that lasted several weeks. Early in October, his sister Iginia, who as Suor Giulia Enrichetta had been mother superior at the convent at Vicopelago near Lucca, died, thus breaking one of Puccini's closest attachments to his own family. His very real grief did not prevent his working on *Turandot*. He had come to realize that there must be a big aria in Act 2, and thus *In questa reggia* came into being.

The recollections of the tenor Giovanni Martinelli shed further light on the development of *Turandot* during early August 1922. At that time the aria *Nessun dorma* existed in sketch, although it was not fitted into the fabric of the surrounding scene until the following year. Martinelli, who had known Puccini from the time of the La Scala *première* of *La Fanciulla*, came to call on the composer and was shown some passages of the work in progress, among them *Nessun dorma*, which he sang to Puccini's acompaniment. According to Martinelli, Puccini was sufficiently impressed with what may

29. Puccini's letter and Gatti-Casazza's reply are preserved in the Archives of the Metropolitan Opera House.

well have been the first performance of this aria that he proposed to Martinelli that he create the role of Calaf. That this important assignment did not fall to Martinelli is explained by the bad feeling between Gatti-Casazza and Toscanini in those years; indeed, Martinelli reports that Gatti told him that if he went to La Scala to sing the *première* of *Turandot* for Toscanini he need never bother returning to New York! This anecdote may well explain why two other tenors, both mentioned later by Puccini as possible creators of Calaf and both under contract to the Metropolitan—Gigli and Lauri-Volpi—did not participate in the *Turandot première*.

Just before he left for Paris to attend the first production of *Gianni Schicchi* at the Opéra-Comique,[30] Puccini conceived one of the crucial ideas in the development of *Turandot*. On 3 November 1922 he wrote to Adami: "I think that Liù must be sacrificed to some sorrow, but I don't see how to do this unless we make her die under torture. And why not? Her death could help to soften the heart of the Princess."[31] The death of Liù the slave girl is such a striking episode in the opera that it seems almost incredible that it did not materialize until twenty months of discussion and work had gone into *Turandot!*

The end of December 1922, Puccini went to Milan for the anniversary production of *Manon Lescaut* at La Scala, conducted by Toscanini. Although they had had their differences of opinion in the past, the great bond between them was emphatically recognized at this time. The high point of this production occurred on 1 February 1923, thirty years after the first performance, when a great testimonial dinner was offered to Puccini. Even on such an occasion as this, Puccini's embarrassment at public functions overcame him at the thought he might have to make a speech. He avoided making one by asking that he and Elvira be seated at an inconspicuous table.

In the early months of 1923 he completed his sketches for Act 2, some parts of which, the intermezzo scene, the riddles, were already in existence. In March he informed Adami that he had some qualms about the changes in Act 3 and asked for still another revision. In late June he started to sketch Act 3 and inserted Calaf's sumptuous aria, *Nessun dorma*. On 12 November, he was so far advanced with

30. *Gianni Schicchi*, without the other members of *Il Trittico*, was first given at the Opéra-Comique on 6 November 1922. It was sung in a French translation by Paul Ferrier, conducted by André Catherine, and sung by Vanni Marcoux (title role), Victor Pujol (Rinuccio), and Germaine Épicaste (Lauretta).
31. Adami, *Letters*, pp. 291-2.

Act 3 sketches that he could tell Adami: "I find that I have no lines
for the death of Liù. The music is all there; it is a case now of writing words for music which is already composed . . . ."[32] And he
goes on to suggest the lines of Liù's last aria as they now appear:
"Tu che di gel sei cinta." As so often had happened with his earlier
operas, Puccini contributed part of the text himself.

On 10 December 1923 he started to orchestrate Act 2. The intensity with which Puccini worked is shown by the fact he was still
working on the intermezzo scene in January 1924, but by 22 February he had completed the whole act. Puccini said he had been
working feverishly, and one can believe it, for he orchestrated all
of Act 3 up to and including the death of Liù in March 1924. And
it was in March that a pain in his throat became a constant source
of discomfort and worry.

Although he had made it plain to his librettists a whole year before that he needed a new version of the final duet, it still was not
forthcoming. Puccini had composed and orchestrated everything
but the final quarter of an hour of his opera. His anxiety for the text
grew, but it was not until 31 May that he saw Simoni's prose sketch
for the end of the opera and approved it. It was not until 1 September that he had the verses to set. He began at once on his sketches
for the conclusion of *Turandot*.

If these last lines of text had been in his hands some months
sooner, and there seems no good reason why they were not, there is
little doubt that Puccini would have finished his opera. Although
his throat bothered him a great deal and he passed through periods
when his will to work evaporated, there was ample time between
March and September 1924 for him to have written the final scene.
As it was, even though his health had begun to deteriorate alarm-
ingly, between early September and 10 October he made quite a
number of sketches for the final duet.

On 6 September 1924 Toscanini came to Puccini's villa at Viareggio to discuss *Turandot*, which Puccini had definitely decided to
give at La Scala. Puccini played the whole opera and discussed his
intentions for the final scene with Toscanini. Puccini's music made
a powerful impression on Toscanini, who took away with him
Puccini's assurances that the opera would be ready for a *première*
in April 1925.

Although Puccini's throat had been bothering him continuously

32. Ibid., p. 301.

since March, and periodically before that, Puccini was unaware that he had a cancer at the base of his larynx. His friends became increasingly alarmed by his condition, and it was arranged that Puccini should be examined by specialists. Tonio was told of the true nature of his father's condition, but both Giacomo and Elvira were kept in the dark. A second consultation with another specialist confirmed the diagnosis, and Tonio was told that the only possible hope lay in leaving at once for Brussels, where a Dr. Ledoux had achieved some remarkable cures in his clinic there. On 4 November 1924, Giacomo, accompanied only by Tonio and Fosca, went to Brussels by train. With him Puccini took his sketches for the final pages of *Turandot*.

At first Puccini was treated externally with X-rays, a regimen that did not keep him confined to bed. On Monday 24 November, Dr. Ledoux performed an operation to insert seven tiny radioactive crystal needles around the tumor. The operation lasted 3 hours and 40 minutes and was carried on with Puccini under only a local anesthetic, so as not to overtax his heart. When his ordeal was over at long last, Puccini could not speak. On a pad, he scribbled: "I feel as though I have bayonets in my throat. They have massacred me."

Puccini's constitution was sufficiently strong that for several days he seemed to rally well after his operation. His condition was judged promising, and hopes for his survival rose. The encouraging news made headlines around the world. Dr. Ledoux's plan was to remove the crystal needles on Sunday, 30 November. Suddenly, however, about 6 o'clock in the evening of Friday, 28 November, Puccini went into heart failure. His agony lasted until 11:30 the following morning, Saturday, 29 November 1924.

The sad news was released to a world that received the announcement almost with incredulity, because of the encouraging tone of the earlier reports. A death-mask of Puccini was made, and his body was embalmed. On 1 December there was a funeral service in Brussels, followed by a second service in Milan Cathedral on 3 December. Toscanini conducted the orchestra and chorus of La Scala in the Requiem from *Edgar*, and Hina Spani sang the phrases of Fidelia, "Addio, addio, mio dolce amor." At the conclusion of the ceremony, Puccini's body was taken by a large band of mourners through a furious rainstorm to a cemetery, where it was temporarily placed in the vault owned by the Toscanini family.

Two years later Puccini's remains were taken to Torre del Lago and placed in a special chapel constructed in the Villa Puccini. Fittingly, his tomb was arranged so that it is just on the other side of the wall from the upright piano at which he had composed so much of his music.

Maria Bianca Ginori, long a friend of the Puccini family, provides the details of how Puccini came to be buried at Torre del Lago.

> Some time not long after Puccini's death, Tonio asked me to go to their house at Torre del Lago because his mother wanted to speak to me. Signora Elvira told me that for all her careful search through the papers left by her husband she had found no clue as to the place where he desired to be buried. Elvira said: "I know that Giacomo talked about many things with you. I have been wondering if he ever expressed a wish in this matter." When I answered in the negative, she asked me what solution I would suggest. After a little thought I proposed Torre del Lago. Thinking of his affection for the place, I hoped I had done the right thing, even though they might reject my suggestion, even though it might mean the quiet of Torre del Lago would be destroyed. . . . Signora Elvira and Tonio agreed with my suggestion straight off. There was only one doubt: would it be possible to obtain permission to build a tomb in the middle of an occupied dwelling. The permission was granted. Then Signora Elvira said to me: "And later, when we are buried here, you will not forget us, *vero?*"[33]

Elvira Puccini was buried in the chapel in 1934, and now Tonio is buried beside his parents.

Shortly before he knew he had to go to Brussels, Puccini had still hoped that *Turandot* would be ready for its world *première* at La Scala in April 1925. Since he had not lived long enough to complete his score, the first performance had to be postponed a year. Having had the benefit of hearing Puccini play the score to him and explain his ideas, Toscanini was determined the opera should be completed so that it could be given as nearly as possible as Puccini intended it to be. To work up the final scene from Puccini's provocative but incomplete sketches Toscanini nominated Franco

33. Letter to the author.

Alfano.[34] It took Alfano nearly six months to work out and then to rework his conclusion to *Turandot*.

The world *première* of *Turandot* took place at La Scala on 25 April 1926. The evening was an emotional one. As is well known, Toscanini halted the performance at the point at which Puccini had stopped orchestrating the score; he addressed the audience briefly, explaining his reason for terminating the performance. The fine cast made a strong impression. It was headed by Rosa Raisa (Turandot), Maria Zamboni (Liù), Miguel Fleta (Calaf), Carlo Walter (Timur), and Giacomo Rimini (Ping).[35] At the second performance and thereafter *Turandot* was performed with the Alfano conclusion. Since the *première* came late in the season, there were only eight performances of *Turandot* at La Scala that spring. It is not generally known that Toscanini did not conduct the whole series; on at least one occasion Ettore Panizza took his place. When the opera was put on a second time at La Scala in November 1926, Panizza conducted all fourteen performances.[36]

The first performance of *Turandot* outside Italy was given at the Teatro Colón in Buenos Aires on 25 June 1926, the chief roles being sung by Claudia Muzio, Rosetta Pampanini, and Giacomo Lauri-Volpi. This run of four performances was conducted by Gino Marinuzzi. The first performance in Germany was at Dresden (in July 1926). At Vienna the following October the opera made a sensation: the first cast was headed by Lotte Lehmann and Leo Slezak, while the following evening their roles were sung by Maria Nemeth and Jan Kiepura. With principals of this calibre to alternate in the chief parts, *Turandot* was the talk of Vienna.

On 16 November 1926, the Metropolitan gave the North American *première* of *Turandot*, enlisting the vocal services of Maria Jeritza and Giacomo Lauri-Volpi and the conducting of Tullio Serafin.[37] The London *première* took place at Covent Garden on

34. Alfano (1876-1954) composed his first opera, *Miranda*, in 1896, but it was not until 1904, with *Risurrezione*, that he made his mark. His other operas of real merit are: *L'Ombra di Don Giovanni* (1914), *La Leggenda di Sakuntala* (1921), *Madonna Imperia* (1927), *L'Ultimo Lord* (1930), and *Cyrano de Bergerac* (1936).
35. The balance of the first La Scala cast included Francesco Dominici (Altoum), Emilio Venturini (Pang), Giuseppe Nessi (Pong), and Aristide Baracchi (the Mandarin). In some performances Franco Lo Giudice replaced Fleta as Calaf.
36. The second edition of *Turandot* at La Scala, 24 November 1926, was sung by Scacciati (Turandot), Zamboni (Liù), Lo Giudice (Calaf), and Taurino Parvis (Ping).
37. The Metropolitan's first cast for *Turandot* also included Martha Attwood (Liù), Pavel Ludikar (Timur), Giuseppe de Luca (Ping), Angelo Bada (Pang),

7 June 1927, where it was sung by Bianca Scacciati, in place of
an indisposed Jeritza, and by Francesco Merli. In the other three
performances of *Turandot* at Covent Garden that summer, Florence Easton replaced Scacciati, who had been suddenly summoned
and as quickly disposed of.[38]

The differences in the reception of *Turandot* in Italy, in England,
and in the United States are instructive. The Italian critics' initial
response to Puccini's final opera was, almost without exception, enthusiastic. Besides the emotional connotations of *Turandot* as
Puccini's posthumous work, they responded to the beauty and im-
pressiveness of the score; they wrote of the great expansion of Puccini's musical and dramatic horizons; they commented on his greater
maturity of style and praised the splendor of his orchestration.
Turandot appeared at a fortunate moment, for just then there were
a number of big-voiced sopranos and tenors to introduce it to the
many opera houses of Italy. Since the beginning of its career,
Turandot has maintained itself in the active repertory. As the vogue
for outdoor performances grew, *Turandot* proved well adapted for
such stagings. On occasion the beginning of the performance has
been timed so that the moon's rising will coincide with the Act 1
Invocation to the Moon.

In England, the initial response to *Turandot* was mixed. At the
first production there were disappointments in the casting, and the
staging was not all it might have been. A devoted band of enthusi-
asts was won over by Puccini's score, but the general public remained cool. In 1928 the English soprano Eva Turner won a great
personal success in the name-part, and this helped turn the tide in
favor of the opera. When it was included in the gala Coronation
Season of 1937, sung by Turner and Martinelli, *Turandot* became
firmly sealed in the English affections, a place it shows no signs of
losing.

In the United States, the vocal splendor of Jeritza's Turandot and
Lauri-Volpi's Calaf made a deep impression, but the critical reception of Puccini's score was decidedly lukewarm. Today it is a little
difficult to tell what caused the critics of 1926 to take a jaundiced

Alfio Tedesco (Pong), Max Altglass (Altoum), and George Cehanovsky (the
Mandarin).
38. Bianca Scacciati (1894-1948) was a classic example of an Italian soprano with
a strong, vibrant voice, well regarded in Italy, and found intolerable in England.
In Italy her Turandot was regarded as the best until Gina Cigna made her mark
in the part. Scacciati continued to sing until 1942.

attitude toward the work. In its first production, *Turandot* survived for twenty-one performances in four seasons at the Metropolitan. Thereafter, for almost three decades it was neglected. Oddly enough the opera did not reach Chicago until 1933, although Raisa, the Turandot of the world *première*, had been a regular member of the resident company there. The New York City Center presented a small-scale production of the opera in 1950. In San Francisco it was given in two seasons during the 1950's.

The great resurgence of popularity came with the revival at the Metropolitan on 24 February 1961. Leopold Stokowski conducted, and Birgit Nilsson and Franco Corelli sang the roles of Turandot and Calaf. With this revival, *Turandot* won enthusiastic acceptance as an integral part of the Metropolitan repertory.

As the account of Puccini's composing of *Turandot* should make clear, the libretto was painfully evolved, only very gradually taking its present form. Although the text ultimately derives from Gozzi's play, the action has been so considerably changed that the version of Adami and Simoni can almost be regarded as an independent work. They replaced the loose, episodic construction of the original with an admirably unified design. The chief things they retained from the play are the exotic Chinese setting, the Princess who takes a dim view of men—Gozzi's heroine is much less glacial and domineering than her operatic counterpart—and the device of the riddles. Some of the other ingredients of the libretto have distant antecedents in the play, but they have been transformed, really re-created, by the librettists.

One way to approach the merits of the libretto is through the characters. First claim to our attention belongs to Turandot. During the first act, she appears only briefly *and silently* to give the order for the execution of the Prince of Persia (an unsuccessful riddle-solver); that is all we see of her, yet she dominates the entire act. At the very opening of the opera, the Mandarin reads her edict, which establishes at once her position and power. Her presence continues to be felt. It is her cruelty that has whipped the blood-maddened crowd into a frenzy. Her pervasive influence even colors the Invocation to the Moon, which has for its central image the simile of a bloodless decapitated head. Her appearance is enough literally to enchant Calaf; once he has seen her, his one thought is to win her. The rest of the action of Act 1 deals with those who try to impede Calaf or to dissuade him from his purpose. The act closes with Calaf striking the gong to announce his acceptance of Turandot's challenge.

Again, Turandot is absent from the opening scene of Act 2, the intermezzo for the three Ministers, but she and her bloodthirsty ways and her demoralizing influence are their chief topic of conversation. When she first opens her mouth, at just about the midpoint of the opera, her domination becomes even more palpable. Those who feel that the equilibrium of the work is upset by the sympathetic character of Liù—an unbalancing due to the coincidence that Puccini lived to complete Liù's death scene, but not the final duet—should remember that Turandot has the power and fascination to attract dozens of men to risk death, that Calaf from his first glimpse of Turandot senses the fires beneath her icy exterior, and that he is really in love with Turandot. There are those, too, who say that the libretto for the final scenes is defective, but this is a judgment I find it difficult to agree with. In the closing pages Turandot's idiom has much the same note of almost ferocious intensity that marks her earlier lines. She is deeply shaken by Calaf's kiss, and her aria *Del mio primo pianto*, which is frequently cut, unfortunately, makes it clear how deeply she is shaken and how ambivalent her feelings toward Calaf have been from the beginning.

> TURANDOT: How many men I have seen die for me!
> Though I scorned them, I was afraid for you!
> In your eyes there was the light of heroes!

Her capitulation is as intense as her previous cruelty had been. The development of her character is consistent.

It has always struck me as curious that many writers about Puccini treat the text of this final scene as though it were spurious or incomplete. This is just not so. Puccini accepted this part of the text, he was pleased with it, and he started to set it to music. The latest date on his sketches is 10 October 1924, less than a month before he left for Brussels.

Calaf is unique among Puccini's heroes because he strikes a genuinely heroic note. He makes no confessions of weakness, no tearful pleas, no outbursts of passionate nostalgia. Calaf sees what he wants and by his own skill, his ingenuity, and the force of his personality he wins his goal. It is important to remember that Calaf does not love Liù. Although he appreciates her faithful service to

his father, he never looks on her as more than an exceptionally devoted slave. There is no inconsistency or callousness on Calaf's part
that as soon as Liu's body is borne sorrowfully away he starts his
serious wooing of Turandot. One important aspect of his true hero-
ism that is often overlooked is that more than gallantly giving
Turandot the chance to guess his riddle (his name), he tells her his
name, thereby throwing himself on her mercy and trusting in the
sincerity of her newly awakened love. This is the most heroic of all
Calaf's acts.

For most people, the role of Liù is the most immediately appeal-
ing and effective in the opera. Yet it is important to remember that
she exists as a point of contrast and indirectly as a means for soften-
ing Turandot's heart. That Turandot is at all affected by Liù's
death must be indicated by subtle acting, for only by one word is
Liù's influence upon her revealed. When Turandot sees Liu's fear-
lessness in the face of torture, she demands to know what power
has given her such courage. When Liù answers, "Love," Turandot
softly echoes the word, obviously much struck by Liù's reply. I
think those critics who like to compare Liù's sacrifice with that of
Butterfly tend to obscure a significant difference. Butterfly makes
her sacrifice as a mother, while Liù makes hers for the memory of a
smile. Nevertheless, the character of Liù, who has her distant point
of origin in Gozzi's Adelma, is a cherishable creation. Both her text
and music are triumphs of understatement.

Adami and Simoni display their greatest originality in the three
masks: Ping, the Grand Chancellor; Pang, the Grand Purveyor; and
Pong, the Grand Cook. Their equivalents in Gozzi's play are the
traditional *commedia dell'arte* figures of Pantalone, Brighella, and
Truffaldino, who take no part in the action but improvise commentary upon it, rather like a comic chorus of three. In the opera,
however, the masks participate in the action as well as responding
to it. Although they exist in one dimension as stylized grotesques,
they possess a core of humanity, which is shown by their homesick
longing to escape from Turandot's endless beheadings and by the
emotion Liù's death generates in them. In spite of their pungent
mockery, as when they try to persuade Calaf that one hundred
women would afford more varied recreation than a single Turandot, and in spite of their sneering at death, even they are susceptible
to the power of heroic love. They always appear together and they
are only partially individualized, but nonetheless their corporate

existence gives them a weight and balance in this libretto that makes them unique in the gallery of Puccini characters.

The libretto's appeal lies in more than these clearly cut characters. Not only are the major characters sharply drawn, but even the more static ones of Timur and the practically centenarian Emperor Altoum. Part of the libretto's success depends on the clear way all the participants are brought together and interact. All of them to some extent are touched by the power of love. But the libretto does more than relate the characters to a powerful underlying theme; it creates a haunting world, legendary and half-barbarous, where these events take place and where these persons live. The plot is further integrated by the limitation of setting to the palace and its garden and by the restriction of time to the events that occur between moonrise and dawn. All the difficulties and frustrations its writing entailed aside, Adami's and Simoni's libretto for *Turandot* is a first-class example of its genre.

The score of *Turandot* is undeniably Puccini's greatest achievement. Its exotic clangor, its virile impetus, and its brilliant orchestration are healthy signs of Puccini's bold breaking of new ground. Yet, at the same time, one can argue that *Turandot* represents a logical progression of Puccini's methods and practices. Surprisingly enough, his hand shows no signs of age, only greater strength and a more mature grasp of aesthetic problems.

If one were to single out two of Puccini's earlier operas which point toward *Turandot* as the culmination of his style, one could turn to *Manon Lescaut* and *La Fanciulla*. Some aspects of the general plan of *Manon Lescaut*, particularly its first act, resemble *Turandot*. The large units of Act 1 of *Manon Lescaut* are somewhat analogous to the movements of a symphony; although the units in *Turandot* are more flexible and varied than those in the earlier score, they can be seen to have an organic relationship. The Mandarin's Proclamation is the introduction; the chorus summoning the executioner, Tu-Pin-Pao, forms one of the main themes of the allegro first movement; the Moon chorus launches the second; the Masks introduce the scherzo; and Calaf's aria *Non piangere, Liù* is the basis of the finale. The monumental grandeur of the first act of *Turandot* constitutes one of the most sustained accomplishments of Puccini's career. Yet, when one views it in terms of Puccini's total output, the only other act that remotely resembles its underlying structure is the opening act of *Manon Lescaut*. With *La Bohème*, Puccini began to use a lapidary technique, constructing an act out of carefully wrought and contrasting details, building up a musical mosaic. This technique served him well, and there are some traces of this approach, even in Act 1 of *Turandot*. But what gives that act its over-all breadth and eloquence is a more spacious development of its materials.

Another striking feature of *Turandot* is the extensive use of the chorus as a dynamic agent. Again this is most clearly seen in Act 1 of the opera, for in Act 2 its use is primarily ceremonial, and in the first scene of Act 3, elegiac. Again, there are parallels with *Manon Lescaut*, with the extensive use of the chorus in Act 1 and its highly dramatic use in the embarkation scene. One thinks also of the exposition of the opening act of *La Fanciulla*, but here the miners often are used as a chorus of comprimarios, rather than the usual chorus. The writing for the chorus in *La Fanciulla*, particularly in Minstrel's Song ("Old Dog Tray") with its widely spaced parts to give greater resonance, resembles the techniques used by Puccini in the more lyrical choral passages in *Turandot*.

The resemblances between *La Fanciulla* and *Turandot* make the latter opera seem the realization of some of the more experimental aspects of the earlier score. The highly individualized orchestration that capitalizes on clashing timbres and unexpected harmonies, as in *La Fanciulla*, is carried much further in *Turandot*. The breezy impetus animating some pages of *La Fanciulla*, such as the brief prelude, is an anticipation of the tremendous energy that seethes through much of *Turandot*. There is a faint parallel between the haunting, nocturnal opening of Act 3, scene 1 of *Turandot* and the finely evocative, economical opening to the last act of *La Fanciulla*. Puccini's gift for creating at once a landscape of the emotions was never stronger than in *Turandot*.

In still another way *Turandot* can be seen as a culmination of Puccini's practice. From Manon and Mimì, through Tosca, Butterfly, Minnie, Angelica, to Turandot, there can be detected a progression in Puccini's demands upon the soprano voice. I am not speaking here of weight of voice, of lyric or dramatic, but of Puccini's demands of range and *tessitura*. The role of Mimì, for instance, except for the pianissimo high C at the end of Act 1, is not vocally a very demanding one—but expressively, very. Not as demanding a role as Tosca, which in the torture scene and the Act 3 description of Scarpia's murder requires power and stamina at the top of the range. The role of Butterfly, because of its length and its many emotional climaxes, is one that exacts a good deal more of a singer than its many 'little' effects would suggest. The role of Minnie requires a soprano with a strong top range, and if one thinks of those sixteen bars, added while Puccini was working on *Turandot*,[39] there is a passage that calls for great facility in the immediate neighborhood of high C. The role of Angelica, particularly the pages following the intermezzo, concentrates heavily on notes above the staff. The soprano Maria Labia, the Giorgetta of the Italian *première* of *Il Tabarro*, claims that she told Puccini to his face that there was "too much screaming" in the final scene of *Suor Angelica*.[40] The demands of the role of Turandot are greater than those of any of these earlier roles.

Puccini's concept of the voice as an expressive instrument and his notion of its range of telling effect was undoubtedly modified by his listening to and studying the soprano roles of Richard Strauss. Not that Puccini sought to imitate the high-flying cantilena of Strauss or the Bavarian composer's melodic structure, which is so idiomatically shaped by German syntax. The lesson that Puccini derived from Strauss, having seen *Salome* first in 1907, *Elektra* in 1909, and *Die Frau ohne Schatten* in 1920, was an increasingly optimistic view of the expressive possibilities and the stamina that could be called for in the upper reaches of the soprano range. Before Puccini felt realigned with La Scala as a result of the anniversary revival of *Manon Lescaut*, he had thought of giving the *première* of *Turandot* at the Metropolitan. In April 1922 he wrote to Gatti-Casazza about *Turandot* and said that he saw 'no other' singer for the title role than Jeritza.[41] Thus, we can assume that Puccini had the voice of Jeritza, which in its prime was practically indefatigable in the upper fifth of its range, in mind when he conceived the *tessitura* of the role of Turandot.

There is a corresponding development in Puccini's demands for the tenor voice. We have only to create a series, consisting of Des Grieux's aria in Act 3 of *Manon Lescaut*, Johnson's confession aria (see Ex. 5, *La Fanciulla*), and Luigi's outburst (see Ex. 5, *Il Tabarro*). Puccini wrote the role of Calaf for a tenor with both

39. See p. 151.
40. Quoted in *Carteggi Pucciniani*, p. 470.
41. Letter in the Archives of the Metropolitan Opera House.

power and ease in his upper register. Consider such a passage as this:

Or this:

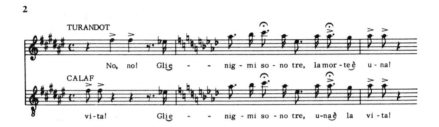

While the three Masks are one of the most delightful and original aspects of the score of *Turandot*, there are some anticipatory
glimmerings of this style in *Gianni Schicchi*. One thinks of the lucid
part-writing in the trio of the women cajoling Schicchi (see Ex. 4,
Gianni Schicchi) and in the ironical little song bidding farewell to
Florence (see Ex. 5, *Gianni Schicchi*). These excerpts show that
the potentiality for this vein and style already existed in Puccini.[42]

To turn from a consideration of *Turandot* as a logical development of Puccini's earlier practice, an examination of some of the
key episodes of the opera show Puccini's great sureness of hand.
The central episode of the plot, the scene of the riddles, is based
upon a sequence of three chords:

42. The women's trio in *Gianni Schicchi* and the Masks in *Turandot* have one
thing in common: in each case the lowest voice is written on top (Zita and Ping,
respectively).

At their first appearance, their striking color comes from the scoring—violas, woodwinds, and muted brass. During the first riddle,
Turandot's lines are practically unaccompanied, except by punctuating chords, until the clarinet starts to double her line and two
solo cellos play a little figure, marked *come un lamento:*

4

This figure bears a family resemblance to the pseudo-lament in
Gianni Schicchi, but here its effect is very different. In *Turandot,*
the sequence is isolated, while in *Gianni Schicchi* it is set in a
bustling context (see Ex. 1, *Gianni Schicchi*). In Example 4 above,
the harmonic pinch of the B-flat against A produces the effect of
an uneasy shudder. This figure recurs during Turandot's asking the
riddles and adds much to the atmosphere of suspense.

In their melodic line Turandot's enigmas closely resemble each
other, each starting with the sequence of Example 3. The suspense
of the third riddle is increased by its being pitched a semitone higher
than the first two. Although the riddles begin identically their ends
differ and each is orchestrated differently. In the second riddle, the
oboe and bassoon double the voice, while muted violins and violas
play tingling runs that alternate with clarinet flourishes. In the
third, the doubling of the oboe and bassoon is reinforced by the
addition of clarinets and English horn, but in the last half of this
last riddle, the tension is increased by doubling the voice just by
two flutes in their distinctive lower register.

Calaf's replies to the riddles are brief and confident. The worrying figure of Example 4 is absent. Much of the feeling of confidence
comes from the prominent note of the dominant sustained in the
next to the last phrase and the resulting sense of a resolute cadence.
Although his answers begin ritualistically with the contours of

Example 3, the orchestration is brighter here, and the ominous thudding chords of Turandot's questions are replaced by impulsive figures for clarinet, violins, and cellos that link the phrases.

Much of the tension of the riddle scene comes from the stylized, ritualistic effect given by the predictable recurrence of Example 3 and from the nerve-wracking harping on Example 4. The suspense created by Calaf's tardy answer to the final riddle further increases the effectiveness of this scene.

The intermezzo scene for the Masks that opens Act 2 is one of the highlights of the score. Although it does not advance the plot, this scene, which lasts about twelve minutes, gives no feeling of delaying the opera; rather it enhances the atmosphere. It contains a wealth of melodic ideas and much ingenious and effective orchestration. It begins with only three bars before the singing starts, but these few seconds of music set the scene and establish the grotesquely Oriental mood.

Here, the bass line echoes the top line at the interval of a minor second producing a clash of harmony that is not so much harsh as brittle-sounding. Much of the distinctive color is given by the pizzicato strings, the bass xylophone, and the snare drum, in addition to the woodwinds and horns. The third beat of each bar gets an unusual stress from harp glissandi, the timpani, and a chord for three trombones. Puccini's mastery of orchestral effect demonstrated here continues unabated, if not always so exotically, throughout this scene.

The greatest possible contrast to the bustling brittleness of the opening of this scene occurs when Ping's thoughts turn lyrically and nostalgically to his home by the blue lake surrounded by bamboo:

6

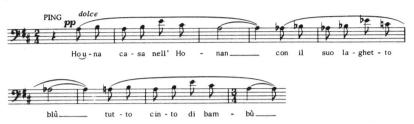

While the start of this episode may seem a little reminiscent of Ravel in an idyllic vein, the way Puccini develops it is highly character-istic of his own style. The orchestration of Example 6 is both deli-cate and evocative, combining two flutes, two clarinets, three-part chords for the celestra, and the harp playing harmonics, while the bassoon contributes a gentle ostinato. This episode is in ternary form, the second section beginning with Pong's thoughts of his forests near Tsiang. In the curtailed final section, Example 6 returns, but now it is played by the flutes, harps, and strings, the violins being directed to play *sul tasto* (on the fingerboard). The whole intermezzo scene is a model of elegant inventiveness. The transitions throughout this episode, and throughout the whole score, are con-ducted with great surety and finesse.

The role of Liù is particularly fortunate in its solo moments. Her musical ambience is in a sense a private one, as her voice, except in the finale to Act 1, rarely overlaps with another. Her private mu-sical world is established from almost the first moment when Calaf asks her who she is. A gentle theme underlies her explanation:

7

(By an odd and probably unintentional coincidence a very similar pentatonic melody occurs when the Masks ruefully foresee the ruin of China.)

8

Liù's music lies extremely well for the voice. Her first little passage ends with a pianissimo high B-flat, sustained over a series of descending chords. Coming after so much that has been fiercely strenuous, this quiet moment sets Liù apart. While her first real aria, *Signore ascolta*, is a strictly pentatonic melody, her two arias before her suicide in Act 3 are both diatonic, and the melodies are very conjunct. Particularly moving is her final aria, *Tu che di gel sei cinta*, and some of its emotional intensity may derive from the words, which are Puccini's own.[43]

9

At the beginning of this aria the voice is doubled by the mournful color of the oboe and bassoon (here very different in effect from their doubling of the second riddle). The off-beat impetus is established by the clarinets. The whole orchestral accompaniment up to the end of this scene is piercingly eloquent. Each time the melody of Example 9 recurs it is differently scored. The choral writing, too, in this episode is extraordinarily moving. A passage that never fails to produce a deep impression is this one, in which the crowd tries to propitiate Liù's shade.

10

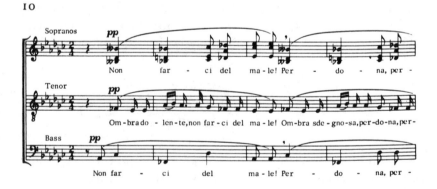

Throughout this opera Puccini's writing for the chorus is of a calibre achieved by few opera composers. With the possible ex-

43. The melody of Liù's aria is almost a perfect inversion of the Prunier–Lisette duet from *La Rondine*, see Ex. 7 *Rondine*.

ception of the Invocation to the Moon, *Turandot* contains no choral passages that produce an effect out of context, such as occur in the early Verdi operas or in *Carmen* or *Faust*. The influence of Moussorgsky can be discerned occasionally in *Turandot*, especially in the overlapping lines of the propulsive chorus summoning the executioner. Again, some of the cries of "Morte! Morte!" give rise to memories of the way Verdi writes choral exclamations in *Aïda*.

The massive ceremonial choruses that open and close the riddle scene (Act 2, scene 2) show a remarkable variety of effect. The various repetitions of the hymn in praise of the Emperor, "Diecimila anni al nostro Imperatore"—one of a number of real Chinese melodies that Puccini adapted to his uses—show Puccini's uncommon resourcefulness in choral writing. Near the end of the scene, the chorus sings the melody jubilantly:

Earlier in the scene, they sing the hymn gently and respectfully:

More than any other of Puccini's operas, *Turandot* repays close study. The details of effective scoring are present in profusion. It is instructive to see how Puccini creates so quickly and smoothly the transition from the peroration of Calaf's *Nessun dorma* to the characteristic tone of the Masks in half a dozen bars. From the grandiose tone of the opening to the deep pathos of Liù's death, *Turandot* encompasses a wide range of moods, each one instantly characterized.

Before leaving the score of *Turandot*, it is important to have a look at Alfano's conclusion. Many harsh words have been written about Alfano's work on it, and this is not surprising, considering the quality of Puccini's work on the score and the tragic circumstances that left it incomplete. If one can put aside a natural resentment that the opera had to be completed by another composer, it is possible, I think, to see that Alfano's music is not an act of desecration, nor is it without merit, although it does not match the rest of the opera.

As is well known, Puccini left pencil sketches for the final episodes. They consist of 23 sheets, 13 of them having music on both sides, making a total of 36 pages of notes in all. From these Alfano worked up his conclusion. Puccini's sketches are in Ricordi's archives, as are *both* versions of Alfano's completion, the first which was returned by Toscanini to be modified, and the present one which is printed in the scores of *Turandot*.

Most people are prejudiced against Alfano's contribution by the opening of it. Following after the exquisite music accompanying Liù's cortege, music of haunting, liquid sadness, the next episode begins with a dismaying blatancy. Yet, Calaf's lines, "Principessa di morte," and their supporting harmony appear in one of Puccini's sketches. One may not like this passage, one cannot be sure that Puccini might not have modified his original ideas when he orchestrated them, but it does represent Puccini's own ideas, not Alfano's. What makes the wrench from the previous episode seem particularly noticeable is the absence of one of Puccini's subtle transitions that shifts tone and mood seamlessly.

The sketches run from the opening of the scene up to the first phrases of Turandot's aria *Del mio primo pianto*, although the first phrase of Turandot's too frequently omitted aria is a halftone higher in the sketches than it appears in the present score. There is a second, briefer, but important, excerpt of twelve bars in Puccini's sketches: this passage runs from Calaf's "Il mio mistero?" to Turandot's "So il tuo nome!" This passage, therefore, includes the important phrase of Calaf's revelation of his name.

Some other things in this final episode should be specified as Puccini's. For instance, the writing of the off-stage wordless chorus of women that is sung against Calaf's phrase, "Oh! mio fiore mattutino!," exists in the sketches. So does Calaf's phrase "La tua gloria," which recurs with such moving effect in Turandot's aria *Del mio primo pianto*. In my opinion, this aria should be retained in performance. Its relatively low *tessitura* provides necessary relief in a scene that is written pretty much at the top of the voice—in both senses. With some release of tension, the scene seems shorter, in fact, *with* the aria than without it. Furthermore, this aria is essential in making Turandot's conversion convincing. Those who reject this aria, who say what does it matter since Puccini didn't write it anyway, are using an untenable argument. Puccini's sketches show that he *did* want the aria, and he left indications of how he wanted it to begin.

Certainly, Alfano's style falls short of the sheen and elegance of Puccini's. Alfano's doubling is more consistent and less varied than Puccini's obvious but carefully controlled use of this device. Most sadly lacking in Alfano's contribution are the shifting inner voices to inflect the harmony and to give a secondary stress to subordinate beats, aspects so characteristic of Puccini's music. A good deal of Alfano's writing strikes the ear as too four-square, lacking the ever-shifting impulses we find in Puccini. The least satisfactory pages are those of the choral conclusion that follows Turandot's declaration that the Prince's name is Love. Even in a *tutti* passage, Puccini carefully controls gradations of instrumental resources; he holds back reserves of power; he surprises with splashes of unexpected color. Alfano's climax starts big and monotonously continues just as big. At this point, he might well have been more daring.

Alfano's task was truly thankless. He could not avoid criticism, no matter how well or ill he did his job. He was not, he could not be, a Puccini. Except for the blaring final pages and a certain uninflected brashness at times, he did his uncomfortable assignment commendably. Above all, he was gratifyingly faithful to the hints and clues and phrases Puccini left.

LIST OF PUCCINI'S WORKS

Operas

Le Villi	First performed (in one act):	Milan, 31 May 1884.
	First performed (in two acts):	Turin, 26 December 1884.
Edgar	First performed (in 4 acts):	Milan, 21 April 1889.
	First performed (in 3 acts):	Ferrara, 28 February 1892.
Manon Lescaut		Turin, 1 February 1893.
La Bohème		Turin, 1 February 1896.
Tosca		Rome, 14 January 1900.
Madama Butterfly		Milan, 17 February 1904.
La Fanciulla del West		New York, 10 December 1910.
La Rondine		Monte Carlo, 27 March 1917.
Il Trittico (*Il Tabarro*, *Suor Angelica*, and *Gianni Schicchi*)		New York, 14 December 1918.
Turandot		Milan, 25 April 1926.

Selected Non-Operatic Works

a. Puccini's religious music, except for a Requiem (1905), was written prior to his entering the Milan Conservatory.

227

b. His choral music includes a youthful cantata, a hunting chorus, "Inno a Diana" (1897), another entitled "Avanti, Urania" (1899). The most important of these is the "Inno a Roma" (1919, publ. 1923).

c. His chief orchestral work is the *Capriccio sinfonico* (1883).

d. His most important chamber music, besides a good deal of student works is found in *Two Minutes* and *Crisantemi* (both 1890).

e. Puccini wrote a number of songs while he was a student, but of his later ones, "Sole e amore" (1888) and "E l'ucellino" (1899) are the most important.

SELECTED BIBLIOGRAPHY

Adami, Giuseppe. *Il romanzo della vita di Giacomo Puccini*. Rome, 1944.

Aldrich, Richard. *Concert Life in New York (1902-1923)*. New York, 1941.

Barberini, Urbano. "Puccini e l' 'Inno a Roma'." *Strenna dei Romanisti*. Rome, 1965.

Bloomfield, Arthur J. *The San Francisco Opera: 1923-1961*. New York, 1961.

Carelli, Emma. *Trent'anni di vita del teatro lirico*. Rome, 1932.

Carner, Mosco. *Puccini: A Critical Biography*. New York, 1959.

Casa Ricordi: 1808-1959. Ed. Claudio Sartori. Milan, 1958.

D'Amico, Fedele. "Una ignorata pagina 'maliperiana' di *Suor Angelica*," *Rassegna Musicale Curci*, XIX (March 1966) 6-16.

Davis, Ronald. *Opera in Chicago*. New York, 1965.

De la Guardia, Ernesto and Roberto Herrera. *El arte lirico en el Teatro Colón: 1908-1933*. Buenos Aires, 1933.

Del Fiorentino, Dante. *Immortal Bohemian*. New York, 1952.

De Schauensee, Max. *The Collector's Verdi and Puccini*. Philadelphia, 1962.

Eaton, Quaintance. *The Boston Opera Company*. New York, 1965.

Eaton, Quaintance. *Opera Caravan*. New York, 1957.

Forsyth, Cecil. *Orchestration*. New York, 1942.

Fraccaroli, Arnaldo. *La vita di Giacomo Puccini*. Milan, 1925.

Gatti, Carlo. *Il Teatro alla Scala*. Milan, 1964. 2 vols.

Gatti-Casazza, Giulio. *Memories of Opera*. New York, 1941.

Giacomo Puccini. Ed. Claudio Sartori. Milan, 1958.

Giacomo Puccini nel centenario della nascita. Lucca, 1958.

Giovannetti, Gustavo. *Giacomo Puccini nei ricordi di un musicista lucchese.* Lucca, 1958.

Hughes, Spike. *Famous Puccini Operas.* New York, 1962.

Karlik, Heinrich. *The Vienna Opera.* Vienna, 1963.

Key, Pierre V. R. *Enrico Caruso.* Boston, 1922.

Kolodin, Irving. *The Metropolitan Opera: 1883-1966.* New York, 1966.

La Scala, December 1958. (The whole issue is devoted to Puccini.)

Loewenberg, Alfred. *Annals of Opera: 1597-1940.* Geneva, 1955, rev. ed. 2 vols.

Marek, George. *Puccini.* New York, 1951.

Monaldi, Marchese Gino. *Giacomo Puccini e la sua opera.* Rome, n.d.

Pagani, Severino. *Alfredo Catalani.* Milano, 1957.

Paladini, Carlo. *Giacomo Puccini.* Ed. Marzia Paladini. Florence, 1961.

Pizzetti, Ildebrando. "Giacomo Puccini," *Musicisti contemporanei.* Milan, 1914.

Puccini, Giacomo. *Carteggi Pucciniani.* Ed. Eugenio Gara. Milan, 1958.

Puccini, Giacomo. *Letters of Giacomo Puccini.* Ed. Giuseppe Adami. Philadelphia, 1931.

Puccioni, Mario. *Cacce e cacciatori di Toscana.* Florence, 1932.

Ricci, Luigi. *Puccini interprete di se stesso.* Milan, 1954.

Rosenthal, Harold, and John Warrack. *Concise Oxford Dictionary of Opera.* London, 1964.

Rosenthal, Harold. *Two Centuries of Opera at Covent Garden.* London, 1958.

Seligman, Vincent. *Puccini among Friends.* New York, 1938.

Seltsam, William H. *Metropolitan Opera Annals.* New York, 1947.

Shaw, Bernard. *Music in London: 1890-94.* London, 1950. 3 vols.

Specht, Richard. *Giacomo Puccini.* London, 1933.

Torrefranco, Fausto. *Giacomo Puccini e l'opera internazionale.* Milan, 1912.

Wolf, Stéphane. *Un Demi-Siècle d'Opéra-Comique: 1900-1950.* Paris, 1953.

SUMMARIES OF OPERA PLOTS

Le Villi (two-act version)
Setting: The Black Forest

Act 1 takes place in a clearing in front of the house of Guglielmo Wulf (baritone). It is springtime and there are tables outdoors laden with food and drink. The foresters are celebrating the engagement of Guglielmo's daughter Anna (soprano) to Roberto (tenor). Because an elderly female relative of Roberto's has left him her fortune, he must go to Mainz to claim his inheritance. After the guests dance a *Ländler*, Anna comes forward with a spray of forget-me-nots which she tenderly lays on Roberto's luggage, with the hope the flowers will make Roberto mindful of their message. Roberto returns and tries to cheer Anna. When she confesses her fears, he swears eternal loyalty, a pledge she joyfully echoes. As the hour of his departure comes, all join in a solemn prayer for his safe journey.

The first intermezzo, "The Abandonment," is preceded by a poem telling how a "siren" at Mainz has so thoroughly seduced Roberto with her "obscene orgies" that he has forgotten Anna completely. Near the end of this intermezzo, Anna's funeral procession is seen behind a scrim. The second intermezzo, "The Witches' Sabbath," is also introduced by a poem, this one describing how the Villis—spirits of abandoned girls—lie in wait for their betrayers and dance them to death. The poem further tells that Roberto's "siren" has jilted him and that at long last he is returning home. This intermezzo concludes with a ballet for the Villis and their attendant will-o'-the-wisps dancing through the wintry forest.

Act 2 opens with Guglielmo's brooding over his daughter's un-avenged death. Guglielmo re-enters his house and the taunting voices of the Villis are heard. Roberto appears, tormented by remorse and hop-ing for pardon, but the supernatural voices make him feel accursed. Anna's spirit appears before him, announcing that she is her own venge-ance. Deaf to his apologies, she tells him of her disillusioning wait and stretches out her arms to him. At once they are surrounded by the whirling Villis. Finally the exhausted Roberto falls and dies at Anna's feet. The Villis sing, "Hosannah!"

Edgar (three act version)
Setting: Flanders, 1302

Act 1 is set in the square of a Flemish village, with its church and tavern and, near by, Edgar's house. At dawn the Angelus sounds, and the peas-ants go off to the fields. Fidelia (soprano) wakes Edgar (tenor), who is asleep at the tavern. As he appears out of sorts, she breaks off a branch of almond blossoms and, kissing it, throws it to him. Edgar fol-lows Fidelia. Tigrana (mezzosoprano), a Moorish waif raised by Fi-delia's father, appears and waits for Edgar, whom she chides for loving the innocent Fidelia. Tigrana points out, over Edgar's furious protests, that his tastes run more toward depravity. With Tigrana's mocking laughter in his ears, Edgar enters his house. Fidelia's brother Frank (bar-itone) reproves Tigrana for her failure to meet him the previous night. When she mocks him, he weeps and rails against the erotic slavery that binds him to Tigrana. Church services begin, and as the congregation sings a hymn, Tigrana sings a decidedly secular song. The people are scandalized by her song and outraged when Edgar defends her. For his part, Edgar is so furious that he sets fire to his house and announces his determination to flee with Tigrana. Frank opposes him, but the pleas of neither Fidelia nor her father Gualtiero (bass) can prevent a duel, in which Frank is wounded. He curses Tigrana as the guilty pair runs off.

Act 2 On the moon-drenched terrace of a sumptuous palace, Edgar describes his disillusionment with his life as a voluptuary and thinks longingly of the innocent Fidelia. Tigrana approaches and tries to re-arouse his passion, but her most beguiling blandishments cannot banish Edgar's feelings of shame and horror. When a troop of soldiers passes, Edgar is astonished to recognize their leader as Frank. As Frank's re-sentment of Edgar has been purged by patriotism, he welcomes Edgar as a comrade. Tigrana tries to prevent her lover's departure, but when he insists on marching off with the soldiers she promises revenge.

Act 3 A catafalque has been erected near the fortress of Courtray. The funeral procession winds through the dusk. Following the coffin are Frank and a monk, his face shrouded by his cowl. The crowd sings a Requiem for Edgar, whom Frank praises as a hero fallen in battle. When the monk tries to stir up the crowd with talk of Edgar's past sins, Fidelia speaks in defense of her only love. Gualtiero leads her away from the bier. Tigrana approaches and kneels to pray, closely observed by Frank and the monk. They offer her splendid jewels if she will speak out against Edgar. The monk condemns Edgar as a traitor, and Tigrana, dazzled by the gems, concurs. Outraged, the crowd tears open Edgar's casket and are amazed to find it contains only an empty suit of armor. The monk throws back his cowl and reveals himself as Edgar. He threatens Tigrana, who barely escapes his wrath. Edgar embraces Fidelia, proclaiming that he has been reborn. Suddenly Tigrana returns and stabs Fidelia. Edgar falls sobbing by Fidelia's body, as the soldiers seize Tigrana.

Manon Lescaut
Setting: The second half of the eighteenth century

Act 1 In a square in Amiens, Edmondo (tenor) sings a mock-pastoral to the delight of his fellow students. When Des Grieux (tenor) appears, Edmondo joshes him about love. Des Grieux declares himself equally susceptible to blondes and brunettes. The student's merrymaking is interrupted by the arrival of the coach from Arras. Lescaut (baritone) and Geronte (bass) descend and help Manon (soprano) to alight. Des Grieux is struck by her beauty, and when her brother leaves her alone briefly he engages her in conversation. He learns that her name is Manon Lescaut, that she is convent bound. When her brother calls her, Manon leaves, but not before she agrees to meet Des Grieux later. He voices his infatuation with Manon, a declaration overheard by Edmondo and the delighted students. They go off, and Geronte tells Lescaut indirectly that he has designs on Manon, a suggestion the venial Lescaut does nothing to discourage. Edmondo returns and overhears the latter part of their conversation, including Geronte's arrangements with the innkeeper for a coach in which to abduct Manon. Edmondo reveals this plot to Des Grieux, who warns Manon of it, but then finding themselves so much in love, Manon and Des Grieux pre-empt the coach for themselves. Geronte is furious to find himself out-tricked, but Lescaut counsels against instant pursuit, for he knows that when Des Grieux's funds are exhausted Manon will welcome a generous protector.

Act 2 In her elegant boudoir in Geronte's mansion, Manon prepares for the evening's festivities. She cannot repress her wistfulness for the modest apartment she shared with Des Grieux. When Lescaut arrives, he guesses her train of thought and tells her he has been teaching Des Grieux how to gamble. Some musicians sent by Geronte entertain them with a madrigal. After Lescaut leaves in search of Des Grieux, Manon has a dancing lesson. Geronte and his friends come in to admire her ability. As Geronte dances with her, the others compliment them extravagantly. When they leave, Manon remains to freshen her toilette. Des Grieux appears and reproaches her for cruelly abandoning him. She confesses her fault and begs his forgiveness so persuasively that all Des Grieux's former love for her returns. As they embrace, Geronte returns. Manon seizes a mirror and shows Geronte his aged face and tells him to compare himself with the youthful Des Grieux. After Geronte leaves, seriously offended, Manon prepares to flee, but she cannot bear to leave all her possessions behind. Des Grieux reproaches her for her self-indulgence and thoughtlessness. Lescaut rushes in to warn them that Geronte has ordered Manon's arrest as a common prostitute and thief. Before the lovers can make good their escape, soldiers arrive and seize Manon.

Act 3 is preceded by an intermezzo. The curtain rises on a square at Le Havre, next to the port and adjacent to the jail where those awaiting deportation are held. In the darkness before the dawn, Des Grieux and Lescaut are outside the prison plotting to help Manon escape. When Lescaut goes to try to arrange her escape, Des Grieux talks to Manon through the window of her cell. Suddenly an alarm is raised, and Lescaut rushes in to tell Des Grieux that their plot has failed. The Sergeant (bass) starts the roll-call of the girls who are to be deported. When Manon appears, Des Grieux makes his way to her side. She urges him to forget her, but he tries to prevent her being led aboard. In despair he begs the captain to take pity on his misery and to allow him aboard as a simple sailor. Moved by Des Grieux's outburst, the Captain (baritone) consents.

Act 4 takes place on "an interminable desert on the frontier of New Orleans." Poorly dressed and close to exhaustion, Manon and Des Grieux appear. Manon has reached the limits of her strength. Despairing, Des Grieux tries to encourage her. She faints, and regaining consciousness she complains of thirst. Des Grieux goes off in a futile effort to find water. When she can no longer see him, Manon gives way to her terror at the thought of dying alone in the desert. Des Grieux returns empty-handed to discover Manon delirious and close to death. Faintly Manon assures him of her undying love. When she falls back dead, the sobbing Des Grieux embraces her body.

La Bohème
Setting: Paris, the Latin Quarter, 1830

Act 1 In their garret studio the poet Rodolfo (tenor) and the painter Marcello (baritone) complain of the winter cold. When they are joined by Colline (bass), Rodolfo tries to alleviate the chill by burning the manuscript of his latest drama. The flames have barely died down, when Schaunard (baritone) bursts in, scattering money and followed by boys laden with groceries and firewood. Schaunard's explanations of his windfall go unheeded by his friends, who eagerly examine the delicacies. Schaunard gives them a share of the money and declares that since it is Christmas Eve they must dine out. The landlord Benoit (bass) comes to demand the overdue rent. Marcello flatters Benoit into revealing an extramarital escapade; then, feigning moral indignation, the friends push him out of the room. When they prepare to leave for the Café Momus, Rodolfo explains that he must put the finishing touches on an article. Alone, Rodolfo starts to write, but soon his fancy flags. A timid knock reveals Mimì (soprano) on the landing; her candle has blown out in the drafty hallway. Rodolfo invites her in and relights her candle. Mimì almost faints and Rodolfo offers her a glass of wine. When she feels stronger she starts to leave, but discovers she has lost her key. Once again, the draft extinguishes her candle, whereupon Rodolfo surreptitiously blows out his candle, too. In the darkness they grope for the key, which Rodolfo finds and pockets; then his hand grazes Mimì's. He tells her about his life as a poet and about his dreams and aspirations. In return, Mimì artlessly describes her life as a maker of artificial flowers and reveals her longing for spring and its warm sunshine. Just then, Marcello and the others call up, urging Rodolfo to hurry and join them at the café. Seeing Mimì radiant in the moonlight, Rodolfo impulsively declares his love. Mimì responds passionately. Over Rodolfo's protests, she suggests they join his friends, They go out arm in arm.

Act 2 Later that evening the streets around the Café Momus are filled with a gay holiday throng. Rodolfo buys Mimì a lace-trimmed bonnet. The friends gather round a table at the café, and Rodolfo introduces Mimì to them. A toy-vendor Parpignol (tenor) passes by with his gay cart followed by a crowd of eager children and disapproving mothers. Mimì shows off her new bonnet. The friends are about to drink a toast when suddenly Marcello catches sight of his former love, Musetta (soprano), who has in tow a wealthy old roué, Alcindoro (bass). While Marcello studiously avoids Musetta, she just as assiduously tries to attract his attention, much to Alcindoro's chagrin and the crowd's amusement. Then in an all-out assault on Marcello, Musetta sings a waltz, a highly provocative bit of self-description. Then to rid herself of Alcindoro, she pretends her shoe pinches and sends him off to buy her a new pair. On one foot Musetta hops into Marcello's eager arms. The waiter now approaches Schaunard, who discovers that he and his friends have squandered their money and cannot pay their bill. Always resourceful, Musetta tells the waiter to add this bill to Alcindoro's. A company of soldiers passes, and the friends go off after them. Alcindoro returns with the new shoes, only to find Musetta gone and a staggering bill waiting for him.

Act 3   At the Barrière d'Enfer, one of the custom-gates of Paris, a group of crossing-sweepers and some milkwomen appear through the dim light of a chill February dawn and pass through the gate. From a nearby cabaret Musetta is heard singing her waltz. Mimì enters and inquires for Marcello. When he comes out of the cabaret and invites her to enter, she refuses when she learns Rodolfo is inside. Mimì pours out her heart to Marcello, telling him of Rodolfo's strange behavior and his jealousy. Marcello tries to console Mimì, who is shaken by a severe fit of coughing. When Rodolfo awakes and calls Marcello, the painter urges Mimì to leave without making a scene, but instead she hides behind a tree, overcome by anxiety and curiosity. Rodolfo comes out of the cabaret and starts to complain of Mimì's flirting. Marcello questions his sincerity; whereupon Rodolfo confesses that he truly loves Mimì, but that he is in despair over her rapidly declining health. This disclosure moves Marcello to pity, while the eavesdropping Mimì is filled with despair by it. A paroxysm of coughing and sobbing reveals Mimì's presence. A sudden outburst of wanton laughter causes Marcello to run into the cabaret to scold Musetta, leaving Mimì alone with Rodolfo. She tells him that she must leave him; she will send for her few possessions, but she will leave him her bonnet as a souvenir. Rodolfo reminds her of their past happiness and begs her not to leave him until spring has fully come. Mimì consents. Musetta and Marcello burst out of the cabaret, embroiled in a rancorous quarrel. They go off shouting at each other, and shortly after Mimì and Rodolfo slowly go off together, arm in arm.

Act 4   On a chill autumn day in their garret studio, Rodolfo is trying to write and Marcello stands at his easel, but their thoughts of the absent Mimì and Musetta make work impossible. Rodolfo gazes at Mimì's bonnet, while Marcello strokes a ribbon that Musetta left behind. Although Schaunard and Colline arrive with only one salt herring for dinner, the friends turn the meal into a facetious occasion. Their entertainment includes dancing for Rodolfo and Marcello and a strenuous mock-duel for Schaunard and Colline. When the fun is at its height, Musetta bursts in to say that Mimì is with her, but she has fainted on the landing. Rodolfo rushes out to carry her in. On a hastily improvised cot, Mimì looks around, pathetically eager to be surrounded by her friends once more. Aghast at their lack of medical supplies, Musetta leaves with Marcello to pawn her earrings so that she may buy Mimì a muff and some cordial. Colline decides to pawn his beloved great coat and takes Schaunard away with him. Alone with Rodolfo, Mimì has only pretended to drop off to sleep. They reminisce about their first meeting, and Mimì reveals that she knew all along that Rodolfo had found her key. Mimì weakens rapidly. The others return with the medicine and report that a doctor will shortly arrive. Delighted with the warmth of the muff, Mimì seems to drift off to sleep. Musetta murmurs a prayer as she warms the medicine over a spirit lamp. Rodolfo arranges Musetta's shawl to shade Mimì's face from the sun. Schaunard discovers that Mimì has died and whispers the news to the others. Turning around at the window, Rodolfo is puzzled by their strange behavior. Suddenly guessing the truth, he rushes to the bed and embraces Mimì's lifeless body.

Tosca
Setting: Rome, 14-15 June 1800.

Act 1   The stage represents part of the interior of the church of Sant' Andrea della Valle. An escaped political prisoner, Angelotti (bass), hurries in and starts to grope around a statue of the Virgin. At last he finds what he is seeking—the key to the Attavanti chapel—and hurriedly unlocks the grille and disappears from sight. The Sacristan (bass) enters grumpily, complaining about the painter who makes such a mess in church. While the Sacristan recites the Angelus, the painter Mario Cavaradossi (tenor) appears, climbs the scaffolding to his easel, and removes the sheet from his portrait of Mary Magdalen. The Sacristan is shocked to recognize it as a portrait of a woman who was praying there the day before. Taking up his brush, Cavaradossi contrasts the blonde portrait with the beauty of his dark-haired mistress, Tosca. The Sacristan's spirits rise when Cavaradossi tells him that he is not hungry enough to touch his well-filled hamper. Rubbing his hands in anticipation, the Sacristan leaves. Cavaradossi remains absorbed in his painting until he is startled by an unexpected noise. Investigating, he finds Angelotti hiding in the chapel. Recognizing the escaped prisoner at last, Cavaradossi greets him warmly. They are interrupted by Tosca calling, "Mario!" Cavaradossi pushes the prisoner back into the chapel and thrusts the hamper into his hands. The opera singer Tosca (soprano) enters, her suspicions aroused by the sound of whispering; she demands to know with whom Cavaradossi has been speaking. He chides her for her suspicions. Mollified, Tosca tells him that she will meet him at his country villa after her performance that evening. Glancing at the portrait, her jealousy surges again when she detects its resemblance to Angelotti's sister, the Marchesa Attavanti. Once again, Cavaradossi calms her jealousy, and she apologizes for her impulsiveness. Leaving, she again urges Cavaradossi to paint the Magdalen's eyes black. As soon as she is gone, Cavaradossi goes to Angelotti, who explains his plan to hide in the church until dark and then escape in the woman's clothing that his sister (the Marchesa Attavanti) had hidden for him. Now Cavaradossi understands why the Marchesa has spent so much time in the church lately. When Angelotti mentions his captor, Scarpia, Cavaradossi, who hates this brutal police chief, agrees to help Angelotti, no matter what the consequences. Just then the cannon from the Castel Sant' Angelo tells them that Angelotti's escape has been discovered. Cavaradossi offers to show Angelotti a safe hiding place in an abandoned well at his villa and to take him there.

No sooner have they run out than the Sacristan bustles in, followed by the choristers. The Sacristan announces gleefully that Bonaparte has been defeated in a great battle and that a special Te Deum will shortly be sung in the church, and that night in the Queen's apartment a cantata to celebrate the victory will be sung with Tosca as soloist. Overjoyed by all this good news, the choristers begin to dance in their excitement. Scarpia (baritone) suddenly appears and sharply denounces such unseemly behavior in church. Brusquely he orders his agent Spoletta (tenor) to search for the escaped prisoner. In short order Scarpia notices the open chapel, the empty hamper, and the portrait of the Marchesa. Even more, he has found in the chapel a fan bearing the lady's coat-of-arms. Tosca enters, come to inform Cavaradossi of the change in the evening's plans. She is both annoyed by Cavaradossi's absence and deeply upset by Scarpia's insinuations that the painter has gone to a rendezvous with the Attavanti. Reduced to tears, she sweeps out. As the church fills for the service of the Te Deum, Scarpia contemplates the execution of Angelotti and his own possession of Tosca. An outburst by the choir reminds him he is in church.

Act 2   That evening in his apartment in the Palazzo Farnese, Scarpia, counting on Tosca to lead him to his prey, envisions both Angelotti and Cavaradossi on the gallows. He orders his other agent, Sciarrone (baritone) to inform him when Tosca arrives at the palace. Musing to himself, Scarpia reflects how much more exciting violent possession is than milk-sop wooing. Spoletta enters and explains, to Scarpia's fury, that he has not found Angelotti, but that he has brought Cavaradossi along for interrogation. Cavaradossi stoutly denies any knowledge of Angelotti's whereabouts. Through an open window Tosca is heard singing the cantata with the choir. When Cavaradossi refuses to talk, Scarpia orders him led off to have the information tortured from him. Tosca enters, and after a menacingly courteous beginning, Scarpia reveals that Cavaradossi is being tortured with a sharp iron band cutting into his head. Unable to endure any more, Tosca reveals Angelotti's hiding place. At Tosca's insistence, Cavaradossi is carried in, and then in front of him Scarpia orders Spoletta to fetch Angelotti from the well. Cavaradossi turns on Tosca, but almost at once Sciarrone bursts in to report that the battle has turned out to be a defeat instead of a victory. Cavaradossi greets this unexpected news enthusiastically and defiantly tells Scarpia the days of his tyranny are numbered. Furious, Scarpia orders Cavaradossi dragged off to be executed. When Tosca demands to know the price of Cavaradossi's freedom, Scarpia at first ironically and then with increasing passion informs her that the price is her acquiescence to his lust. Horrified, Tosca refuses and begs him to have pity on her in her hour of grief. Scarpia tries to seize her, but she eludes him. When Spoletta returns with the news that Angelotti has committed suicide to avoid capture and to inquire what disposition is to be made of Cavaradossi, Scarpia looks questioningly at Tosca, who can only nod her assent. Then Scarpia gives Spoletta ambiguous orders, making it sound as if Cavaradossi's will be a mock-execution. To stall for time, Tosca insists on a safe-conduct, allowing her to flee the Papal States with Cavaradossi. While Scarpia writes the paper, Tosca searches for some means to evade consummating her bargain. Her eye falls on a fruit knife on the table, which she snatches up and conceals behind her back. When Scarpia comes toward her with outstretched arms, she stabs him to the heart. After she is sure Scarpia is dead, she looks for the safe-conduct and is aghast to discover it still clutched in his hand. After she gingerly extricates the paper from his dead fingers, she places candles around the corpse, puts a crucifix on Scarpia's chest, and steals out of the room.

Act 3   The setting is the topmost platform of the Castel Sant' Angelo. Just before dawn the voice of a shepherd (boy soprano) is heard singing a nostalgic song. The bells of Rome strike the hour. Soldiers lead Cavaradossi in. He asks the Jailer (bass) if he may write a final letter to Tosca. He starts writing, but soon he cannot continue, so dear is the thought of her and so deep is his despair at the thought of his dying. Tosca hurries in and jubilantly tells him how she has gained his release by murdering Scarpia. They plan their escape, but Tosca tells him first they must go through the farce of a mock-execution. Uneasily, she watches the firing squad march in, fire, and file out. She calls Cavaradossi and is horrified to discover the execution has been a very real one. Her grief is interrupted by the arrival of Spoletta and some soldiers, come to seize her for Scarpia's murder. Tosca eludes them by throwing her long cloak over Spoletta; then she climbs the battlement and leaps.

Madama Butterfly
Setting: Nagasaki, the present (1904)

Act 1 The marriage-broker Goro (tenor) discusses with Lt. Pinkerton, USN (tenor), the arrangements made for the American officer's forthcoming marriage to a geisha. Pinkerton is amused by his house, by three kow-towing servants, and by the composition of the wedding party. The U.S. Consul Sharpless (baritone) arrives, out of breath, and takes a more serious view of the impending marriage. When Pinkerton explains the favorable terms of the marriage-contract, which lasts for 999 years but may be rescinded any month, Sharpless tells him he overheard the girl at the Consulate and was struck by the deep sincerity of her voice. Unheeding, Pinkerton proposes that Sharpless drink with him to the real American girl he will marry some day. Just then Goro runs in to announce the arrival of Butterfly (soprano) and her friends. As she slowly climbs the hill, Butterfly describes herself as the happiest girl in Japan, even in the whole world. Sharpless begins to question the bride. Guilelessly, she tells him about her family's reduced circumstances, which caused her to become a geisha, and confesses to being just fifteen. Moved by the girl's artlessness and perturbed by Pinkerton's crass infatuation, again Sharpless warns him that the girl takes the marriage seriously. Butterfly shyly shows Pinkerton some of the objects she carries in her sleeves: handkerchieves, an opium pipe, some cosmetics, the dagger with which her father committed hari-kiri, and little figurines of Japanese gods. These last Butterfly discards, explaining to Pinkerton that she has gone to the mission to receive instruction in his religion. The brief wedding ceremony is performed by the Imperial Commissioner (baritone). When the officials leave, accompanied by Sharpless, Pinkerton proceeds to celebrate his marriage with his exotic new relations. The festivities are cut short by the angry voice of Butterfly's uncle, the priest, or Bonze (bass). He is furious that Butterfly has renounced the Japanese gods and curses her. All her friends and relations turn on her and renounce her. They hurry away, their angry voices audible for some time. This unexpected rejection reduces Butterfly to tears, and Pinkerton comforts her. Smiling through her tears, she tells him that although they have renounced her she is happy nonetheless. While Pinkerton waits impatiently, she puts on her wedding *obi*. As night falls, Pinkerton declares his love and eagerness with increasing impetuosity. At first a bit shy, Butterfly is swept away by Pinkerton's ardor. He draws her into their house.

Act 2 Three years have passed, and Pinkerton has been called back to sea duty. Waiting in their house for him, Butterfly expresses her complete confidence in his return, even though her maid Suzuki (mezzosoprano) has real doubts about it. Pinkerton has told Butterfly that he would come back when the robins rebuild their nests. She describes to Suzuki just how she will behave when he finally returns. Sharpless appears, obviously somewhat ill at ease, and Butterfly gives him a ceremonial welcome. Each time Sharpless tries to speak, Butterfly interrupts him with polite questions and offers of hospitality. She gives him a cigarette; she wants to know when the robins nest in America; she tells him that Goro has been trying to get her to marry again. Just then, one of Goro's clients, Yamadori (baritone) comes to pay elaborate court to Butterfly, but she treats him with easy irony, explaining that she still regards herself as married to Pinkerton. Goro whispers to Sharpless what he already knows: that Pinkerton's ship will soon enter the harbor. Yamadori makes a dejected exit, Butterfly laughing at him behind her fan. Alone with her at last, Sharpless explains that he has a letter from Pinkerton to read to her. Butterfly is overjoyed, but again she keeps interrupting. When he reads Pinkerton's words that perhaps Butterfly doesn't remember him, she protests, scandalized. When she takes the letter to mean that Pinkerton will return, she is so excited that Sharpless cannot continue. Cursing Pinkerton, he stuffs the letter in his pocket and bluntly asks what Butterfly would do if Pinkerton never returned. Stunned, Butterfly whispers that she could become a geisha again, or, better, die. Sharpless asks her why she does not accept Yamadori's proposal. Further shaken, Butterfly forces herself to regain her self-control and hurries off to return with Pinkerton's child in her arms. She has not mentioned him because she wanted to surprise Pinkerton with his son, but now she thinks the child's father should learn of his existence. She tells the child what Sharpless has said to her and reveals her tragic forbodings. Much moved, Sharpless prepares to leave, promising Butterfly that he will tell Pinkerton about the child. He asks the child's name, and Butterfly explains that now his name is Trouble but that when his father returns his name will be changed to Joy. After Sharpless departs, Suzuki's angry voice is heard shouting at Goro. When Butterfly learns that Goro has been saying that nobody knows who is the father of her child, she threatens him with a dagger. Goro makes his escape, and Butterfly tries to comfort the child. A cannon shot is heard announcing the arrival of a ship, and through her spyglass Butterfly sees that it is Pinkerton's ship. Butterfly is sure all her faith is justified. With Suzuki's help, she proceeds to decorate the house with all the flowers in the garden. As they prepare themselves for Pinkerton's return, Butterfly touches up her cheeks with rouge and puts on her wedding *obi*. As darkness falls, she pokes three holes in the paper wall, one for the child, one for Suzuki, and one for herself to watch through. They begin their vigil, and mysterious voices are heard humming in the distance.

Act 3 After an intermezzo that describes the night-long vigil and the coming dawn, the curtain rises on the child and Suzuki sleeping, while Butterfly stands rigid just as she was at the end of Act 2. Butterfly picks up the sleeping child and carries him off to the next room. Pinkerton and Sharpless arrive, much to Suzuki's joy, but she is shaken to see an American woman in the garden, and horrified to learn that it is Pinkerton's wife. Sharpless explains that they have come early hoping to find Suzuki alone because they are anxious to make suitable arrangements for the child. Pinkerton is filled with painful memories by the house where nothing has been changed since he left it. Sharpless pushes Suzuki out into the garden and turns to Pinkerton, bitterly reminding him that he had tried to convince him of Butterfly's sincerity at the time of the wedding. Remorse overcomes Pinkerton, and he hurries away, leaving Sharpless and Kate Pinkerton (soprano) to confront Butterfly. When Butterfly returns, at first she believes Pinkerton is hiding from her. Gradually she guesses the truth: that Kate is Pinkerton's wife, that they have come for the child. With a powerful effort at self-control she tells them to return in half an hour for the child. When they leave, Butterfly collapses in broken sobs. She orders Suzuki to stay with the child. Then she takes her father's dagger from its lacquered sheath and reads the motto inscribed on it: "It is better to die with honor than to live without honor." She is about to stab herself when Suzuki pushes the child into the room. Butterfly takes an agonizing farewell of the child, blindfolds him, and gives him an American flag to wave. Then, behind a screen, she commits hari-kiri and, with a final effort, struggles to crawl toward the child. Pinkerton rushes in, too late.

La Fanciulla del West

Setting: The Sierra Nevada Mountains of California, during the days of the Gold Rush.

Act 1 The setting is the Polka Bar, adorned with Indian blankets and animal pelts, furnished with rustic chairs and tables; on one wall is a poster offering $5000 reward for the capture of the bandit Ramerrez, and signed Wells Fargo. Near the bar is the barrel in which the miners deposit their gold for safe-keeping. When the curtain rises, however, the bar is dark. All that can be seen is the glowing tip of Sheriff Jack Rance's cigar and through the windows the snow-capped Sierras tinged violet and gold in the sunset. From outdoors comes the distant shouting of approaching men, and a baritone voice is heard trolling a snatch of nostalgic song. The bartender Nick (tenor) appears with a lighted candle and lights the lamps. Three miners, Joe (tenor), Harry (tenor), and Bello (baritone), enter boisterously and join Sid (baritone) for a rowdy game at the faro table. Soon Rance (baritone) is wondering what can be detaining Minnie. Sonora corners Nick to ask: "Has Minnie definitely decided on me?" When Nick roguishly confirms his hopes, the elated Sonora orders cigars for everyone. A moment later, Trin (tenor) asks if he has not been chosen by Minnie, and when Nick confirms that hope, the equally elated Trin orders whiskey for all. Jake Wallace (baritone), the camp minstrel enters, singing a song of home. The miners join in the poignant song, which reduces Larkens (bass) to tears. He begs the men to send him home, and they pass the hat for him. Larkens thanks them brokenly and stumbles out. The gambling resumes, but soon Bello is accusing Sid of cheating, and at once the men threaten to hang him. Rance restores order by pinning a card over Sid's heart and by telling him never to touch another card. Now the Wells Fargo agent, Ashby (bass), enters and tells Rance that the bandit Ramerrez still eludes capture. When Nick proposes a toast to Minnie, Rance corrects him by saying he should have proposed the toast to the future Mrs. Rance. Sonora takes violent offense at Rance's words, and the two men start a bitter exchange of insults. Sonora draws his gun, but just then Minnie (soprano) appears and separates the men.

The miners greet Minnie affectionately and offer her gifts. As they gather around her, Minnie produces a Bible and proceeds to hold her "school," explicating a verse that holds out the promise of redemption for even the most sinful of men. Ashby approaches Rance and tells him that a certain Nina Micheltorena has agreed to lead him to her lover Ramerrez's hiding place. Ashby hurries out. Rance declares his love to Minnie. She reminds him he is already married and tells him she prefers her single life. Swearing he has never really loved anything before, Rance offers her a treasure for a single kiss. Minnie reminisces about the warm natural affection that existed between her mother and father and wishes that some day she might know such a love. A stranger (tenor) arrives, who soon announces that he is Dick Johnson from Sacramento. Rance eyes him suspiciously, particularly as he and Minnie are soon reminiscing about a previous encounter on the road to Monterey. Jealous, Rance tries to turn the men against Johnson, but Minnie personally vouches for him. Johnson asks Minnie to dance with him, and, while they are waltzing in the dance-hall, Ashby returns with the captured half-breed José Castro (bass). One of Ramerrez's band, Castro has given a start when he recognizes Johnson's saddle inside the door. Fearing his leader is in danger, Castro does his best to put Ashby off the scent. Castro offers to lead a posse, hoping to gain time. Before he leaves, Castro manages to whisper to Johnson that his men are near by and that at the signal of a whistle they will help him steal the miners' gold. Rance, Ashby, and all the miners leave with Castro.

Alone, Minnie and Johnson converse easily. He admires her courage at remaining alone to guard the gold. Anyone who came to steal the gold, she tells him, would have to kill her first. Moved by her staunch straightforwardness, Johnson ignores Castro's whistle, assuring Minnie that no one would dare to rob her. She invites him to visit her later in her cabin so that they may continue their talk. Leaving, Johnson tells her that she has the face of an angel. Minnie is so stirred by this that she hides her face in her hands.

Act 2 Less than an hour has elapsed since Act 1. In Minnie's cabin the squaw Wowkle (mezzosoprano) sings a lullaby to her papoose. Billy Jackrabbit (bass) tells Wowkle that Minnie is eager that they get married to make the baby legitimate. Entering, Minnie dismisses Billy and orders Wowkle to tidy up the cabin. Minnie dresses in her best for Johnson, who soon arrives in good humor. At first, Minnie is ill at ease and wonders why he had come to the Polka Bar, asking if he had mistaken the road to Nina Micheltorena's. Johnson's evasive answer is to compliment Minnie on her snug cabin. Minnie tells him how immensely she enjoys her solitary life. Wowkle serves them. When Johnson tries to kiss Minnie, she gently puts him down. She sends Wowkle home, although it is snowing hard now. Again, Johnson demands a kiss, and this time Minnie consents. Johnson starts to leave, but Minnie warns him the snow has covered the trail. Just then three shots ring out, and Johnson agrees to stay. Minnie gives him her bed and curls up in front of the fire with her bearskin. Through the wind howling outside, Johnson believes he hears men shouting.

There is an abrupt knock at the door, and Nick warns Minnie that Ramerrez has been seen near by. Minnie hides Johnson behind the bed curtains and opens her door to admit Nick, Rance, Ashby, and Sonora. They are relieved to find her safe. With obvious relish, Rance tells her that Johnson is none other than the bandit Ramerrez. Minnie is deeply shocked, and more so when she discovers that Johnson's "woman," Nina Micheltorena, has given Rance a photograph of Ramerrez, which Rance shows to Minnie. Without revealing his observation to the others, Nick notices Johnson's cigar in the ashtray. He offers to stay with Minnie, but she refuses. When the four men leave, Minnie confronts Johnson with her knowledge. He confesses the truth, but assures her that ever since he first saw her he has longed to become an honest man. Indignantly, Minnie tells him that she can forgive him for being a bandit, but she cannot forgive him for stealing her first kiss. She orders him out. Johnson leaves in the howling storm. A moment later a shot rings out and the sound of a body falling against the door is heard. Beside herself, Minnie drags him inside and confesses that she really does love him. With a superhuman effort, she manages to push him up a ladder to a hiding place in the loft. Rance knocks at the door and enters, pistol in hand. After ransacking the place, vainly looking for Johnson, he suddenly seizes Minnie and kisses her. Minnie fights him off. A few drops of blood from the loft splash on Rance's hand. Looking up, he realizes the situation and orders Johnson down. Minnie helps the wounded man to the table, where he promptly faints from loss of blood. To save his life, Minnie offers to play a game of poker with Rance. Momentarily distracting Rance's attention, she stuffs some cards into her stocking. They start to play. Minnie wins the first hand; Rance, the second. When Rance lays down his winning third hand, Minnie pretends to faint and asks Rance for a drink. Unobserved, she draws the cards from her stocking and throws down her hand, which now is higher than Rance's. Rance grabs up his hat and coat and leaves without a word. Minnie bursts into overwrought laughter; as she embraces the unconscious Johnson, she starts to sob hysterically.

Act 3 It is early dawn in a clearing of the forest. The great trees are shrouded with mist. By a fire sit Rance and Nick; Ashby is lying full-length on the ground, some distance off. Although Nick wishes Johnson had never disrupted their lives, he compliments Rance on being a man of his word and not betraying Johnson's presence in Minnie's cabin. Rance declares with a sneer that he cannot understand how Minnie could love such a man. Distant voices shout. Ashby jumps up and exclaims that the posse is closing in on Johnson. As Ashby is directing the manhunt, he cannot understand the sheriff's recent behavior. When some of the men rush in, Ashby tells them he wants Johnson taken alive. Ashby jumps on his horse and leads them off to join the posse. Although Rance has kept his word, he cannot help rejoicing that Johnson is about to be captured and that a noose awaits him. After some more frenzied comings and goings, Sonora gallops in with the news that Johnson has been caught.

As a noisy crowd gathers, Billy Jackrabbit slings the rope over a branch of a tall tree. As the miners look forward to the hanging, Nick comes unobserved to Billy and gives him some money, telling him not to make the noose until he is ordered to. As Nick hurries off, Johnson is led in, pale and disheveled. Ashby turns Johnson over to Rance and the men, for them to administer justice. The miners angrily accuse him of murder, but Johnson proudly claims he never stooped to killing. It is clear that they chiefly resent his having stolen Minnie from them. Calmly, Johnson asks them to get the hanging over with quickly, but he asks to speak briefly of the girl he loves. The others protest, but Sonora insists he has a right to speak. Johnson asks them to let Minnie believe that he got away free to live the better life she had made him long for. Furious, Rance strikes Johnson in the face, violence that shocks the men. Johnson goes to the tree, but just then a wild shout is heard, and Minnie gallops in, her hair wind-blown, a pistol between her teeth. Although Rance orders the men to proceed with the hanging, Minnie defies him. She reminds the men of their old comradeship and tells them that Johnson is hers, a man redeemed, worthy of leading a new life. Sonora is the first to relent. Minnie turns to the others and reminds them of her past kindnesses to them. She throws away her pistol, swearing that once again she wants to be their loving sister. After some inward struggle, the men yield. Sonora cuts the ropes binding Johnson and turns him over to Minnie. Arm in arm Minnie and Johnson slowly leave, bidding farewell to this part of the world. The men remain dejected. Rance sits grimly by the tree.

La Rondine
Setting: Paris and the Riviera, during the Second Empire

Act 1 Magda is the mistress of the rich banker Rambaldo. One day in her elegant salon she is pouring tea for her guests. Three girls, Yvette (soprano), Bianca (soprano), and Suzy (mezzosoprano), laugh at the poet Prunier (tenor), who is holding forth on his grotesque theories of love. When he speaks approvingly of sentimental love, Magda's maid Lisette (soprano) tells him he doesn't know what he is talking about. Prunier is offended, and Magda (soprano) dismisses Lisette. Prunier insists that at this time everyone is prey to romantic love; it is a regular epidemic. To prove his point, he starts to play and sing a poem about Doretta. When Prunier admits he does not know how to finish his song, Magda improvises a second verse. Everyone is charmed by her performance; Rambaldo so much so that he gives her a handsome pearl necklace he had intended to give her later. Magda's gratitude is cool. Lisette rushes in to announce a stranger who has been at the door time and again inquiring for Rambaldo. Rambaldo asks Magda for permission to receive the son of an old school-friend. As Lisette bustles out, Prunier asks Magda how she can put up with such a windmill. Magda says she finds her diverting. Looking around Magda's handsome establishment, the girls wonder what need she has of diversion As a reply, Magda describes a youthful escapade at a dance hall, where she met a charming young man with whom she drank bock beer and had a delightful flirtation. For her, the memory is unforgettable. The girls suggest Magda's story to Prunier as the subject for one of his songs, but he retorts that he prefers perverse heroines, like Berenice and Salome. Next, Prunier takes the girls to one side for a demonstration of his knack for palmistry. While the palm reading is going on, Lisette shows in young Ruggero Lastouc (tenor), whom Rambaldo greets, and then reads a letter from Ruggero's father. Meanwhile, Prunier tells Magda that she is like a swallow, eager to migrate across the ocean toward the sun, toward true love. When Rambaldo discovers that Ruggero has never been to Paris before, he calls on the others to suggest suitable entertainment for a young man's first evening in town. Prunier advises the young man to go straight to bed. Lisette interrupts, insisting that the occasion should be a gala one, and gets Ruggero to write down the names of famous dance halls. Lisette particularly recommends Bullier. When Ruggero leaves, Magda, carelessly swinging her new necklace, chides the others for making fun of the nice young man. When her guests leave, Magda tells Lisette she will not be going out, but after a moment's reflection on Prunier's simile of the swallow she impulsively decides to go to Bullier herself and hurries off to change. Soon, Lisette comes tiptoeing in, all dressed up to go out; Prunier is waiting for her and kisses her. When he tells her he dislikes her hat, even though it is Magda's best, Lisette obediently goes to change it. When she returns he approves her appearance and kisses her again before they steal out together. A moment later Magda appears, dressed like a simple *grisette*. She puts a flower in her hair and pauses at a mirror, wondering who could possibly recognize her.

Act 2 At Bullier that evening a pleasure-seeking crowd fills the place with animated chatter. Suddenly the crowd's attention is caught by Magda, who enters shyly. Some young men crowd around her, hoping to gain her favor, but she manages to escape them and hurries over to Ruggero's table. She apologizes and explains that she will leave him as soon as the young men are no longer watching. Ruggero gently urges her to stay. She is not, he goes on, like the others, but more timid, more like the girls back home in Montaubon. She answers him casually, but soon he is urging her to dance and tells her that she dances even better than the girls back home. Magda gives herself over to the pleasure of the waltz, obviously taken with Ruggero. Soon the dance floor is crowded. Prunier and Lisette appear. They are having an argument because of Prunier's insistence on trying to turn her into a lady, and Lisette leaves him, angry. Magda and Ruggero return to their table. When Ruggero orders two beers, Magda is filled with memories of her youthful escapade. When they drink a toast, Ruggero asks her her name. "Paulette," Magda replies, and writes her name on the marble-topped table. Ruggero signs his name beneath hers, telling her that her name is engraved on his heart. He will fall in love only once and then forever, he assures her. Their mutual attraction grows in intensity, and soon they are lost in a kiss. Lisette turns up again, now convinced that Magda is her mistress, a deduction that Prunier pretends not to believe. To prove his point he takes Lisette and introduces her, but Magda tries to preserve her incognito. The two couples sit at the same table and soon are toasting their love in champagne. Suddenly Prunier catches sight of Rambaldo. Upset, Magda begs Ruggero to leave her alone for a few minutes. When Rambaldo demands an explanation, she answers that he has seen it all already, she has nothing to add. Rambaldo asks her to leave, but Magda refuses, swearing she loves Ruggero. When Rambaldo leaves her, the hall is deserted except for Magda. Ruggero brings her her shawl, and the two of them exit slowly together, very much in love.

Act 3   For some months Magda and Ruggero have been leading an idyllic existence on the Riviera. Ruggero informs Magda that he has written to his family not just for money to pay their many debts but also for their consent to his marriage to Magda. Knowing that she is unacceptable to Ruggero's family, Magda suffers as she listens to Ruggero's loving picture of wedded bliss in the bosom of his family, his hopes of the child they may have one day. When Ruggero goes to see if an answer has come from his parents, Magda is torn between her desire to tell Ruggero the truth and her wish to avoid hurting him. Lisette and Prunier appear. Lisette is distraught because Prunier has tried to convert her into a music-hall singer and the night before at Nice she was a fiasco. The whistling of the audience still rings in her ears. Prunier is outdone with her because she is immune to his "improvements"; Lisette only wants to return to Magda. When Magda sees them, she welcomes Lisette back, who happily runs off to resume her duties. Prunier gives Magda an oblique message from Rambaldo, who will be happy to take her back on any terms and to serve her in any way. When Lisette puts on her apron again, Prunier feels all the old attraction and wants to know when she will be off-duty that evening.

Ruggero returns with his mother's letter, which he gives to Magda to read. In a trembling voice, Magda reads of Ruggero's mother's hopes that her son has chosen a virtuous woman who will be a worthy mother of his children. Unable to keep silent any longer, Magda reveals her past to the stunned Ruggero, telling him that while she can be his mistress she can never be his wife. Ruggero protests and begs her not to leave him, but Magda insists he hear her out: he must return home and the day will come when he may even think of her with gratitude. Ruggero slumps down, his head in his hands, while Magda walks away, leaning heavily on Lisette.

Il Tabarro
Setting: Bank of the Seine, Paris, 1910

Michele's barge is tied up to a landing-stage, and stevedores unload the cargo. Giorgetta (soprano) tells her husband Michele (baritone) that the men need a drink to help them finish the long job. Michele agrees, but when he tries to kiss his wife, she draws back. When Luigi (tenor), one of the stevedores, complains of the heat, Giorgetta, with a meaningful glance, promises him some relief and goes to fetch wine. Luigi and his fellow workers, Tinca (tenor) and Talpa (bass), drink to Giorgetta's health. An out-of-tune barrel organ starts to play, and Tinca dances with Giorgetta. When he steps on her feet, she breaks away and starts to dance with Luigi. Michele returns, and Giorgetta shivers, blaming it on the autumn chill. A song-vendor (tenor) passes along the quay, singing about Mimì, the girl who lived and died for love. La Frugola (mezzosoprano) enters, looking for her husband Talpa, and shows Giorgetta what she has scavenged that day. Frugola has found a bit of beef heart for her cat, whose contented purring she describes. When it is quitting time, Tinca announces he is going to get drunk, as it is better to drink than to think too much. Luigi agrees with him, saying that thought is too painful for a man who can only live by being a sweating beast of burden. Frugola declares that her dream is to have a little house in the country, where she and Talpa and the cat can snooze all day in the sun. Giorgetta's ambitions are different. She longs for the excitement of the city, the feeling of the sidewalk beneath her feet. Luigi, who like Giorgetta was born in Belleville, seconds her sensual celebration of city life. The others leave, Luigi remains behind with Giorgetta on the pretext of having to speak with Michele. In an urgent undertone, Giorgetta tells her lover to be careful of Michele, but she cannot resist telling him how the memory of last night's kisses makes her tremble. Michele comes back on deck, and Luigi, to allay suspicion, asks about the chances of work in Rouen. Michele gives him a discouraging answer and goes below to fix the barge's lights. Alone together again, Luigi tells Giorgetta how terrible it is to have to share her with another man and how he longs to go away with her. She, too, hates her present life. Luigi agrees to return within an hour, wearing rope-soled shoes. He will come aboard when she gives their usual signal: lighting a match. As Luigi hurries off, Giorgetta meditates on the difficulty of finding happiness.

Michele reappears, carrying the trimmed lamps. He reproaches her with not loving him any more. She tries to avoid this conversation by saying it is cold and she is sleepy. Michele tells her he has noticed she does not sleep much any more. When he mentions their dead child, she can not bear the memory. Trying to stir some warmth in her, he reminds her of their former happiness, of the days when he would shelter her beneath his cloak and she would drowse on his shoulder. Giorgetta says that they both have changed and goes to her cabin. Watching her go, Michele calls her a whore. As Michele hangs the lanterns on either side of the barge, two lovers (soprano and tenor) pass by, promising to meet the following day. Michele looks through the cabin window and sees Giorgetta sitting there still dressed and wonders whom she is waiting for. Miserably, he goes over in his mind the various possibilities and rejects them, even Luigi. Then he savagely imagines the joy of strangling her lover. His outburst over, he sinks back and automatically lights his pipe. Mistaking the signal, Luigi approaches stealthily. Michele leaps on him and, wringing from him a confession that he loves Giorgetta, strangles him. Giorgetta is aroused by the struggle and calls out, whereupon Michele quickly covers Luigi's body with his cloak. Giorgetta comes on deck, frightened, and tries to come close to Michele. Michele suddenly pulls back the cloak, seizes Giorgetta, and forces her down on Luigi's body. Giorgetta screams.

Suor Angelica

Setting: A Tuscan convent, toward the end of the seventeenth century.

From the chapel to one side of the cloister come the voices of the nuns singing an "Ave Maria." When the service ends, the sisters come out of the chapel, bowing to the Abbess. They gather around the Monitress (mezzosoprano) who questions them for their sins of commission and omission and assigns their penances. Suor Genovieffa (soprano) tells them it is again that time of year when the setting sun gilds the fountain, and the sisters rejoice that it is May once more. The Mistress of Novices (mezzosoprano) approves their simple joy. When the sisters begin to discuss the wish of a recently deceased sister, Suor Angelica (soprano) declares that while wishes are the flowers of the living, they do not bloom for the dead. Severely, the Monitress tells them that nuns have no business having wishes. Suor Genovieffa, who used to be a shepherd, timidly describes her longing to pet a baby lamb once more. Fat Suor Dolcina (soprano) acknowledges that she, too, has a wish, but the other sisters knowing her love of good food, laugh. Suor Angelica, speaking for herself, denies that she wishes for anything. Now the other sisters are shocked, for they know Angelica has told a lie; they all know that she longs for news of her noble family. The Nursing Sister (mezzo-soprano) enters to announce that Suor Chiara has been stung by wasps and asks Suor Angelica, who understands how to cure such things with herbs, to concoct a remedy. Two Alms Sisters (soprano and mezzo-soprano) arrive, bringing with them a donkey-cart laden with donations of food. They report seeing an elaborate coach at the gate. Suor Angelica questions them eagerly about the crest on the coach, hoping that at long last there may be a visitor for her.

The Abbess (contralto) enters and motions to the sisters to retire; then she tells Suor Angelica that her aunt the Princess has come to see her. Angelica's agitation increases. When the proud, black-clad Princess (contralto) enters, leaning on her ebony stick, she avoids looking directly at her niece, although Angelica has knelt before her. The estate of Angelica's late parents is to be divided, since Angelica's younger sister is to be married, and the Princess has brought a document to be signed. When Angelica asks whom her sister will marry, the Princess sternly replies that it is a man who will forgive the stain on the family honor. Angelica calls her aunt inexorable, a judgment that deeply offends the Princess, who tells her that she must continue to atone for her sin. Unable to restrain her anxiety any longer, Angelica begs for news of her baby, of the son she had seen only once. The Princess tells her that the child died two years ago. With a cry, Angelica falls to the ground. The Princess summons the Abbess, and Angelica recovers herself sufficiently to sign away her inheritance. When the Princess leaves, Angelica breaks into prolonged sobbing. In the distance, the nuns can be seen lighting the lamps on the graves in the convent cemetery. Angelica can think only of her child, who died without his mother near, and she longs to be reunited with her baby. At a signal, all the nuns retire to their cells, but Angelica soon reappears, carrying a little pot. She gathers herbs and brews a poisonous decoction, which she drinks. No sooner has she poisoned herself than she realizes she has committed a deadly sin. Frantically, she prays to the Virgin for forgiveness, begging to be saved for love of her son. Angelic voices are heard from the chapel. The doors swing open, and the chapel is seen to be filled with angels. The Virgin appears in the doorway, guiding a child by the hand, and she gently pushes the little boy toward the dying Angelica.

Gianni Schicchi
Setting: The bedchamber of Buoso Donati, Florence, 1299

All Buoso's relatives are present, supposedly to mourn his death, but they are really concerned with his will. There are rumors that the richest parts of his inheritance have been left to the monks. The relatives start a feverish search for the will. Rinuccio (tenor) finds it, but before he will hand it over to his Aunt Zita (contralto), he asks that if they should turn out to be Buoso's heirs may he have permission to marry Gianni Schicchi's daughter Lauretta. Zita grants his request, providing everything turns out as they hope. Rinuccio whispers to his young cousin Gherardino (boy soprano) to run and fetch Gianni Schicchi and Lauretta. Buoso's will is now opened, and as the relatives read the document their expressions become more and more grave. All of them— Simone (bass), Ciesca (soprano), Marco (baritone), Betto (bass), Nella (soprano), Gherardo (tenor), Rinuccio, and Zita—are horrified to find their worst fears confirmed: the monks get the cream of the bequests. Soon they are all wondering if there may not be some way to circumvent the will. Just then, Gherardino rushes in to announce that Gianni Schicchi is on his way. The relatives all turn on Rinuccio for bringing in an outsider at a time like this. Rinuccio emphatically disagrees with them. He speaks of the flourishing state of Florence and points out that it is just such shrewd men as Gianni Schicchi who make such prosperity possible.

Gianni Schicchi arrives and wonders what the gloomy faces mean. Rinuccio's joy at seeing Lauretta vanishes when Zita tells him that without a dowry a match between them is impossible. While Schicchi and Zita roundly insult one another, Lauretta and Rinuccio see their dreams of future happiness evaporate. Rinuccio begs Schicchi to see what he can do about the will. At first Schicchi refuses to help the Donati family in any way, but Lauretta begs him to think of her, for she really loves Rinuccio, and if she cannot have him she would rather die. Schicchi decides finally there may be a way out of the difficulty. After sending Lauretta out on the balcony to feed the birds, Schicchi assures himself that no one but the relatives knows of Buoso's death. Gianni's scheme has its first test when the doctor, Spineloccio (bass), comes to look in on his patient. Slipping into bed and imitating the dead man's voice, Schicchi tells the doctor that he fells much better and urges him to return later. The relatives are delighted with Schicchi's impersonation. He explains that they must summon a notary and that he will disguise himself as Buoso and dictate a new will. Rinuccio goes to fetch the notary. As the female relatives dress him in Buoso's gown and night cap, they offer Schicchi bribes to favor them in the new will. Schicchi reminds them of the penalty for falsifying or abetting the falsification of a will, a penalty that entails the amputation of the right hand and permanent exile from Florence. Rinuccio returns with the lawyer, Ser Amantio (baritone), and two witnesses (basses). Schicchi dictates the new will, leaving something to each of the relatives, but keeping the best things for himself. The relatives are furious, but helpless, as Schicchi keeps reminding them of the penalty for fraud. When the lawyer and the witnesses leave, the relatives turn on Schicchi, but he drives them out of the house. They try to carry off everything they can get their hands on. Rinuccio and Lauretta, on the terrace, embrace and pledge their love. Now there is no impediment to their marriage, as Schicchi has provided Lauretta with a dowry. Then Schicchi, cap in hand, addresses the audience directly, asking them not to think too badly of him.

Turandot
Setting: Peking, legendary times

Act 1 Outside the Imperial palace, the Mandarin (baritone) reads the proclamation that the Princess Turandot will marry whoever succeeds in answering her three riddles, but whoever fails to answer them must forfeit his head. The crowd, their blood-lust up after many beheadings, howls for more victims. In the milling throng, a slave-girl Liù (soprano) cries out that the old man she is accompanying has been knocked down. The old man is Timur (bass), the deposed King of Tartary. Liù and Timur are assisted by a young man, whom they recognize as Timur's long-lost son, Calaf (tenor). Liù is moved to see Calaf again, having loved him ever since he smiled on her one day years before. The headsman Tu-Pin-Pao appears, and the turbulence of the crowd increases. When the moon rises, the people are filled with superstitious awe and compare the moon's white disc to a severed, bloodless head. A funeral procession consisting of guards and priests in white mourning leads the proud young Prince of Persia to his fate, for he has failed to answer the riddles. At the sight of the unsuccessful suitor, the crowd begs mercy for him. The Princess Turandot appears, silent, on the balcony and gives the signal for the execution to proceed. Calaf is transfixed by Turandot's beauty. So great is his instant resolution to win her that he is deaf to the pleas of Liù and Timur. Calaf tries to make his way to the great gong to signal his intention to take up the challenge, but he finds himself surrounded by three Ministers: Ping (baritone), Pang (tenor), and Pong (tenor). With heavy irony, they do their best to dissuade him from accepting Turandot's challenge. They speak of the graves of his many predecessors; they point out that Turandot is only, after all, a woman. Calaf is resolute. The voices of Turandot's maids are heard demanding silence so that Turandot's sleep will not be disturbed. The Ministers continue their warnings to Calaf. Mysterious voices of the spirits of the dead aspirants for Turandot's hand faintly proclaim that their love for her transcends the grave. Timur asks his son if he wants his father to die alone on the road of exile. Liù humbly explains that she is at the limits of her strength and weeps. Calaf asks her to continue to watch over his father, but tells her that now he can smile no more. Once again everyone joins in trying to dissuade Calaf, but he pushes his way to the gong and strikes it three times.

Act 2, scene 1   Inside a little pavilion, Ping, Pang, and Pong bemoan the slaughter that has followed Turandot's proclamation of the riddles. They are barely over the last execution when here comes another fool to try his luck. Things have come to such a pass that they are reduced to being no more than Ministers of Execution. They think longingly of their homes in the provinces. Ping has a little house on a blue lake in Honan; Pong has forests near Tsiang; Pang, a garden near Kiù. Their thoughts return to all the bloodshed, and they imagine how pleasant it would be if a prince would solve Turandot's riddles and rid her of her hatred of men. How happy China would be then! They are roused from their dreaming by the trumpets announcing the trial of the stranger.

Act 2, scene 2   In the courtyard of the palace the throne of the aged Emperor Altoum is placed at the top of a long flight of steps. The crowd prostrates itself before the Emperor (tenor), who tries to persuade Calaf to give up the enterprise. The young Prince is determined to undertake the trial. Turandot (soprano) appears and explains how long ago her ancestress Lo-u Ling was ravished by invaders, and now Turandot feels herself the personification of her vengeance. She proudly swears that no man will ever possess her. She asks the first riddle, which Calaf confidently answers "Hope!" With only slight hesitation he answers her second riddle: "Blood!" Turandot poses her third riddle, and only after an agonizing wait Calaf gives the correct answer: "Turandot!" While the crowd exults at Calaf's success, Turandot goes to her father and begs him to release her from her oath. The Emperor claims his word is sacred. Moved by the passionate intensity with which Turandot addresses her father, Calaf offers her a riddle of his own. If she can discover his name before the following dawn, he will die. The Emperor hopes that with the new day he can greet the stranger as his son. Once more the crowd praises the Emperor.

Act 3, scene 1   It is nearly dawn in the garden of the palace. The voices of heralds repeat Turandot's commands that tonight no one must sleep in Peking, that the stranger's name must be discovered. Listening to these voices, Calaf meditates upon the approaching morning and the joy of winning Turandot. Ping, Pang, and Pong approach and tempt Calaf with lascivious maidens, with wealth, if only he will save their necks. Calaf refuses. The crowd howls that they will all be killed if the stranger's name is not found out, and they turn on Calaf, their daggers upraised. Just then soldiers drag in Liù and Timur, shouting they have found two who know the stranger's name. Turandot enters, and Calaf swears he does not know the two prisoners. Torturers seize old Timur, but Liù cries out that she alone knows the name. Calaf tries to help her, but he is held and bound. Liù says that she would rather die than reveal the prince's name. Turandot wonders what power has given the girl such courage; Liù tells her that it is love. Liù's love is secret, but nonetheless sweet, and the only reward she asks of her love is that it enable her to withstand torture. Turandot summons the executioner. Liù approaches Turandot and predicts that the princess will come to love the stranger. Then with a sudden movement she snatches a dagger from her guard's belt and plunges it into her heart. The crowd cowers in terror, for they believe that someone who dies unjustly may turn into a vampire. A veil is placed over Turandot's face. Timur laments Liù's death, as slowly and tenderly the crowd picks up her body and bears it away.

Left alone with Turandot, Calaf tries to arouse her passion, but she repulses him icily. He tears the veil from her face, but she swears that to touch her would be a profanation. Calaf takes her in his arms and kisses her long and passionately. Turandot is softened, bewildered. She weeps and admits that from the first she knew he was more of 'a hero than the others. She begs him to leave with his mystery still intact. He throws himself on her mercy by revealing his name. The trumpets proclaim the hour of the new trial. Confident, Calaf goes off with Turandot.

Act 3, scene 2 Once more the court is assembled, and the Emperor is upon his throne. Turandot goes up to her father and announces that she has learned the stranger's name: it is Love. Calaf goes to her and embraces her, as the crowd rejoices.

INDEX